LOSING TIME

LOST TIME BOOK ONE

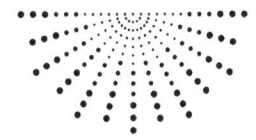

NICOLA CLAIRE

❀ Created with Vellum

CONTENTS

ABOUT THE AUTHOR

Nicola Claire lives in beautiful Taupo, New Zealand with her husband and two young boys.

A bit of a romance junkie, she can be known to devour as many as half a dozen books a week if she drinks too much coffee. But her real passion is writing sexy, romantic suspense stories with strong female leads and alpha male protagonists who know how to love them.

So far, she's written well over 50 books. She might have caught the writing bug; here's hoping there's no cure!

For more information:
www.nicolaclairebooks.com
nicola@nicolaclairebooks.com

ALSO BY NICOLA CLAIRE

Kindred Series

Kindred

Blood Life Seeker

Forbidden Drink

Giver of Light

Dancing Dragon

Shadow's Light

Entwined With The Dark

Kiss Of The Dragon

Dreaming Of A Blood Red Christmas (Novella)

Mixed Blessing Mystery Series

Mixed Blessing

Dark Shadow

Rogue Vampire (Coming Soon)

Sweet Seduction Series

Sweet Seduction Sacrifice

Sweet Seduction Serenade

Sweet Seduction Shadow

Sweet Seduction Surrender

Sweet Seduction Shield

Sweet Seduction Sabotage

Sweet Seduction Stripped

Sweet Seduction Secrets

Sweet Seduction Sayonara

Elemental Awakening Series

The Tempting Touch Of Fire

The Soothing Scent Of Earth

The Chilling Change Of Air

The Tantalising Taste Of Water

The Eternal Edge Of Aether (Novella)

H.E.A.T. Series

A Flare Of Heat

A Touch Of Heat

A Twist Of Heat (Novella)

A Lick Of Heat

Citizen Saga

Elite

Cardinal

Citizen

Masked (Novella)

Wiped

Scarlet Suffragette Series

Fearless

Breathless

Heartless

Blood Enchanted Series

Blood Enchanted

Blood Entwined

Blood Enthralled

44 South Series

Southern Sunset

Southern Storm

Southern Strike (Coming Soon)

Lost Time Series

Losing Time

Making Time

Finding Time (Coming Soon)

The Sector Fleet

Accelerating Universe

Apparent Brightness

Right Ascension

Zenith Point

The Summer O'Dare Mysteries

Chasing Summer

Sizzling Summer (Coming Soon)

For:
Mrs Stead, my high school English teacher,
who barged on into my fifth form year
and gave me a new appreciation of the English language,
and a female role model to look up to.

I applaud you!

"Fideliter"

"Lost time is never found again."

Benjamin Franklin

PROLOGUE

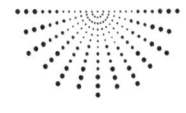

MIMI

*I*t's funny how things happen. How the unexpected can catch you by surprise. How your life can have meaning and the world can be bright, the future an impossible to believe promise.

And then everything is taken in a flash of blinding light.

The dream wasn't the same dream I'd been having for so many months now. It didn't start with the grinding sound of metal twisting. Or the flash of orange as flames erupted into a darkening sky. Or the startling thud of a bullet ejecting from a gun. Or the multitude of other imagined ways my parents could have died.

It started with a kiss.

I'd thought I'd had my share of surprises. I'd thought my once glistening future could never have looked so bleak.

Until *he* invaded my dreams.

But it's not the dreams we should worry about. It's not what's to come, but what has been.

But when you're talking about temporal paradoxes, those causal loops that mix up Time, where a future event is the cause of a past event, well...

Maybe we should just fear everything.

EVEN DREAMS COULDN'T CHANGE THOSE SORTS OF THINGS

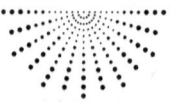

MIMI

*I*t was a scream that woke me. So desperate and full of fear. For a moment, I couldn't tell where I was. Who had made the sound. What the wretched cry could mean. I sucked in a breath of air; noticed the rawness of my throat, which led me to believe it had been me screaming and not some other person, and then felt a jolt rock through my body, followed by a rumble filling my ears. Panic and disorientation took a moment to subside. And then a careful hand grabbed my wrist and whispered, "Hey, sleepyhead, we're here."

I blinked, the vision of a water-filled car and distorted faces slowly vanished, replaced with a United Airlines Airbus A330 plane.

"That guy over there was watching you," Carrie said conversationally. "I thought it was because you look sexy when you sleep. And then I noticed the drool."

"Gee, thanks," I muttered.

My sister watched me from the corner of her eye as I rubbed two hands over my face and tried to settle my heartbeat. It always thundered inside my chest when I woke from the dreams. The nightmares. I stared at the blank screen in the seat in front of me; aware Carrie hadn't stopped her furtive glances yet. She wouldn't ask. She didn't need to.

We both knew what my sleeping mind had seen.

"So, what are we doing first?" Carrie asked, hugging her small carry-on backpack to her chest and jumping up and down in her seat. She stared out the window at the tarmac as the plane slowly lumbered down the runway. "Universal? Disney? I know! The Everglades."

She turned and looked directly at me, a smirk twisting the edges of her lips. Blue eyes the mirror image of mine stared across at me; blinking widely, innocently. She raised her eyebrows and then wiggled them suggestively.

"All those rugged airboat captains," she purred. "Smooth southern accents telling you just what they want. Big muscles from wrestling the alligators wrapped around your body." She winked. "Just what the doctor ordered, I think."

That was Carrie, full of joie de vivre. If it wasn't for the dark smudges under her eyes and the occasionally haunted look staring out of them, you'd think Carolyn Wylde didn't have a care in the world.

"I know, I know," she said exasperatedly. "NASA. It's all about the science."

"Well, I am one, so…"

"Yeah, not recently."

"I have my degree," I argued.

"You have," she agreed good-naturedly, then ruined it by adding, "and a half written Ph.D."

"We're not here to discuss that," I griped, slumping back in my seat and wondering when they were going to park this damn thing. How long did it take to drive from one end of a runway to the other and hook up to a terminal?

I looked out the window at a stunning blue-sky day and saw three other United Airline planes parked up on the runway before us. Stationary.

Great. No avoiding Carrie.

"We've got time," Carrie offered, always acutely aware of what I was thinking.

That's the thing with twins; they've known you since conception. They have a connection right to your inner thoughts and feelings.

"Carrie," I said softly, a hint of defeat entering my tone.

She was silent for a while and then she asked tentatively, "How did it happen this time?"

The nightmare. My mind's effed up way of making sense out of something that didn't.

I'm a scientist; I like answers. If I can't see an immediate solution to a problem, then I search for one. No stone unturned. My mind had decided there was an answer somewhere. I just happened to have a very creative mind while asleep.

In stark contrast to my mind when awake.

I sighed. "Car accident." I shifted uneasily. "Into a river."

"The Neva?" she asked. St. Petersburg was the last location we'd heard from them.

"Yeah," I said, as the plane started moving forward.

Her small hand reached over and clasped mine. It was cold. Like the icy waters of the Neva. "It'll be all right, Mouse," she said softly. "We'll be all right."

I wasn't sure if she was saying that more for herself or me.

"Yeah," I agreed, and let out a slow breath of air that hurt deeply.

We didn't talk again while we went through customs. Both of us lost to our heartache. When would it feel better? When would these incessant dreams cease? Not for the first time, I wished for something normal. For a life without this aching melancholy.

The lines zig-zagged back and forth for what seemed like miles, but we finally made it up to the immigration officer and handed over our passports. Armed security guards stood behind the wall of welcome signs, their eyes hard, their postures alert. I'd never been fingerprinted before, but then I'd never been to America either. Not that I'd ever considered one being synonymous with the other.

The officer asked a few questions, Carrie trying valiantly not to hop around excitedly listening to his accent and no doubt thinking up raunchy things, and then we were through. And our chariot awaited.

It was a Cadillac. An Escalade. It was bigger than my studio apartment.

"We're not in Kansas anymore, Toto," Carrie mock-whispered to me in the back of the vehicle. There was something akin to a rugby field between us. I shot her a shut-up look.

The driver glanced at us in the rearview mirror but didn't say anything.

I closed my eyes and tipped back my head, not wanting to sleep, but too tired to face the craziness of American driving. Every time we'd turned a corner onto the wrong side of the road, I'd cringe. It was bizarre enough that the car had the steering wheel on the left of the vehicle.

Which only made me think of the foreign vehicle that had been in my dream. I'd been sitting on the right, the driver's side. As if I had caused the accident, not them. Did they drive on the left like us in Russia? I didn't know. My nightmares were vivid, but not necessarily accurate.

Something that should have made it easier to breathe.

Carrie bounded out of the SUV when we arrived at the resort, jumping down from the enormous rear seat with unending enthusiasm. That was Carrie; full of beans even after more than a day of travel. Sometimes her energy sustained me. Sometimes her upbeat personality was enough to brighten my day.

It's not that Carrie didn't miss them or grieve them. I could see the wear of their loss on her face. But Carrie and I had a symbiotic relationship. When she was down, I'd pick her up. And when I was, she'd be the clown for me.

Lately, though, I'd been down more than up. I resolved to stop that immediately.

"We can't go straight to bed," I announced after we'd searched every inch of our condo; you never knew what you'd find in a closed drawer. Carrie was lounged out on the sofa, a glass of water in one hand, the resort's information folder in the other.

"Did you know you can order in groceries?" she said, absently.

"Like, to the door?"

"Yeah. And get this: There are thirty different types of beer."

"We do have beer at home too, Carrie."

"Yeah, but not in aluminium bottles."

"You're kidding?" I exclaimed with excessive enthusiasm. Her eyebrow twitched.

"I want one with dinner."

"OK. Then let's go," I said, reaching for my wallet. "There's a restaurant and bar down by the pool."

Carrie slowly placed the folder down and stared off into space. I stood in the centre of the lounge and watched her for a minute. Then moved and sat down beside her, taking her hand.

A tear trickled down her cheek.

"They've got Samuel Adams," she whispered. Dad's favourite beer. He had to buy it online; the local Liquorland didn't stock it. But every time there was an All Blacks match on TV, he'd stock up with his Sam.

"It's going to be all right," I said softly. A pale reflection of her earlier words. Because when Carrie said it, she believed it. Carrie believed in life, wholeheartedly. But when I said it, I was pretending.

How could it be all right? Our world, my world, had ended.

Carrie leant over and rested her head on my shoulder. "I miss them," she admitted. Her voice cracked.

"I do too," I said, my words barely above a whisper.

We stayed like that for several long minutes, and then Carrie donned her sunshine superhero cape again and dashed away the tears.

"Do you think they'll serve us Starbucks at the restaurant?"

"Carrie," I said, shaking my head. "We have Starbucks too, you know." She smirked.

"I did peek at the menu," she said mischievously. I couldn't stop my returning smile. "You can order a NASA Nachos," she announced.

"Um…" I said.

"With Apollo Dip."

"As opposed to Guacamole?"

"It's better than Armstrong Dip."

"Armstrong for avocado," I guessed. My sister was so lame.

She sniggered. "You wanna taco 'bout it? Or do you wanna eat?"

I snorted. She beamed back at me.

"I love you, sis," I said with meaning.

"Nah, you just like my lame-ass jokes."

"Well," I hedged.

She slung her arm through mine and walked us toward the door to the apartment. "You don't have to eat the Nachos. You can save all that for tomorrow."

"Tomorrow?"

Carrie gave me an "Oh, please" look. "As if we're going anywhere other than the Kennedy Space Center tomorrow."

I offered her my own smirk. "I am a scientist," I agreed.

"It's nacho degree that's taking us there," she said straight-faced.

"Carrie!" I groaned, trying not to smile.

"Bad, huh?"

"Terrible."

The door closed with a snap behind us and the warm Florida air wrapped around our bodies. I shivered.

"It'll be all right, Mouse," she whispered as we navigated the pathways.

"I know," I said, and maybe part of me agreed. "But, Carrie?"

"Yeah, Mouse?"

"It's just us now." I swallowed down the agony. "The last two Wyldes."

She didn't say anything for a while. Not until the festive lights dotted around the pool area came into view, and soft music from the bar and restaurant reached out to greet us.

"A promise is a promise, Mimi," she announced as the happy faces of the other resort tourists danced all around us. Their features wavered in the twinkling lights, as my vision blurred with tears again. I blinked them away and tried to breathe.

She stopped and turned to look at me, her face so much older than her twenty-five years. As if she'd lived a lifetime in the past year, just like me. She brushed my hair back and smiled. It was sad, not the Carrie that used to be.

"We reach for our dreams," she said quietly, the hubbub of the poolside surrounding us, but not touching us inside our little bubble.

"And then we return to our lives. You return to your Ph.D," she said with conviction.

I nodded my head. A promise was a promise.

But secretly I knew the scientist in me couldn't let it go. My parents were still missing. Presumed dead.

Even dreams couldn't change those sorts of things.

2

YOU COMING?

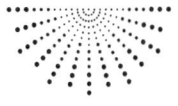

MIMI

"**C**ome on, Mouse! You know you want to."

I most definitely did *not* want to, and Carrie knew damn well.

"We were told to stay together," I hissed back.

"And we'll be together," she insisted. "Like always."

"This is not what they meant, and you know it."

Carrie had always been the adventurous one. Her dream had been Nepal and Mount Everest. Mine had seemed grander at the time, but I realised now that the Outer Space I'd dreamed of since I was a small child was not as vast as the world's tallest mountain.

Unattainable things rarely are.

"How many times have you talked about this?" she asked. We'd talked about it only last night. Over NASA Nachos and Apollo Dip. "And here you are. At last." All thanks to my incorrigible sister. "Just think," she added, laying it on thick now; I could tell, she'd adopted the sing-song voice and whimsical hand motions of an evangelist; an evangelist wearing a sunshine superhero cape, "Neil Armstrong walked here."

"Not quite," I grumbled, kicking my Converse into a mound of sandy dirt. "He would have been on a bus." Not unlike the bus beside us, currently spewing steam out of its innards and fogging up the windows. My dream was off to an inauspicious start.

"My point exactly!" Carrie agreed, moving in for the finale. Her arm snaked around my shoulders, and she swung me to face Launch Pad 39A. She didn't say anything. She just let me look. No words could have convinced me more. This had been my dream. The dream I hoped would conquer my fears when I sleep.

But still…

"There's a reason why they bus us around here," I muttered.

"And there's a reason why our tour bus broke down right beside the one place it all began."

Slightly dramatic, but that was Carrie, too; full of life and wonder and ever-present optimism.

I looked across at my younger-by-three-hundred-seconds - her words, not mine - sister, and saw the strain of the past few months, hidden beneath the thin veneer of our promise. Dark blonde hair, like me. Blue eyes, like me. Five foot five, like me.

Dark rings beneath long lashes adding shadows to high cheek-bones, just like me.

I saw that promise she'd made me. And my reluctant promise to her in return.

The weight of it felt heavy. Living when your heart felt dead was even harder than it seemed.

"OK," I said. "You win."

"I always win, Mouse," she said softly, giving me a tight squeeze, and then looking around surreptitiously. We were standing slightly apart from the other misplaced tourists, but close enough to be seen.

This was so going to backfire. I could feel the handcuffs on my wrists already.

"Quick," Carrie announced suddenly. "The replacement bus is almost here."

I glanced up to see a glint of light reflected off an approaching bus grille, the angle of the sun momentarily blinding.

"Now or never," Carrie whispered urgently, tugging on my arm and pulling me away from the safety - and sanity - of the rule following crowd.

"And how will we get back?" I whispered frantically in reply, second thoughts assaulting me much too late for my intrepid sister to notice.

"We'll wing it," Carrie said excitedly. And for a moment I saw her, the Carrie I'd known all my life. Fun, upbeat, wild. The yin to my yang.

Protests drowned a silent death on my tongue. Sense evaporated on the warm Florida air. And I followed like I'd followed her here, to my dream, not hers.

My chest tightened, and the ever-present threat of tears almost became too much. But I dashed them away with an angry hand and took one last brief look over my shoulder. The group we'd been with were lining up like good little soldiers, waiting to board the new bus and resume their tour from behind the safety of glass walls.

My heart missed a beat, and for a second I felt truly alive again. For a small moment in time, I felt weightless.

I rushed to follow my sister's darting frame as it ducked around a coarse clump of bush out of sight of the bus driver and potential handcuff-wielding officials. My feet felt three sizes too big for my body to make for stealthy manoeuvring, but somehow we made it. Fate, as my mother used say, lending a hand.

Fate and Carrie's penchant for adventure. She'd never met a challenge she couldn't beat.

With a huge grin on my face, I came to rest beside her, bright blue eyes shining wickedly back at me. The world momentarily complete.

And then the roar of the bus's engine reached us and the reality of what we'd done sunk in.

"If I get arrested in America because of you, Carolyn Wylde, I'm gonna haunt you until you die a dastardly death," I said steadily.

Carrie snorted. "Nice Kiwi girl like you in the state penitentiary could do quite well, you know."

"This is insane," I insisted.

"No, Mouse," Carrie said softly. "This is living."

For a heartbeat the past few months caught up with us again, both of us quiet as we remembered our own battle with shock and grief. Perhaps if our parents hadn't have been such big personalities, it wouldn't have hurt so much.

Who was I kidding? It would hurt no matter what. We weren't special, our family. Eccentric, maybe. But not unique.

I blinked away tears, again, and cleared my throat.

"So, are we doing this?"

"Look at you," Carrie teased. "All fired up for your big adventure. I'm so proud. You're practically all grown up."

I play punched her on the upper arm.

"Just don't get used to it. Scientists aren't known for their sense of adventure."

She simply laughed; a sound I hadn't heard enough of recently.

"Come on then, Madame Curie. Let's run an experiment. How exactly did they walk in those space suits?" She started stomping towards the launch pad in an exaggerated Michelin Man gait. Rocking side to side, legs wide, arms outstretched. Armstrong would have been mortified.

I felt my lips spread into a wide grin, my heart healing a little, even as my breath hitched inside my chest. Why did everything hurt so damn much? Why did laughter feel like guilt?

The towering hulk of the launch pad scaffolding cast striped shadows across the concrete towards us as we passed beside the giant liquid hydrogen tank. Until then, most of the details of Launch Pad 39A had been only visible through the digital zoom on our phone-cameras, but as the towers grew in height, and the globe-like tank passed us by, it became obvious that gaining entry into the launch zone itself would be impossible.

Despite the knowledge that we were trespassing - a pastime I had never before attempted - I felt disappointment settle deep inside as we stared up at the security fence. Still a good fifty metres away from the actual place Neil Armstrong, Buzz Aldrin and Michael Collins strapped themselves into Apollo 11 and rode a Saturn V rocket to the moon.

"So close," I whispered, my fingers wrapping themselves around the thankfully not electrified wire fence.

I could see where the water tower released its gallons and gallons of water across the launch pad in an effort to suppress sound. I could see prior scorch marks in the concrete deflection trench, where the blast from ignition would go. I could see how the pad had been modified for the Space Shuttle programme, making it almost unrecognisable to an Apollo astronaut today.

But I was close. So close. Closer than a bus full of tourists.

"It's all right," I said, as much for myself as for Carrie. "It's enough."

"You see," my sister drawled from the *other* side of the security fence, "that's always been your downfall. Dissection you can do. Chemical combustion you're a whizz. But lateral thinking? Hopeless!"

"How did you...What are you...Huh?"

"Now's not the time to impress me with your language skills, Mouse. Get on your knees, sister!" She indicated a hollow barely big enough for a child to crawl through under the fence several feet away. I glanced at it. Glanced at her, noting the dirt stained hands and broken fingernails. And then glanced back at the hollow.

"Are you mad?" I all but screeched.

"Undoubtedly. But that's beside the point, don't you think?"

"Beside the point? Until now, we could have claimed we got lost while taking a pee. This..." I shook my head. "No, Carrie. This is breaking and entering."

Carrie snorted and then started skipping. Away from me.

"Where are you going?" I hissed.

She waved over her shoulder, covering distance like an effing gazelle. In seconds she was beside the launch pad. A minute later she was knocking on the Fixed Service Structure Tower.

I was equal parts impressed, jealous, and out of my mind with worry. I gnawed on my bottom lip.

"You coming?" she mouthed, stroking the scaffolding as though it was the bunched muscles of one of those airboat captains she'd talked about yesterday.

I shook my head and took a step backwards. Away from her.

The look of disappointment on her face was brief but telling. I was never an adventurer like Carrie.

She smiled softly, forgiving me my foibles so easily. And then let go of the tower, taking a step back towards the fence line.

Then she stopped. Her head turned sharply, then cocked at an angle to the side, as if better to see something. She raised her hand to her eyes, as though to shield herself from a bright light. But I couldn't see any light from where I was standing. I couldn't see what had made her pause, at all. Then she took a step forward. Slowly. Hesitantly. Reluctantly, but not.

As though she was being drawn inexorably towards something. Something only she could see.

"Carrie?" I said, not nearly loud enough for her to hear.

I watched as my sister took one more step.

And then I watched as she walked completely out of sight. Not behind a structure. Not hidden by shadow. But simply out of sight.

My breath held. My chest tightened. The wire on the fence dug into each finger on my hands.

Sounds seemed distorted, but I could have sworn I heard a roar and then utter silence.

"Carrie!" I shouted in earnest now, diving for the hollow.

3
THIS WASN'T HAPPENING

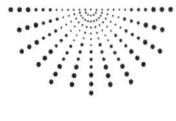

MIMI

*M*y butt was too big; I could feel the wire from the bottom of the fence tearing my jeans. Holes appeared on my knees where I used them for leverage, shuffling and squirming like a landlocked eel. I grunted and groaned, spitting the odd expletive out with the odd bit of sand along with it. Who'd have thought Florida soil could be so vexing?

Dragging myself out the other side, I thanked Carrie's digging skills and cursed the soil composition in this part of the world. Easy to dig. Just as easy to collapse again. But I'd made it. And I was on Launch Pad 39A. I dusted myself off and then started running.

In seconds, I'd made it to the spot where Carrie had disappeared. Searching frantically, breathing erratically, sweating profusely. And finding absolutely nothing to indicate where she had gone to.

Not. A. Damn. Thing. At. All.

"Carrie?" I called out, albeit quietly. I have no idea why I was whispering. "If this is some kind of joke..." I didn't finish the threat. It didn't feel right to.

Nothing about this place felt right.

Which was ridiculous. This was *the* place. *The* launch pad. Apollo

11 had flown from here. Not on wings, but a rocket. This spot. Right here.

And I couldn't even enjoy it.

Panic had taken hold.

"Carolyn Abigail Wylde!" I snapped, walking the same area again and again. "This is not funny!"

There was no reply.

"God damn it, Carrie," I said, my voice cracking. I started searching farther afield. Walking beneath the massive FSS, and then its neighbouring RSS. Both the Fixed and Rotating Service Structures hid nothing. Minutes ticked by as I scoured every inch of the launch pad, long minutes - it was effin' huge! - getting up close and personal with a site not too many people got to see so intimately.

But as much as I would have exploded with happiness under different circumstances, it was sheer angst that propelled me across the pad, down onto the crawler-transporter platform area, and even up into the tower itself.

Finally, I had to face the truth; a not unusual hardship for a scientist, even one who refused to finish her doctoral degree. But this truth lacked reason. And without reason what was I?

Carrie had gone. Like my parents had gone. Simply vanished.

I walked slowly back to where I had last seen her, staring sightlessly down at a non-descriptive concrete slab.

This didn't make any sense. But I had no alternative hypothesis to work on. Not even an effing clue where to start.

I sank to my butt on the surprisingly warm concrete and tried, for the hundredth time the past few months, not to bawl.

And that's where they found me.

Their arrival was heralded by a spray of grit from spinning tires and blue flashing lights on top of an oversized vehicle. It skidded to a stop several metres away, the world skidding to a stop along with it, and two bulky figures jumped out as though they'd trained for this exact moment...Repeatedly.

My hands were in the air before the first gun was levelled on me; a deeply unnerving sensation taking hold in my gut. Those guns were real.

"Don't move!" one man ordered. I froze. Hell, I might have danced the Macarena if he'd asked it of me right then. "Where's the other one?" he yelled, making me want to flinch and ruin the whole not moving part of this scenario.

"She's g..gone," I managed to stammer, my hands still held aloft, my neck craning to look up at the approaching threat.

I could see the handcuffs hanging from his belt from here.

Shit!

The officer talking nodded for his partner to move forward while he continued to aim that *real* gun at my chest. The other one replaced his own weapon in its holster on his hip, velcroing it in place - it's strange what you notice at times like this - and then retrieving the handcuffs from farther along his thick belt.

I looked around frantically for my sister, half crazy with fright and a whole lot pissed off at the situation. I could just imagine Carrie watching from the White Room laughing her arse off.

The cold bite of steel did it. I started to cry.

How had my life become so surreal? How had my world turned upside down? They'd never accept me into the astronaut training programme now.

A hitched breath - halfway between sob and laughter - left me, as the officer hauled me to my feet and led me to their truck. I realised on closer inspection that it wasn't a police car; more like Kennedy Space Center Security minus the KSC logo. Nice. Keeping it all low key.

Maybe I could avoid official arrest, after all.

The ride was silent and uncomfortable. I couldn't find my balance what with my hands tied behind my back. But the distance, at least, was short. Even if any childhood dreams of joining NASA's space programme were now well and truly thwarted, I'd at least made it to the Launch Control Center. Right next to the VAB.

I snuck a glance in through the massive over-height doors of the

Vehicle Assembly Building and saw a jagged, smoking hole in the side of the building, leading away toward Launch Pad 39A.

No wonder they weren't talking arrest; they'd just had a major incident and civilians had been caught in the crossfire. The threat of a lawsuit was probably forefront on their minds.

My stomach churned as the puzzle pieces came together. Carrie had been taken out by my dream.

My eyes landed on the sixty-three-metre high American flag painted on the side of the VAB and the reality of what had happened hit hard. Carrie was gone. And I was in a foreign country. I might have grown up with American culture in TV shows and movies. I might have dreamt of one day working here and being part of that American Dream. But even though I spoke their language, this land was still so very foreign to me. The sheer might and vast power of the place dwarfed me. Made it hard to breathe.

I automatically moved to rub my temples, my head pounding; only to fall over sideways when my wrists met resistance and consequently tangle myself up in the seatbelt.

One look from the officer who opened my door said it all. What planet had I landed from?

What world had I arrived in?

The officer extricated me with surprising care and assisted me down from the super-sized vehicle. Then led me towards the Launch Control Center. Even as my eyes darted everywhere trying to take in each minute detail of this iconic building, my mind reeled attempting to make sense of what had happened. Of what might still happen once I got inside there. I'd been in police stations before, rescuing Carrie and her friends from protest rally mix-ups. But visiting them as a rescuer was a different thing altogether than walking into one in handcuffs. Of course, this wasn't a police station, but it sure as hell had the appearance of one.

X-Ray machines and security gates. Closed circuit video cameras and surly looking receptionists. More of the same uniformed officers as the two escorting me. Hard eyes landed on my face as we progressed through the entrance area. Some scowled. Some rested their hands on their holstered weapons. If they were afraid of being sued, then they had a strange way of avoiding inflaming a situation.

I hunched my shoulders and kept my head down, not even taking in the LCC in all its glory.

The officers took me to a small room straight out of *Law & Order: Special Victims Unit*. The requisite harsh lighting, small table and two chairs made up the entirety of the whitewashed room. I sat down without having to be told, the handcuffs removed in utter silence. Other than the two sentences shouted at me when they'd arrived at the launch pad, the officers hadn't said a word.

The door clicked shut behind them, and I waited. My mind running over the turn of events and Carrie's bizarre disappearance unsuccessfully. No matter which way I looked at it, I couldn't make sense of a damn thing.

One minute she was there.

The next she was not.

The minutes ticked by and became hours. I knocked on the door demanding attention and received none. If I was being watched, I couldn't see the camera or two-way mirror. Eventually, I gave up hammering on the locked door and yelling myself hoarse and sat down in the chair resting my head on the table.

And that's where they found me. Two suit wearing men who screamed FBI or NSA.

I was in so much trouble.

I sat back and took in the hard glint in the eyes of the dark blue suit wearing official. The salt and pepper ex-military haircut. The chiselled jawline they write about in books. Next to him was a slightly scruffier version, with a slightly less officious look, in a brown suit with equally short but somehow not military-esque hairstyle, this time in brown. To match the suit.

Brown suit was FBI, then.

Blue suit was the one to be wary of.

"Miss Wylde," brown suit began. "I'm Special Agent Carter. FBI."

Bingo. "This is Special Agent Dawson from the NSA." Two for two. "Do you understand what we are?" His question was delivered with a friendly smile. I didn't trust it.

"Federal agents," I said quietly.

"Do you understand what we do?" Still in that friendly tone I didn't trust.

I shook my head.

"We investigate domestic criminal activity." It sounded so simple, save for that one word.

"Am I the criminal in this situation?" I asked, working hard to keep my voice level.

Carter pulled out the opposite chair to mine and sat. Dawson remained mute, aloof, and threatening.

"You tell me," Special Agent Carter asked.

"My sister..."

"Yes," Carter interrupted. "Carolyn Abigail Wylde. Twenty-five years old. Native of New Zealand. What about her? Care to tell us where she went?"

If he was aiming for all-knowing and creepy, he was nailing it. The fake friendly smile only increased the *Twilight Zone* feel.

I clenched my fists in a sudden spurt of rage. Both men noticed. But I'd had enough. It happens.

"She was fine until you lost control of one of your rockets!" That hole in the VAB *had* to have been caused by something.

Carter leant forward. Dawson remained statue still.

"What rocket?"

I snorted. "Great. You're going to deny it. What? My word against yours? And I'm not backed by the U.S. Government."

"What rocket, Miss Wylde?"

I shook my head and firmed my lips into a thin line.

Carter sighed. "I can't help you if you don't talk."

I made a scoffing sound. Carter frowned. The first time his facial expression appeared remotely believable.

He stared at me for a long moment and then shrugged, standing up from the table and moving into the corner of the room. I worked hard on not showing a reaction. But when Dawson came forward and sat himself down where Carter had been, it was almost impossible to hide my fear.

He pulled a file out of nowhere and proceeded to open it, flipping through pages methodically.

"A Master of Science from the University of Auckland." I blinked. "Double major in Chemistry and Biology. Part way through your Ph.D. Quite impressive." I was sure he'd been impressed by greater things than my degree. And probably greater things than my still unfinished Ph.D.

"Did you use a bomb?" Dawson suddenly said, breaking into my musings with the power of a sledgehammer. Or C4 explosion.

"Wh...what?"

"To damage the Vehicle Assembly Building," he said conversationally. "What did you and your sister have planned for Launch Pad 39A?"

"I..."

"We've got you on camera," he added. "No bags, so we assume the bomb was placed earlier, and you were planning your next move. But we don't understand why the bomb went off now. Before you had a chance to sabotage the launch pad."

This was crazy. Completely insane.

"Make a mistake, Miss Wylde?"

"What? No!"

"Your sister then? Is that why you had a falling out?"

"We didn't fall out..."

"Did she sabotage your plans? Desert you? Leave you to take the blame."

"She vanished..."

"And set the explosion off while you were still there."

"She didn't explode anything!"

"So, you admit the bomb was all yours?"

"What? No!"

21

"You keep saying that, but your sister is missing, and there's a hole in the side of the VAB. And the only person left standing is you."

I started shaking my head.

"You have the skills and knowledge," Dawson insisted. "You came directly to the Kennedy Space Center upon landing in Florida. You haven't even visited a theme park."

"I like science. NASA."

"Then why sabotage Orion?"

"I didn't..."

"Three people are dead, Miss Wylde." Oh, God. "Because of you."

"No!"

"No?" He shook his head, abruptly stood up, and produced a set of handcuffs from his back pocket.

I admit I flinched when he snapped them on.

"Let's see if we can jog your memory," Dawson said harshly, dragging me from the relative safety of the interview room.

We passed no one. The entire ten-minute walk was devoid of people.

Until we got there. To the VAB.

It was huge. Enormous. I could picture Saturn V rockets standing tall inside its enormous walls. The largest building by volume in the world and I was dragged unceremoniously into it without an ounce of fanfare. My hands cuffed securely at my back, Special Agent Dawson of the NSA fisting the collar of my shirt tightly. Carter now the brooding, silent one at our backs.

People stopped what they were doing and watched; the looks I received here so much more lethal. These people wanted me dead. Dead like the three tarpaulin covered forms on the scorched concrete.

Dawson tugged me over towards the bodies and the hole in the wall. It was big, bigger than me. And yet on the side of the Vehicle Assembly Building, it seemed tiny.

"Is this what you and your sister wanted?" he demanded. "Death on U.S. soil? A halt to Orion? What's your endgame?" He shook me roughly. "Who do you align with?" Another shake. Another teeth clattering rough-up. "What's your manifesto?"

Words and demands spewed out of him, too quick for me to translate. My brain was on shutdown, my eyes glued to the still forms under the sheets, a humid breeze slipping in through the gaping hole on the side of the structure, but unable to touch me.

"You'll be lucky if you ever see New Zealand again," Dawson hissed in my ear.

I looked up at him. I saw no softness there. They thought I was a terrorist. They thought I'd done this. They thought I had a message to deliver to the world.

Something had happened here that they didn't understand. And if *they* didn't, then how could I? Carrie was missing.

Three men were dead.

And I was about to be locked away for a very long time for something I had no hand in.

"I want a lawyer," I said numbly.

Dawson sneered. "I thought you would." He spun me around and started to drag me away, but another agent approached; halting us in our tracks. Shoving me to my knees, making the hard concrete bite into flesh, he growled, "Stay put."

I bit back a cry of pain, but he'd already turned away.

I realised I was panting slightly; my wrists were chafed raw where the too tight cuffs had dug in. Bruises were forming on my knees, my upper arm where the agent had gripped me, and deep inside my chest. My head hurt. My heart ached. I felt so very alone.

The weight of accusatory glares weighed down on me, bowing my back, hunching my shoulders. Making it even harder to catch my breath.

This couldn't be happening. This was a nightmare.

Carrie. Carrie and her stupid dream chasing.

Oh, God. Carrie.

Then on that wretched thought, bizarrely and suddenly, a billowing, surreal cloud started to form around me. I blinked rapidly, but the vision didn't waver. Rust reds and deep mauves, shot through with sunlight yellow. I was sure I was hallucinating. It flowed mesmerisingly, billowing up as high as the one-hundred-sixty-metre tall roof. I stared at it dumbfounded. It engulfed me, little pinpricks of dazzling bright lights blinding, sparkling behind my eyelids.

I couldn't breathe.

And then a roar of jet-like engines engulfed me, followed by the eerie and utter silence of space.

4

MOUSE

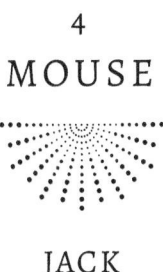

JACK

*T*he communicator buzzing woke me from a vivid dream. So real I could have sworn I felt her. I shook my head, trying to dislodge the disquieting sensation of realism where reality did not exist and reached for the device on my bedside table.

"Yes?" I said into the mouthpiece; experience of abrupt awakenings having me sounding far more alert than I actually was.

"Dr Evans," a voice said clearly in my ear. "We've got a rip in the fabric. It's...It's rather big, sir."

"Bigger than yesterday's?"

"The biggest we've seen yet. Dr Crawford thinks it might be an originating tear."

"Does he?" I queried doubtfully. Clive Crawford would have us believing our troubles were almost over every other day. I knew better. "I'll be right there." The communicator chirped as the dispatcher disconnected without another word.

Clearly ruffled.

I scrubbed a hand over my face, trying to dislodge the sensation of disquiet which had invaded my mind since waking. The dream didn't help. They never did. Making quick work of freshening up, I was dressed in a standard jumpsuit and striding down the hallway to control. If this was a category one rip, then we needed to fly immediately.

I walked into utter chaos. Which wasn't saying much, RATS was often in chaos.

"What have you got?" I said, moving to the dispatcher's screen.

"The rip appeared five minutes ago, sir," she replied curtly. "It set off all the alarms immediately."

I studied the sinusoid on the screen feeling unsettled. Something about this one was going to be big. Not just the height of the curve, nor the length. It was the colour. Bright orange. The same International Orange as our flight suits.

"I don't like the look of this one, Jack," a gruff voice said from over my shoulder. I swung a gaze towards my colleague, but my eyes were soon back on the sine wave on the screen.

"Crawford," I said in way of greeting.

"That colour," he murmured, mirroring my thoughts exactly.

"Well, only one way to find out," I offered. "My team?" I asked the dispatcher. I always seemed to forget her name. Susan? Sarah? They changed so often.

"Your Intern is Rafe Hoffman. Your Novitiate Sally Groves."

I nodded my head, accepting the printout she handed me, as Crawford said, "Do you think it wise?"

I arched a brow in question. Clive Crawford could talk in riddles until the cows came home.

"Training on a mission such as this," he clarified.

"It's standard procedure," I argued.

"This hardly looks standard, Jack, and you know it." He huffed out a breath, flapping his jowls in consternation. My gaze drifted back to the screen.

"Is there ever anything standard about what we do, Clive?"

He humphed good-naturedly, but I felt his disquiet. I recognised it. It matched mine.

Why did the wave have to be orange?

Why now? After *that* dream.

Dreams weren't unusual for Surgeons. But such vivid ones? I could swear I still smelled her perfume.

"Are the others ready?" I asked the dispatcher.

"Meeting you on the pad, Doctor."

"Will you watch the launch from here, Clive?" I asked the RATS Chief Surgeon. "Or from the pad itself?"

Clive met my eyes, the worry and concern I saw before shielded behind his usual affable façade.

"Wouldn't miss it, old boy!" he said jovially, slapping me on the shoulder and picking up his walking stick. I followed him from the room, as he limped away from me, his gait more pronounced than normal. Perhaps his way of reminding me just how wrong missions could go.

The hangar was chilly this early in the morning, but hardly sleepy. Technicians hustled to and fro, tablet computers or simple screwdrivers in hand. Excitement ripe on the air. Even a few Surgeons who weren't scheduled to fly were gathered in the observation room. Crawford offered a firm handshake and then limped towards them. His presence alone heightening the mood.

I let out a slow breath of air and approached my flight crew.

"Good morning," I said in greeting, catching the attention of Rafe Hoffman and Sally Groves.

"Dr Evans," the Novitiate greeted. "It's a pleasure to be assigned to your command, sir."

I returned her smile out of habit, accepting Hoffman's silent handshake while I did it.

"Have you seen the colour?" Rafe asked.

"Yes." I studied the MPCV, then started to make my visual preflight check. Hoffman and Groves followed as I walked the circumference of the Vehicle.

"Do you think..?" Rafe began.

"We won't know until we plot the course," I said, interrupting him.

"Sure," he offered, but I heard the unsaid. He was worried too.

Why did it have to be orange?

"It's not likely to be anything too dangerous, though, is it?" Groves stated. I halted in my tracks. Rafe pretended he hadn't heard her and kept on walking.

"I mean," she said, "you wouldn't take a Novitiate with you if it were. Would you?"

I studied her for a moment. She'd been trailing Bryan Fawkes for the past twelve weeks, doing rather well from what he'd relayed. But this line of questioning was a concern.

"What is it we do here, Miss Groves?" I asked quietly.

"We mend Time, sir."

"And of the many trips you've undertaken with Dr Fawkes were there any in which things did not go well?"

She bit the side of her lower lip in consideration, a wisp of her tightly coiled brunette hair floating down over hazel eyes. She was petite and pretty. And from all reports highly intelligent. But intelligence only got you so far at RATS. Playing Surgeon to Time took courage.

Miss Groves needed to prove to me she had it. Perhaps that was why Fawkes had handed her off all of a sudden.

"Well, sir," she said. "No."

I frowned. Lucky bugger. Bryan owed me a beer or two, then.

"Be prepared for anything, Miss Groves," I instructed. "Time is fluid. Rips disturb the flow. If the tear is big enough, it can destroy it. And any Surgeon who happens to be close."

I continued towards the door to the Crew Vehicle, slipping inside and finding Rafe at the controls. The time rip's sine wave was displayed on one screen, the bright orange noticeable as soon as you entered the main cabin. A still shot took up the majority of the second screen, salient points in regards to location and customs were listed beside it. All in International Orange.

"A category one rip, then," I commented quietly.

Rafe met my gaze. "It's an origin tear, Jack. Maybe *the* origin tear."

"Why wasn't it picked up in Dispatch?" a small voice said from behind me. I stepped to the side, allowing Miss Groves ingress.

"Because the event is unravelling in real time," Rafe explained, inputting coordinates, and handing me his equations to check.

Groves stepped closer to the screen and narrowed her eyes.

"Bloody hell," she muttered. "That's..."

"Yes," I said, handing Rafe the co-ordinates back with a nod. "Cape Canaveral, Florida."

"And th..the time?" she asked on a stutter.

Rafe looked at me but said nothing; he was letting me field this one.

"1969."

"Thank goodness," she said on a breath of air. "Prior to the first Origin Event."

What the hell had Fawkes been teaching her?

I raised an eyebrow at Rafe; this one was all his for the taking. And then turned to the open door. Reaching out, I waved up at the viewing room, catching the shielded look of concern on Crawford's face, and then accepted the door as it was closed by a technician. I'd checked the locks by the time Rafe had explained a few basic tenets to Miss Groves.

"The wave indicates possible planes, you see," he was saying. "At any given point, Time can shift."

"But we're going past the OE."

"In linear time, yes. But the location is also a dimension. And a major contributing factor in a temporal paradox."

"What is a temporal paradox, Miss Groves?" I asked, taking my seat at the helm.

"A causal loop, sir. A paradox of Time. Where a future event is the cause of a past event." Recited verbatim.

"And where are we going?" I asked, starting our pre-flight internal checks.

"Cape Canaveral," she said quietly.

"Buckle yourself in," I ordered just as quietly, allowing the girl to settle her nerves with the familiar. Once checks had been completed, and our Novitiate sat securely in her seat, I turned to her and said, "The original Origin Event occurred decades after 1969, as you know. But it occurred at The Kennedy Space Center."

"Yes, sir," she said, attempting to raise her voice above a whisper.

"You'll be fine, Groves," Rafe offered. "Jack's never lost a Novitiate yet."

I was quite sure I heard a very subdued, "There's always a first."

I grimaced. Flicked the last remaining switch bringing power to our boosters. And said, "Relax. This isn't my first rodeo."

The MPCV shuddered, the lights flickered, outside a dense nebula would have formed, miniature stars shining brightly, and then we shifted.

Usually a rather smooth motion, but this time the entire Crew Vehicle vibrated, the sound of grinding alloys deafening to the ears, followed by a reprieve of space-like silence. And then the entire module convulsed, our seat belts - which rarely saw any use - straining, sparks flying, the console flickering, and dear sweet Miss Groves screaming above it all.

I actually held my breath.

With a screech and a horrendous thud, felt right through to the seat of my pants, the Vehicle stuttered, trembled, and then spluttered. Blackness engulfed us momentarily, and then the blinding brightness of a thousand stars.

When it all righted itself again, I let a slow breath of air out.

"Everyone all right?" I asked.

"All clear," Rafe said immediately. "Time corresponds with calculations. We're in 1969. Location fits too."

"Good," I said as if I'd expected little else.

Truth be told, that had been an extremely rough flight, and we'd be doing extensive checks before attempting another. We might be in 1969 for a while.

"Miss Groves?" I queried, turning in my chair to check on the Novitiate.

Who was staring wide eyed at the back if the MPCV. I followed the trajectory of her gaze and felt the blood drain from my face, leaving me embarrassingly light headed.

"Has that ever happened on one of your rodeos before, sir?" Groves asked, pointing at the object of my bloodless fascination.

"What's that now?" Rafe queried, turning in his own seat. "Bloody hell!" He all but fell off his perch in fright.

Dishevelled, handcuffed it would seem, and stunned immobile. But I would have recognised her anywhere. I'd not long ago been rather close to her in my dream.

"Who are you?" I asked, surprised I could voice a single thing.

"Why is she here is the better question," Rafe exclaimed.

No. I rather thought I knew why. Origin Events never go smoothly.

The woman looked around the Crew Vehicle eyes wide, expression beyond confused, and then her gaze landed on me. Or more precisely my flight suit. She showed absolutely no shock at the colour or design; I could have sworn she recognised it. Our roots at the Academy were very deep.

"Who are you?" I demanded abruptly, making Groves jump in her seat and Rafe reach for his sidearm.

Tension, thick and heavy, enveloped the module.

"Your name?" Rafe reiterated, his weapon aimed at her chest.

She squeaked. The handcuffs rattled.

And then she whispered, "Mouse."

5

BLOODY HELL, INDEED

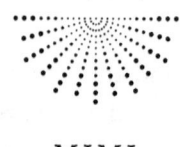

MIMI

The world turned topsy-turvy. Lights and colours flashed around my head. They sped up. They slowed down. Fast. Slow. Fast. Slow. Fast. Fast. Faster. My body revolted. Three Gs. Four. Five. There was no way to tell, but my head was spinning, and my mind was a blur.

I felt sick to my stomach, but more importantly, I felt like this might just be the end.

I cried out, but no sound was made. I tried to move my hands, but whether the cuffs restricted movement, or the centrifugal force made that impossible, I didn't know.

Within seconds, I think, it was over, and I was sitting unceremoniously on a rather cold metal floor.

I'd been on concrete, hadn't I? Or maybe not. The room spun, lights flickered, and then everything slowed down and kept slowing down, like a spinning top losing kinetic energy.

I sucked in a breath of air, thankful to still be breathing, and then blinked away spots. I was dizzy, nauseous, and a little spacey; as if I'd drunk too many Margaritas at Cocktail Hour.

Nothing looked right. Nothing made sense. For what felt like minutes, I stared at a scene that simply did not compute.

Lights and dials, switches and screens, wires and toggles. I couldn't identify more than that, but I did know one thing.

I wasn't in the VAB.

It smelled different for starters. Closed in and stuffy. A hint of overworked electrical wiring met my nose, the tang of perfume mixed with sweat. Aftershave? Something spicy.

I blinked again, making out figures. People. Chairs, like astronaut seats; moulded to the body. I swallowed, tasted aniseed. Aniseed? Then felt the world contract, expand, and finally settle.

"Miss Groves?" a voice said.

Who the hell was Miss Groves and what the hell had happened to Carter and Dawson?

My eyes watered with the effort to focus, but slowly details became clearer. The voice belonged to a man, sitting in what had to be the command chair. Tall, if the length of those long legs tucked under the instrument panel would indicate, thick auburn hair, brushed back from his face, broad shoulders covered in the brightest shade of orange available. Rescue Orange they called it or considering he was wearing NASA coveralls, International Orange.

Test pilot? Technician? Astronaut?

How the hell did I get here?

My head spun, my stomach flipped, and I'd had just about enough of that, thank you very much. Today just did not make any sense whatsoever.

I blinked up at the guy in orange, vaguely aware there were other people in here with us as well, when a female voice said, "Has that ever happened on one of your rodeos before, sir?"

My still slightly blurry gaze had naturally tracked to the female, also in orange, but with a tight brown bun on top of her head. Her eyes were as big as flying saucers.

Much like the man's were when I felt myself drawn back to his face.

His nose was crooked, just slightly, giving an air of roughness to an otherwise striking face. There was a small scar along his jawline, bisecting a day's worth of dark stubble, which I hadn't noticed before then. It was stark white, much like the rest of his pale skin.

"What's that now?" the third occupant of the room said. But I didn't look away from the first man. I'm not sure I could have.

"Who are you?" the first voice asked, tone steady.

"Why is she here is the better question," the other man said, something I would have dearly liked the answer to, as well.

"Who are you?" the original man repeated, this time with a hint of demand in his tone.

My heartbeat faltered. I could feel myself beginning to sweat. Oh, God. Not again. First Carter and Dawson, and now these people.

"Your name?" the second man ordered, and that's when I noticed the gun.

I squeaked. The handcuffs rattled.

And then I whispered, "Mouse."

"Mouse?" the one clearly in charge asked. "You're going with that?"

Sometimes, when I'm pushed too far, when things just get too much, I snap. It takes a lot. It's not my go-to setting. I'm usually more analytical than that. But it *can* happen. Carrie has a unique way of drawing my darker side out. She calls it my Hyde-side. And woe betide anyone who is faced with it.

Hearing the condescension in his tone, I went all Hyde.

"*What* exactly does *that* mean?"

"The entire gamut of names to pluck from thin air and you choose a rodent," he said equably.

"It's a nickname," I growled in defence.

"Pardon me?" He was British, I realised. Pompous and an arse. How had NASA accepted this one? They had a certain advocacy to uphold, astronauts. They were the face of the Space Program; they needed to be charming.

This one might have fitted the role of handsome and buffed - there were muscles under that flight suit, I had checked - but charming was not a word I'd associate with him. At all.

I narrowed my eyes and shook my hair back off my face - better to

34

glare at him - a movement that caused me to lose balance. Stupid handcuffs.

"Mimi," I said, grinding my teeth. "My name is Mimi." I dared him to laugh with a lift of my chin.

Carrie had lucked out on the name front. Taken the smidgeon of normalcy my parents had and claimed it for herself. Being the second born sometimes had its benefits. My parents tried everything out on me. Those three-hundred seconds might as well have been months for all the good being a twin did me.

The guy just stared for a suspended moment and then cleared his throat.

"Mimi *Mouse?*" he asked. "That's even worse."

The other guy snorted but didn't lower the gun. The girl just attempted not to smile.

I took a deep breath. It didn't work. It had been a very tiring day. And then I snapped. Mimi style.

With infinite precision, I said, "Eff you!"

"Ah, the mouse has claws," he drawled. Sarcastic bastard. "I wasn't aware many young women in the 60s used such language."

"She is in handcuffs," the gun wielder pointed out.

"She's not from the 60s," the girl immediately offered.

The one in charge stilled.

"What day is it?" he asked, looking at me.

"Tuesday," I offered.

"Date. Date," he snapped back.

"Eff. You," I helpfully supplied.

He let out a huff of air and pinched the bridge of his nose for a moment. Eyes closed. Head down. I was intrigued, I admit it. I shouldn't have been. For any number of reasons. But he carried an air of command that drew the eye, mixed in with a smattering of vulnerability.

I think my presence here had thrown him off kilter.

Well, welcome to the club.

"What date do you think it is?" I asked. It was a peace offering, but

I'm not sure he realised. He lifted his head and looked at me, but no one uttered a sound, let alone replied.

I let out a frustrated breath of air.

"You know, I dreamed about coming here," I said, noting the way the man in charge frowned. "I used to drive my sister crazy with stories about space ships. *Apollo 13* is my all-time favourite movie. I made her watch it a dozen times."

The silence from all three orange jumpsuit wearing strangers was almost defeating.

So, I forged on. I was beyond caring if *anything I said could be used against me*, now. That boat had long sailed. Maybe that was Special Agent Dawson's plan. Frighten me beyond reason, wear me down completely, confuse the hell out of me, and then throw me in here - I took a brief moment to look around the confined space and orientate myself; a command module, possibly an Orion capsule, I realised - with the object of my supposed evil fixation.

"And finally I get here," I said with a handcuff rattling shoulder shrug for emphasis. "After, you know, a shit year. Carrie insisted we come to Florida first. See the sights. Walk where Armstrong walked. All that jazz. Only to have you lot act like a bunch of Nazis, just because we dug a little hole under the chain link fence to get better pictures of 39A."

The handcuffs clinked loudly again, drawing everyone's eye to my shrugging shoulders. My sigh was louder. Perhaps nonchalance was not the most appropriate behaviour, but along with a sudden onset of Hydism, from time to time, I also tended to overdo "not bothered".

"And now she's gone," I finished. A full stop if ever there was one. "And none of you even care."

"*Apollo 13*," the gun wielder suddenly said, looking at something on his screen. "Released in 1995 by Universal Pictures."

The one in charge swallowed thickly.

"She's out of time," gun wielder added.

And I squeaked again, all semblance of nonchalance forgotten, shuffling backwards, feeling the hard edge of something metal at my back.

"I've co-operated!" I shouted. "I didn't mean to trespass. I just wanted to walk where Armstrong had walked. You know, live the dream. We had nothing to do with the bomb!"

The gun came back up again; I hadn't realised it had lowered at all until then.

"What bomb?" the prick in charge said.

"The hole in the side of the VAB," I rushed to say. "The hole you think we made."

They all shared a look. The girl blanched considerably. The gun wielder tightened his hold on the gun.

"What do you want to do, boss?" he asked, confirming who exactly was in charge here.

The boss looked at me. His steady gaze enough to still my rapidly beating heart. Ridiculous, but that whisky shade seemed safe, somehow. Where everything else screamed danger. Our eyes locked. Time stopped. Or that's what it felt like to me. I have no way of knowing what it felt like for him. As far as I know, he could have been contemplating how to remove bloodstains from orange jumpsuits.

"What date do *you* think it is, Mimi the Mouse?" he asked softly, surprising me. "What century?"

I felt the fight drain out of me, my shoulders relaxed, giving my poor scraped wrists a much-needed break.

The guy could do voodoo with that gentle tone of his.

I licked my lips. His eyes followed the movement. Then flicked back up to mine. He raised an eyebrow. Cocked his head. Waited patiently for my reply.

"Twenty-first," I finally said, the words drawn from deep within, it felt.

"Bloody hell," gun wielder said.

"I don't understand," the girl offered. On closer inspection, I thought she might not be too much younger than me. A year or two at most. Hardly a girl. But the way she cowered made you think naïve, innocent, frightened. Even I wanted to protect her.

"Do your checks, Dr Hoffman" the leader guy finally said, his steady gaze never leaving me. "Write up the log, Miss Groves. An accurate reflection of what has transpired, if you please."

"I'm not sure I understand what *has* transpired, sir," she admitted with some reluctance.

"Retell it how you see it, Novitiate."

"Yes, sir," she replied and turned away toward a small screen.

That left the leader looking at me.

"Do you have a surname, Mimi?" he asked in that gentle tone that seemed to unlock something inside me. "Or must I continue to use...Mimi?" He said my given name as though it were a joke.

The lock snapped shut again. If I'd been able to, I would have crossed my arms over my chest in defiance.

The rattle of the handcuffs caught his ear. He frowned.

"Are you a criminal?"

"She *did* use the word 'bomb,'" the one called Hoffman helpfully supplied, not turning around from his own screen.

"Yes, thank you," his boss said. "I was also present at the time."

"Just making sure we don't forget the 'bomb,'" Hoffman offered.

"Would you stop saying 'bomb,'" the girl, Miss Groves he'd called her, pleaded.

"Mimi?" the one in charge pressed. "And for God's sake, tell me your real name."

Hoffman snorted. Groves grimaced. Both looked pityingly upon their boss.

I smiled sweetly.

"Mimi Blossom Wylde," I said, articulating each name with the utmost care. "My parents were hippies. Three-hundred seconds later they reformed."

"Reformed?" he asked, looking faintly aghast.

"My twin sister is named Carolyn Abigail," I explained, enjoying his reaction.

"Ah," he murmured. "I think I might understand 'Mouse' better now."

I attempted to smile, but I wasn't sure if it reached my eyes. I missed Carrie.

"And the handcuffs...Mimi?" I did smile then. Of course, he was too uptight to use "Mouse."

"Launch Pad 39A."

"Nothing in the data banks," Hoffman supplied. "Whatever transpired was either mended or was kept quiet."

"Orion was in its infancy," the boss said.

I rolled my eyes at the mental moniker I'd assigned him and said, "Er, what's *your* name?"

He blinked. Then nothing.

"He's Hoffman." I nodded at the man in question. "She's Groves." Same head nod for the woman. "You're their boss." Another nod, this time to him.

He smiled. "You picked that up rather quickly. What else have you learned?"

"That you're dodging the question."

"Oh snap!" Hoffman muttered under his breath, but we all heard him. Groves chuckled, then looked mortified that she'd made a sound. And the bossman scowled.

It looked good on him.

I raised an eyebrow when his gaze returned to mine.

"Jack Evans," he said. "Surgeon," he added and winced.

Hoffman did snort at that.

"For NASA?" I asked. "And they put you in command? I thought surgeons were specialists only. Can you fly too?"

"Ah," Jack Evans, Surgeon, replied. "That's all rather irrelevant, right now. What we need to know is more about this..." He shot a look at Hoffman, who offered a wide grin in reply. "Bomb," Evans said with a sigh. "More about the bomb, Miss Wylde, if you please."

I looked at Hoffman and then at Evans and finally flicked a glance towards Groves. All three blinked owlishly back at me.

"Where *have* you been?" I said slowly. Groves smiled sympathetically. Hoffman remained mute, but there was a softening around the eyes.

Evans said, "Consider us new arrivals, Miss Wylde. We were...in transit and missed all the action."

"In transit from where?" I pressed. Something wasn't right.

"That's classified," Evans offered. I flicked a glance at Hoffman, but he wasn't scoffing this time.

"Classified, huh?" I murmured. "Just tell me one thing, did Special Agents Dawson or Carter put you up to this?"

"NSA and FBI, respectively," Hoffman said quietly, reading off his tablet screen.

"I guess not, huh?" I whispered.

"Miss Wylde," Evans started.

"Mimi," I offered, feeling so very tired all of a sudden. I guess there's a limit to how much confusion a body can take. I'd reached mine. "Or Mouse, if you've got the courage," I added, stifling a yawn.

Evans smiled. It looked good on him.

"It's been a rather long day, I would assume," he murmured quietly. "You look exhausted." I was.

I started to lean over to the side. Evans stood from his chair, rummaged around inside a cabinet, and then produced a fluffy white pillow and soft brown blanket. With infinite care, he made me comfortable.

"Sweet dreams, little mouse," he whispered, and I started to drift.

"What the bloody hell has happened, Jack?" I heard Hoffman ask softly, his words distant but still audible, in that space between sleep and wakefulness.

"Origin Events tend to unpredictable," Evans replied, his voice a lot closer still.

"I thought we established this rip was farther back in linear time," Groves argued.

"And have you forgotten the existence of temporal paradoxes, Miss Groves?" Evans asked.

"No, sir. But I still don't understand. The OE did *not* happen in 1969. Even if it did happen right here. I realise there is a connection, but why her?"

The blanket shifted, getting tucked in tighter as though I was a child on a soft bed, not a hostage on the floor of what had looked suspiciously like a Multi-Purpose Crew Vehicle.

"Because," Evans murmured, "I suspect she *is* the Origin Event."

"Bloody hell," Hoffman muttered.

"Bloody hell, indeed," Evans agreed, his voice moving farther away.

It was only as sleep finally took me that I realised he hadn't undone the cuffs. He didn't trust me. Even though he'd tucked me in as though he cared.

The sound of metal rattled insistently throughout my dreamless sleep.

That and the deathly quiet of space flight.

6
BUT THERE'S ALWAYS A FIRST

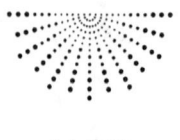

JACK

*S*he looked beautiful while she slept. Even forced to do so at such an odd angle. Those cuffs needed to come off, but the commander in me prevented such a concession. If this woman was the cause of the original Origin Event, then she could be anyone. Anything. On any side.

Not necessarily on ours.

She didn't sound Russian. But then neither did Sergei, really. And we all knew that Sergei had been particularly good at recruitment in the beginning. How else had he managed to steal Orion?

"Is she snoring?" Rafe asked.

"If it's her first time travelling via MPCV then you'd expect her to be tired," Groves offered.

"Who's to say it's her first time," I murmured, still unable to look away from our visitor.

"You can't be serious," Groves demanded. *That* managed to garner my attention. From the moment Miss Groves had greeted me, she'd been more a mouse than Mimi.

Mimi. What a ridiculous name. Mimi Blossom. I almost wanted to laugh.

"And you are naïve, if you believe everything that you see, Miss Groves," I advised the Novitiate.

"You suspect she's a plant?" Rafe queried.

"I'm not sure what to think," I admitted, returning my inspection to the sleeping woman. "Miss Groves," I said suddenly. "Please turn out her pockets."

It was undoubtedly best if I didn't touch her. I could still feel the softness of her skin from my dream.

"Y..you want me to search her?" Groves asked, voice high with alarm.

"Would you rather I did it?" I pressed.

"But..."

"Just do as he says, Sally," Rafe offered quietly, his eyes on my face and neither woman. I arched an eyebrow at him. He raised me one in return.

Groves moved forward and started going through the woman's pockets, drawing the attention to the tightness of Mimi's jeans. They might as well have been painted on. I looked away, and Rafe chuckled. Gladly, I turned my scowl on him.

"There's a wallet, sir," Groves advised after a few seconds. I accepted the purse and started to open it.

"This doesn't feel right," Groves muttered. I didn't bother reprimanding her; I could see Rafe giving her a purposeful stare. The mousey Miss Groves retreated to her own seat and stayed quiet.

"New Zealand Driver's License," I said, pulling out her identity card which placed the woman's age at twenty-five. If it and she were to be believed. "The name matches."

"You mean she wasn't lying about Mimi Blossom?" Rafe asked with obvious humour.

"That's if the license is real."

Rafe grunted in reply. I was guessing he wanted to believe her. But believing Miss Wylde meant she'd somehow been caught up in our flight path, and *that* was definitely something new.

"Say she isn't lying," I said. "Then how do you explain her existence?"

"I can't," Rafe admitted. "But you said it yourself; Origin Events are unpredictable."

"I haven't read about this type of thing happening before," Groves offered.

I shook my head. "It hasn't."

"Then let's break it down," Rafe said, turning his chair away from the main screens and looking at the woman. We all were now. And still, she slept the sleep of a newly minted Novitiate after their first trip through Time. "It's the biggest OE we've ever faced. Which would lead you to think the rip is more extensive than any we've encountered before, too."

"Which would lead to the conclusion that the nebulous power required to travel to this plane point was extensive, as well," I added.

"Which could lead to this," Rafe finished, waving a hand towards Mimi.

"But how? Why her?"

"What about the bomb?" Miss Groves asked reluctantly.

"Now you want to talk about explosives?" Rafe teased. She offered a small smile.

"She did act as though she'd been accused of setting a bomb off inside the VAB," Groves offered. "Something must have happened prior to our arrival. She was already in handcuffs."

I lifted my gaze to the Novitiate. "Valid point, Miss Groves. Perhaps the tear we're chasing?"

"My thoughts exactly, sir," Groves stated, becoming more animated as the conversation evolved. "What if this isn't a natural Event. What if this has been manufactured by someone."

"By the girl?" Rafe asked, staring down at the sleeping woman with new eyes.

"No," Groves whispered. "I was thinking more along the lines of..."

"Our opposition," I finished for her. Miss Groves was developing into a very nice addition to the RATS team, I was thinking. "The reason why we're keeping her handcuffed."

"No, sir," Groves insisted. "That's not what I mean."

"Then what exactly do you mean, Miss Groves?" I asked pleasantly. She paled. Perhaps my pleasant wasn't for everyone.

"Well," she licked her lips, eyes darting around the MPCV, then coming to rest reluctantly on me.

There it was. The courage I thought she'd been lacking. Maybe there was hope for the mousey Miss Groves after all.

"Well," she repeated, lifting her chin. "I've been reading a lot about causal loops and how some scientists believe the loop is in fact not closed."

"The very definition of a loop is closure," I pointed out. "Retro-causality cannot occur unless event one causes event two, which was the original cause of event one."

"And you wonder why we're considered crazy," Rafe muttered.

"Yes, sir," Groves agreed, whether to Rafe or myself, I couldn't tell. "But there is an argument that some loops can become...warped. That if a bulge or warping of the loop occurs, not only does event one cause event two, but it can also cause event one-point-one, which may interfere with the creation of event two."

"What's that now?" Rafe demanded. "She's lost me."

"Hence the reason why you've still not progressed to Surgeon," I offered with a softening smile. He just rolled his eyes at me.

I returned my attention to the very surprising Miss Groves.

"Valid point again, Miss Groves," I conceded. "But if we are dealing with a warped, as you put it, causal loop, then how do you explain the original rip we're responding to? If event two has in fact been altered by the creation of event one-point-one." I indicated the sleeping form of the woman on our Vehicle floor. Or the sleeping form of event one-point-one.

"Temporal paradox, sir," she said with a crooked smile. "The Origin Event didn't occur until Miss Wylde entered the equation."

Rafe groaned, but my mind began to spin with possibilities. That was the problem with time travel; it could unravel and create an abso-lute mess in your head. Temporal paradoxes were not linear. That's why they were called loops. But a malfunctioning loop was an altogether different beast. A malfunctioning loop had an infinite number of possible outcomes.

I glanced towards the sinusoid on the main screen. If it had altered since we'd picked up our unexpected cargo, I couldn't see it. Or perhaps, as Groves insisted, the sine wave was already perfected despite the event not yet occurring, because event two could only exist in its current form if event one-point-one did.

Chicken and egg analogies had nothing on temporal science.

I let out a frustrated breath of air. "It still doesn't explain how she just happened to appear in our Vehicle."

"It doesn't have to, sir," Groves pointed out. "She's as much a part of the rip as we are now." She paused, the hesitation making her head tilt to one side as she considered her next words. "Of course, there is one other theory."

Rafe's groan was louder this time. We both ignored him.

Groves looked down at the woman, a small crease marring her brow.

"What if there was an event one-point-one-point-one?"

Silence. It was quite stunning. MPCVs were not known for their peaceable atmospheres.

"Why would you say *that?*" Rafe finally asked, in all honesty, sounding quite miffed at the possibility.

"To explain why she is *here.*"

"I thought you said it wasn't necessary," I pointed out, just to encourage her thought processes. She might well have been on to something, and part of commanding a training mission was to aid the Novitiates to think.

"Well," she said again. "The rip was caused by *something*. Be it natural or not. And we've never experienced anything like this." She indicated the woman still sleeping. "So, could it be possible that we're caught up in a new type of causal loop? Or even two causal loops intersecting?"

"Two loops would mean two Miss Wyldes," I said, and then stilled. "Didn't she mention a sister?"

Rafe turned back to the computer and entered a command. A few taut seconds later Mimi's voice came over the speakers.

"And now she's gone. And none of you even care."

"The bomb," Rafe muttered.

"The hole in the VAB," I added. I looked down at the handcuffs on Mimi's wrists, noting for the first time the hint of abrasion beneath. I bit back a curse. "Get those off, would you, Dr Hoffman."

"Of course, sir," he said and moved without delay to our tool cupboard. They'd have to be cut, but Rafe had a steady hand with the laser.

"Two loops," I said, pondering the significance of this discovery.

"Have you ever come across *that* on one of your rodeos…sir?"

I smiled at Groves. I was beginning to like the girl.

"No, Miss Groves, I have not. But there's always a first."

7
DOCTOR

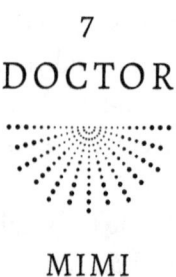

MIMI

I was dreaming. And *he* was in it. But he wasn't wearing a NASA jumpsuit. In fact, he was wearing very little at all. I struggled to get a fuller picture, but like with so many dreams, it was abstract in parts. Realistic in others. The part where he was wearing no shirt and flexing his muscles as he leant on his arms above me was all a little fragmented. But the part where he was sitting inside an Orion Multi-Purpose Crew Vehicle was not.

Rotating images, one after the other, of the MPCV, and bulbous clouds of red and blue and yellow, and sine waves on surprisingly large screens, and a woman with her hair in a bun kept flickering before my closed eyelids.

But I knew I was dreaming, which was saying something. Usually, you're just part of the dreamscape and not existentially aware. I should know. I dream. A lot. But I knew the flickering images now were part of a greater dream which featured *him* in all his natural glory.

Even as I knew I'd never actually seen him bare-chested in my life before.

My mind proceeded to tell me otherwise. He felt real even though his presence was abstract in parts. The MPCV bright and vibrant and clear, much like my parents' car submerged in water had been clear, felt less authentic at that moment than the hazy image of him smiling. Naked. Above me. As if...

I pushed away from that thought abruptly, realising I had a semblance of control over this dreamscape thing. That was a first. I couldn't make the images more focused, though, but I could decide if I wanted the abstract parts or the realistic ones to prevail.

I seriously considered the abstract for a moment, which in a dream could be all of a split second, but felt like a few minutes of heated mental debate.

But the MPCV won out.

I'm a scientist. I analyse data. Naked chests did not feature in my thesis.

Perhaps they should have. I might have returned to it already.

I turned my dream mind to the conversation in the command module instead, homing in on one point of fact in particular.

"She's out of time," Hoffman had said. For some reason, my dreamscape mind decided to fixate on that.

She's out of time.

Again and again, the words repeated, the look on Jack Evans' face flaring before my eyes. Shocked. That's what it had been. Shocked, with a healthy dose of surprised.

She's out of time. What did it mean? My dream mind couldn't decide, choosing to mix those words up with Carrie. Carrie on the tour bus. Carrie drinking Bud Lights from an aluminium bottle at the resort last night. Carrie at my parents' wake. Carrie on the aeroplane sticking drinking straws up her nose to make me laugh. Carrie in a cloud of colours, starbursts twinkling in her eyes.

Carrie out of time.

I felt adrenaline surge. The dream began to shatter. And then the cool, hard feel of metal against my cheek registered, just as the smell of burning electrical wires met my nose. It smelled so much worse than before. I reached up and rubbed my face, taking a few precious seconds to orientate myself.

And then it hit.

My hands were free.

I sat bolt upright, eyes blinking, lights flashing, the module spinning, and then proceeded to vomit all over my jeans.

"We've got a geyser," someone said enthusiastically.

"Oh, no!" a woman cried. A bucket suddenly appearing under my chin.

"That is truly disgusting. I'd forgotten about that side effect." Hoffman. It was Hoffman and Groves speaking.

I felt myself redden, embarrassment flushing up my cheeks even as I dry heaved again.

A cool, wet cloth was placed in my hand.

"Here," Evans said softly. "You're OK."

Was I? *She's out of time.* Me? Carrie? It was all messed up inside my head. The dream had seemed clearer. Reality was the abstract.

I pressed the cloth against my face, blocking out the world, my other hand resting on the metal floor of the module. The grooves were smooth, like little dimples in the alloy. My fingers rubbed back and forth across each ridge and hollow.

Slowly the nausea passed, and I chanced a look at the Vehicle. Hoffman sat in his seat, Groves beside him, now in the command chair. And Evans...Evans was crouched down at my side, watching me intently.

"Are you with us, Miss Wylde?" he asked. I nodded, causing a slight pounding to start up behind my eyes. "It will pass. Much like motion sickness, you get used to it."

"Or you could take an anti-emetic," Hoffman offered. "I find Gin works best. Mixed with a little tonic."

"Your solution to travel sickness is unique," Evans offered, "if not always effective. Gin as *Dutch Courage* is rather dependent on volume. And I have seen how much you put away, Rafe."

"Ah, but have you ever seen me get travel sick?"

"Not since Waterloo."

"Now that was an unfortunate trip, Jack. But a bloody good night out, too."

I stared at them, my mind like mush; unable to parse a word.

"I'm fine," I said. My throat was dry, my stomach felt off kilter, and I was sure I had started to smell slightly whiffy.

It had been an effing long day.

"What did I miss?" I decided to ask.

"I like your approach, Miss Wylde," Evans announced, shifting to his feet. "And you have missed very little. We have secured our location and confirmed our destination on all planes. At present, the MPCV is running a self-diagnostic; our landing left a lot to be desired."

None of that made a lick of sense.

He sighed. God knows what he'd seen on my face.

"For some reason, we have picked you up on our travels, and now you are somewhere else."

"I'm no longer at Cape Canaveral?"

He shook his head and moved to a chair nearby. Not Groves', but another. The Vehicle could carry four seated personnel, I noticed. The number seemed significant somehow. He sat down and leant forward, resting his elbows on his surprisingly thick thighs, hands together between his knees. I tried not to compare the bulging muscles in his arms with the flexing biceps I'd seen in my dream.

I failed. They looked too much alike.

"Not where. When," Evans supplied.

I blinked. "Excuse me?"

Evans started tapping his long fingers together as though considering his next words carefully. Hoffman and Groves watched him with equal measures of interest. The MPCV ticked away quietly, a soft hum in the background indicating the circuitry was active, or NASA computers were working or who knows what was transpiring behind the smooth, dimpled metal of the module.

I struggled to ignore where I actually was. With whom I actually was. And concentrated on why I wasn't on the floor of the VAB in handcuffs staring up into Special Agent Dawson's hard eyes.

I sucked in a breath and reached for my wrists. No handcuffs. I hadn't imagined that then.

Evans raised his eyebrows at me, then turned back to the console behind him and picked up something. He spun around and held it out for me to accept.

"My wallet," I said, mystified, taking the object from his outstretched hand. I made sure not to touch his fingers.

And then I forgot them altogether as anger hit. Hard.

"You went through my pockets?"

"Miss Groves did," Evans said pleasantly. "We needed to confirm your identity."

"And you believe my ID isn't forged?" I queried with a huff of unamused air.

Evans smiled. "Not at first, no," he admitted.

"And now?"

"Perhaps."

"What changed your mind?" I asked, shoving the wallet in my back pocket, trying valiantly to ignore the way Evans watched my every move intently.

I couldn't decide if that was a good thing or not. My body had ideas my mind severely disagreed with. So I decided to just roll my eyes.

Hoffman chuckled. Evans looked away, chagrined.

"Miss Groves came to your rescue," he said, not looking back at me.

My eyes found the young woman's. She smiled shyly. But I caught the intrigue in her hooded lid stare. Secretly she was fascinated by me. Rather than make me feel secure in anyway, it left me feeling disorientated. *Why* was she fascinated in me?

"Hi," I said in way of greeting.

"Hi," she squeaked back.

"Lovely, we've all said hello…" Evans announced.

"Well, you haven't," Hoffman offered.

"…Can we please just get on with it."

"Yes, sir," Groves replied, straightening. "You," she raised her voice as if I might be hard of hearing, "are part of a causal loop. A temporal paradox, if you will."

"No need to yell, Miss Groves," Evans said softly. "She's out of time not deaf."

There was that phrase again. *She's out of time.* I had a sinking feeling it didn't mean what I thought it did. Which should have relieved me. But it didn't.

"Sorry, sir," Groves immediately replied at a normal volume. Evans just nodded for her to continue. "Well, you see," she said leaning forward with obvious excitement. "We believe you got caught up in a temporal paradox. Possibly a second loop on top of the first. Which, of course, considering it was also an Origin Event, anything was made quite possible. So, as far as we can tell, we've somehow picked you up as we've travelled through your plane to get to our destination. It's really quite fascinating," she chirped. "We've never picked up a passenger before."

Silence. They were all staring at me.

"OK," I said slowly.

Hoffman barked out a laugh. "She's got no bloody idea what you're saying, Sally."

I shifted in my seat, my eyes staring at the metal floor, the dimples catching my attention.

"Retrocausality," I murmured.

"I beg your pardon?" Evans asked.

"It doesn't exist," I added.

"You've heard of it, though?"

I nodded. My head reminding me that wasn't such a good idea.

"Physics wasn't my major, but it was fun to read up about it," I explained. "Especially," I added, "when incorporated into fiction."

Evans let out a long breath of air.

"Let's not get too technical, shall we?" Who was getting technical? Certainly not me. "Consider temporal paradoxes real. Add to that the fact that you are now onboard our Vehicle with us." OK, I'd give him that one. Extrapolating a conclusion to *that* dilemma had so far been impossible. "And mix in our current time."

"Current time?" I asked, but the words were whisper-quiet.

I wasn't going to like this, I just knew.

"Miss Wylde," Evans said softly. I started shaking my head; I did *not* want that soft tone used on me. Not now. Not here. I was thinking, perhaps, not ever. "Miss Wylde," he repeated, more firmly, but still with a softness to his tone. "You are out of time."

"What the *eff* does that mean?" I demanded. Hyde in full force in lightning-fast fashion.

"Easy," Hoffman urged. He hadn't gone for his gun, but he was considering it.

My head hurt. I kept shaking it. I wished that I'd stop. But I couldn't. My fingers found the hair at the side of my temples, and I pulled on the strands. Rubbed the skin. Tried to stimulate blood flow. Eliminate the agony and confusion.

"Where am I?" I whispered.

"Cape Canaveral," Evans immediately replied. "But that's not the question you want to ask."

"Am I still in the VAB?"

He looked momentarily disappointed. "In a manner of speaking."

"Did I pass out? Is that how you got me from the concrete floor of the VAB into this command module?"

"You know that's not true."

"Isn't it? I was there, and now I'm here, and you say it's still in the VAB."

"Think," he instructed.

"I am effing thinking! You're just not making any sense."

"She's got you there, sir," Hoffman offered.

"You're not helping," Evans muttered. "Miss Wylde, what did you see before we appeared?"

"You didn't appear."

"What did you see?"

"Nothing."

"Stop lying to yourself. What did you see?

A stretched pause.

"Clouds."

"And?"

"Colours."

"Anything else?"

I shook my head in defeat. This was madness.

"Stars."

"Yes," he whispered. "Stars and a nebula. You saw Time manifesting."

"In a cloud of gas and dust in outer space?" I asked, incredulously.

He smiled. Damn it for looking so good.

"In a manner of speaking."

"You're not making any sense," I repeated.

"I know, and I wish I could explain it to you fully, but we don't have time, and there would be little point." He sighed, looking remotely saddened, and then said, "You're simply out of time, Miss Wylde. Believe me, when I say this, it's a first for us. But it *is* possible."

"What is possible?" I whispered.

He held my gaze, a compassionate look crossed his face. Oh, I was so not going to like this.

"You believe it is the 21st century, is that correct?"

I closed my eyes but nodded my head.

"We're currently in 1969," he said quietly.

I shook my head. Thumped a hand down on the metal floor. And then started to laugh.

"And I thought Special Agent Dawson was a card," I muttered.

"The bomb," Evans said. He wasn't letting any of this sink in. Maybe because it was all utter bullshit, I don't know. But he was on a mission, and it sure as hell was not a mission to Mars. "Can you describe exactly what happened, please?"

Manners. The guy *could* be charming when he tried. I opened my eyes and took in the steady looks on the faces of Hoffman and Groves. They were both in on the act. Not so much as a laugh line to be seen.

I shook my head. Again. Rubbed both hands over my face. And then lifted my hair off the back of my neck, fanning the skin there.

"The bomb, Miss Wylde," Evans pressed.

"You're a persistent bastard," I muttered. Even Hoffman didn't laugh.

"What happened to your sister?"

Of all the things he could have said, that was the one single question that would reach me.

"Carrie," I gasped, my body shaking.

"It's OK," Evans rushed to say. "We'll figure it out."

I stared blindly around the module and then found myself anchored to his face. His eyes. Whisky. Amber. Soothing.

"Who the hell are you?" I murmured.

"Jack Evans," he simply replied.

"You are not a NASA Surgeon."

"No, Miss Wylde. Just as you are not a terrorist."

"I didn't plant that bomb," I agreed.

"It wasn't a bomb, and I think you know it."

"You're talking about something that doesn't exist."

"Not in your time, no."

"You're crazy," I insisted.

"What happened?" he replied.

I sighed. Eff this. I was screwed whichever way I looked at it. I might as well see how it all panned out.

"Carrie disappeared." The words were slow in coming. The scientist in me rebelling. "She saw something. I couldn't see it. And then she started walking towards it. Like she couldn't help herself. And then…and then…"

"And then?" Evans softly enquired.

I shook my head.

"Just say it," he urged. "Better out than in."

I looked down at my now disgustingly soiled jeans. No wonder it reeked in here.

"We'll get you a change of clothes shortly," Evans offered. "But I need to know what happened to your sister. Time is, quite literally, running out."

This day was the day from hell. When would reality return?

Along with my sister.

"Carrie disappeared," I said. Forcing the words out. "There one minute. Gone the next."

"Is that all?"

I glared at him. His turn to shake his head. "Everything, Miss Wylde. I must know everything to understand."

"I didn't see anything on the launch pad..." I started, then rushed to finish before he prompted me with that damn soft voice again. "But I thought I heard the sound of engines roaring."

"Roaring?"

"Like a rocket."

"Followed by silence?"

"Yes," I admitted reluctantly.

"The silence of outer space?"

That's what I'd thought the second time I'd heard it. When the nebula had formed, and I'd ended up in here. At the time that Carrie disappeared, though, I'd not been able to work through anything. It had happened so fast, and I'd seen nothing. But I had questioned what it was I had heard.

"I think so," I finally said. "Look, when I saw that hole in the VAB, I thought maybe the sound had originated there. But Launch Pad 39A is a fair distance from the Vehicle Assembly Building. Whatever caused it would have had to have been expelled by a massive force to get whatever it was to cover that sort of distance and reach Carrie. And even then I didn't see anything."

Evans just smiled. It was more grimace than grin.

"Besides, when I mentioned a rocket to Special Agents Dawson and Carter, they clearly did not agree." I looked toward Hoffman. "The bomb scenario," I offered.

"Jerks," he suggested cheekily.

I smiled. I liked him. And then the absurdity of the situation hit home again.

"Either I'm mad, or you're mad," I offered.

"None of us is mad," Evans replied.

"Speak for yourself. I think Winchester has a screw or two loose, at least." Evans just stared at Hoffman. Yeah, like that would shut him up. I had the feeling there was more to their relationship than boss and subordinate. Hoffman could hold his own.

"And this all happened before you woke up in here?" Groves asked, calling all our attention back to the discussion.

I huffed out a breath of laughter. Like this was an intelligent, sane conversation. I wish.

"Yep," I said. "Maybe three, four hours before I was dragged to the VAB in handcuffs and then suddenly found myself inside here."

Silence.

"And that's when you heard a second engine roaring followed by complete silence?" Groves asked.

"Yes."

She looked towards Evans.

"I know," he said, his eyes meeting hers momentarily. "Two loops."

"Unheard of," Hoffman muttered.

"But why?" Groves added. They were losing me again.

"What's happened?" I demanded. "Can you please just speak in plain English. What the hell has happened to my sister?"

Evans brought his focus back to me and sighed.

"The exact same thing that has happened to you I fear."

He feared. Well, so did I. Because I still had no effing idea of what was transpiring.

"She will be out of time, too," he added. There it was. But this time, it meant so many different things.

"If I'm with you," I said slowly. "Then who is Carrie with?"

Hoffman looked away. Groves stared at the floor.

Evans was the only one to meet my eyes.

"I'm afraid I could not say, Miss Wylde." I opened my mouth to argue; God alone knows how. When he added, "But my guess would be she is in 1969. As we are in 1969."

Madness. This was all madness.

But a part of me was agreeing. Accepting.

That part of me was clearly not made up of actual science.

I shook my head.

He smiled. It was in no way reassuring.

"Shall I convince you?" he said.

"You haven't so far," I pointed out; even if that might have been becoming a lie.

Evans laughed. It suited him.

"What do you know about the sixties, Miss Wylde? In particular, the race to reach the moon and Cape Canaveral?"

I raised an eyebrow at him. And then smiled.

"What don't I know, Mr Evans?" I replied.

"Doctor," he corrected and then immediately grimaced.

This time it was me who laughed.

8
WITHOUT THE NEURALYZER

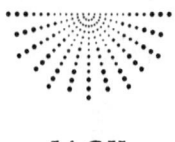

JACK

*T*his was a monumental mistake. I knew it, but for some reason, I couldn't seem to stop it from transpiring. It had been *my* suggestion to take Miss Wylde out of the MPCV and into contemporary time. But God alone knows what Clive Crawford would be saying if he could see what was happening now. I swallowed my disquiet, along with my sanity, and looked up as the water closet door opened.

"It's way bigger in there than I expected," Mimi said, brushing hands over her dress as though uncomfortable.

The late sixties and early seventies hadn't been my favourite of times. I'm more a fifties man at heart. But one look at the extremely short hem of Miss Wylde's dress and I conceded I might have been a little too quick in dismissing this era from my mind.

She had lovely legs. Long despite her modest height. Well defined, as though she ran a lot. Slender and tanned. My throat felt parched, the MPCV felt too small all of a sudden, and I was acutely aware of Rafe watching me from the corner of my eye.

I cleared my throat and stood from my seat. "Ready?" I asked. Too bloody bad if she wasn't, I needed out of this closed in space.

"One last thing," Groves rushed to say, coming forward and handing Miss Wylde a scarf.

"Um, what do I do with this?" Mimi asked.

"It's for your head. A bit of a big thing leading into the seventies."

"Oh," Mimi said, and just stared at the slip of material in her hand.

"Here, let me," Groves offered and took the offending article, shaking it out, then folding it in half diagonally, and moving behind Miss Wylde to place it over all her glorious golden hair.

I was staring again. I shook myself awake and turned towards the screens.

"Everything set?" I asked Rafe.

He snorted but thankfully didn't comment on my Neanderthal behaviour.

"If you're sure you don't want me to accompany you, sir."

"I'd rather Groves isn't left alone, and as we're using her outfit for this excursion, she cannot accompany us into contemporary time as is."

"Agreed. But…"

"Out with it, Dr Hoffman."

Rafe looked pointedly at Mimi.

"Are you *sure*, sir?"

I followed his line of sight as if drawn there magically. That dream had done a number on me, it seemed. I refused to believe it was the woman herself. God alone knows she wasn't my type. But that dream.

Damn it! That dream had been too real.

"If she is tied up in this Event, then she needs to be present to mend it," I pointed out.

"I concur," Rafe allowed. "But shouldn't we carry out a reconnaissance first, before we drop an unknown into a potentially dangerous and unstable situation?"

"Time is ticking, Dr Hoffman. Do you seriously believe we have enough of it spare?"

"You intend to mend the rip on this excursion?" He sounded more than a little alarmed.

"If the opportunity presents itself, then yes."

"Jack…" he warned.

My eyes found Miss Wylde again. Could she be trusted? She was tied up in this somehow. Slap bang in the middle. And let's not forget the possibility of her sister. We had no reason not to believe what she'd told us, and Rafe *had* confirmed a sister existed in Mimi's time, but that didn't mean we weren't being played.

Attraction aside, I needed to stay focused.

"I'll be careful, Rafe," I murmured, as Groves finished up last minute dress adjustments to Mimi's outfit.

"Of course, sir," Rafe muttered, not sounding one bit convinced.

I admitted to myself that I wasn't either.

Mimi walked over to where I was standing, which in a Crew Vehicle only took three steps or so to achieve. She smiled shyly at me, almost as though this was some sort of date. I felt my cheeks redden, almost as though I agreed.

Then I cleared my throat and said, "You do as I say when I say, no questions asked."

The smile fell from her face like autumn leaves tumbling. Replaced with a hard stare.

"I am not your subordinate."

"In this, Miss Wylde, you are very much in my care," I pointed out. "Should things become…challenging out there, I am responsible for your welfare. Entering another plane affected by a rip is not a walk in the park, I might add. You'd be wise to remember that you are out of time."

"There you go with those words again," she growled. "It's not my fault you lot picked me up on your haphazard flight through Time." She snorted, crossing her arms over her chest and cocking a hip. I worked hard on not smiling. She could be so bloody feisty sometimes. "Who was piloting this thing, anyway? You?" She glared at me, and all thought of smiling was immediately forgotten.

"I *am* the commander," I said pleasantly.

"Let me guess; this is where you remind me you're a surgeon, too. What does that even mean?"

I took a step towards her, entering her personal space and ignoring the clean scent of soap she'd used in the bathroom, the hint of toothpaste. Ignoring everything else as well.

"Not everyone can become a Time Surgeon, Miss Wylde. It takes a certain character, hard work, and many hours. I doubt you'd have the stamina or conditioning required."

She brought out a finger and jabbed it into my chest, punctuating each word with a hard thrust.

"I am the epitome of character, hard work, and many hours, *Doctor*. I'll have you know I hold a Masters in Science, and am part way through my doctorate, as well."

"Intelligence is not the only prerequisite to time travel, Miss Wylde." I refused to acknowledge the surprise I felt at her admission. Or the excitement. "And I'd argue your character lacks an essential requirement."

She crossed her arms over her chest and scowled.

"What requirement?" she demanded as if she'd get right on that and acquire whatever was needed to meet the standards required.

I laughed. It wasn't in any way humorous. "Control of one's temper," I snarled.

The MPCV sounded unusually quiet all of a sudden.

And then she smiled. Bloody hell, could she smile when she tried.

"And that's Jenga!" she said triumphantly.

"I beg your pardon?" I asked.

"It's from a movie: *Paul*."

"Released in 2011 by Universal Studios," Rafe said quietly.

We both spun to look at the Intern, realising belatedly that we hadn't been alone throughout that entire embarrassing dialogue. I closed my eyes. Took a deep breath. And then turned back to the object of my ire.

And fascination.

"Mending Time is a precise undertaking," I said softly. "One slip and Time can be lost forever. Our jobs are vital in maintaining history."

My eyes met hers; she was listening. Not fighting. I liked her fight; I'm not sure she was aware how alive she became when riled.

"That is what we do, Miss Wylde. We mend Time. Catch it. Stitch it. Make it. We are Surgeons of Time. And you're about to go where no layperson has ever gone before. So trust me, when I say I am responsible for you. And believe me, when I say your presence alone could fracture or restore Time."

She didn't say anything for a long moment and then she let out a slow breath of air.

"I feel a little like Alice in Wonderland," she murmured. "Too far down the rabbit hole to get out."

My lips tipped up in a small smile.

"Don't worry," I said, regretting the words even before I'd uttered them. "We'll get you back to your time."

"And Carrie?"

"Your sister, too." I did smile then. "We can't have two unexpected passengers running around in a century that is not their own, now can we? Fixing this mess is the only way to fix Time."

"So, we'll find Carrie," she confirmed, "then you'll take us both back to the 21st century"

"Yes."

"Will you wipe our minds with a neuralyzer?"

"A what?" I asked.

"You know, flash something in our eyes like the agents in *Men in Black* to make us forget what we've seen."

"Let me guess, another film?"

"Released in 1997," Rafe muttered. "By Columbia Pictures, this time."

I stared at the woman before me, seeing more than I'd seen before now. More complex than I'd realised. More layered than she'd at first appeared. Intelligent, conservative, and yes, just a little wild. A dichotomy I fervently wanted to explore, but rules were rules.

She was out of time.

"Come on, Miss Wylde," I announced, reaching for the door. "Let's find your sister and return you to your time."

I looked down at her; the world might have stuttered.

And then I recovered and offered her a wink. *"Without* the neuralyzer."

9

AND ALL I COULD DO WAS SQUEAK

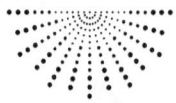

MIMI

*W*e weren't in the VAB. That was the first thing that shocked me. The second was far more profound. Palm trees and a light layering of sand drifting over concrete roadways on a soft, warm breeze, piling up against the storefront of a Piggly Wiggly. The restaurant next to it was called The Moon Hut. Across the road was the Sea Missile Motel. My eyes darted from structure to structure; all lit up in a plethora of bright neon colours. The sand tapped away at my bare ankles, drawing my eye to the drifting grains. I watched as they pooled around a newspaper dispensing machine just to the side of a drug store.

The newspaper behind the glass had a picture of Nixon on it.

The date in the top right-hand corner said July 10th, 1969.

"Did you plan this?" I asked in a numbed voice. "To have us appear, right here, in front of *all* of *this*?"

Evans cleared his throat, seemingly as surprised as me.

"In a manner of speaking," he said softly, using that gentle voice to hide the lie beneath.

"Where did you think we'd appear?" I asked, calling his bluff, the buzz of neon lighting making the hairs on my arms stand up. "Inside the VAB?"

"It is not always possible to be accurate. Time has a way of corrupting things. Especially if the tear is significant."

"But why here?" I pressed. "Why Cocoa Beach?"

"You recognise it?" He sounded surprised.

"How could I not?" I argued, spinning around in a slow circle and taking in the falling sun as it glinted off pristine waves, the salty sea brine laced with a lushness that should not have been, and the references to a moon launch on every available surface that in my time had happened decades ago, but here was an anticipatory thing.

"This location means something," Evans advised, looking about the street we were on with interest. "The MPCV is programmed to follow the rip, and as it is unfolding in real time, our destination is not always static."

"What does *that* mean?" Nothing about any of this made sense. Try as I might, time travel was still an anomaly.

"The rip started at the VAB, but has progressed to here," Evans explained.

"So, the MPCV followed it?"

"Yes."

"And where is our ride home now?" I couldn't even spot the blasted command module. I would have liked to have seen what it looked like from the outside. Whether it matched the one on display at the Kennedy Space Center. Whether the size it appeared to be on the inside corresponded to the size of the Vehicle when viewed from without.

I was guessing there would be no real correlation. Time travel made little sense.

"It will have withdrawn to another plane. When we need it, it will reappear."

"Now you're just making this shit up," I muttered.

Evans smiled. It was temptation wrapped up in a puzzle. I'd always liked puzzles.

I blinked away, watching a group of young people out on the town, dressed much like myself and the good doctor, walking down the opposite side of the street. One of the women wore a scarf similar to mine. The hem of her skirt was even shorter. The belts were large. The patterns were bold. The colours almost clashing. It was a different world. A different time. Or an exceptionally well put together pageant.

"Time is the fourth dimension," Evans was saying. "But what makes up the first three can include any combination."

"Combination?" I asked as the group pushed through the door to a brightly lit Soda Fountain Diner.

"Length, width, height, breadth, and depth," he said in rapid-fire speech. "Whichever three the tear appears in will be where the MPCV travels. But in order to remain undetected, it simply replaces one dimension of the first three, thereby removing itself from the known plane. Or universe."

I turned to look at him, noticing he was watching me closely. I shook my head. I'd learned about the concept of three-dimensional space plus time equalling the known universe and all the matter that exists in it.

I'd hated mathematics.

But what Evans was suggesting here was not quantifiable. Even Stephen Hawking questioned the possibility of time travel. Warped dimensions or not.

"So, what now, Doctor?" I asked, feeling like the world was suddenly so much bigger than it had been.

Before, I'd only had to deal with the present and the thought of a future. Something that could transpire on a linear line before me. Something I could effect with a simple change in the path I was taking.

Now there was so much more to contend with. The past. Where the past occurs and on what plane. And a fourth dimension that screws with it all.

"Now we find out where the rip actually is, and catch it before it tears this time apart completely."

I was caught in a bad b-grade movie.

"And my sister?"

"I'd hazard a guess she'll be near the tear, too."

"Why?"

"Because she or you hitched a ride on it. And as you're with me, and I was chasing the rip after the fact, I assume she caught a lift on the Origin rip itself."

I looked around Cocoa Beach. If Carrie was here, I couldn't see her. Would she be dressed in 1960s fashion? Or would she stand out in jeans and mid-drift baring singlet tee?

"Who is she with, Jack?" I asked suddenly. He knew too much. He was definitely holding something back. The question was why? When I'd be returning to my time and would no longer have the ability to mess with his precious fourth dimension.

Of course, I wasn't sure how I had been caught up in all of this to begin with, so the potential for repetition did exist.

"I couldn't say, Miss Wylde. Any number of factors may have occurred."

"Take a guess. Your best shot. Who's most likely picked up my sister?"

His eyes darkened with the onset of evening. No longing glinting amber in the golden glow of sunset. He narrowed them slightly, assessing me. Then looked abruptly away and sighed.

"Rips are caused by outside influences, Miss Wylde. In some instances, a natural phenomenon can cause a tear large enough to affect Time."

"And in other instances?"

"Someone rips Time apart for a reason."

I blinked up at him. Not liking where this was going.

"Look at where we are," he urged.

I glanced around Cocoa Beach. I couldn't see it in the waning light of day, but I knew it was there. Right across the water. A mere few miles away. Cape Canaveral stood somewhere out there in the darkness. Launch Pad 39A visible when rockets took off into space. The VAB a mere half hour away.

"Remember what you used to get here," Evans added, the air thick with meaning.

"An Orion Multi-Purpose Crew Vehicle," I whispered.

"Yes. Cape Canaveral is an Origin Event location. And July 1969 an important step along the path to reach Orion."

"The Apollo 11 launch."

"Indeed, Miss Wylde. This rip is not accidental. This rip has been caused by someone who wishes to control Orion."

"And my sister's with them?"

"Possibly."

What other explanation was there? It all fit, in a bizarre, my world is out of whack, kind of way.

"We have to find her."

"Yes," he said.

"Stop them."

"Yes."

"Who are they?"

I'd hoped the rapid fire conversation would have loosened his tongue. But Evans just turned away.

"Cocoa Beach became extremely popular during the Apollo Program," he advised, starting to walk down the street. "Its economic growth, however, suffered significantly by the time of the Shuttle. Right now, it was the place to see and be seen, if you were a famous astronaut about to walk on the moon. Especially," he added, "if you drove a Corvette."

He'd stopped outside the Holiday Inn, where three Chevrolet Corvette Stingrays stood front and centre, a group of excited people milling around, flashbulbs flashing, cameras clicking, a happy, chaotic mess of reporters and groupies and three wide smiling astronauts.

My breath left me in a rush of unexpected excitement as I recognised just who exactly the astronauts were.

"It's less than a week 'til the launch," I breathed, taking a step forward as if drawn to the scene, to the people, to the inexplicable.

Evans' hand came down on my shoulder, halting forward motion. "They had a photo shoot today. Sponsored by General Motors. The picture becomes iconic in the pre-launch build-up. It's already happened," he said. "This is just the remnants of a world on the brink of change. Anticipation and excitement the hallmarks of the Space Program. This is where it will happen."

"What will happen?"

"The rip."

"But it's already happened," I argued, getting frustrated.

"Temporal paradox, Miss Wylde. We're in one."

"I don't understand."

He looked down at me, pulling his eyes away from the surreal scene before us.

"Come now," he urged. "You're a scientist. Think."

I couldn't think. I couldn't reason any of this out. I was in 1969. Watching Neil Armstrong, Buzz Aldrin and Michael Collins celebrate their Corvette Stingrays and the upcoming launch to the moon. I was right here in Cocoa Beach where so many of those who worked for NASA chose to live. Where the Space Program was epitomised. Where hope and exploration combined to create the future of NASA. America's golden years of space travel.

I was right here.

And so was Carrie. Somewhere. I started looking around the group of people, ignoring those taking photos, and those calling out questions. Forcing myself to ignore the astronauts and their shiny new vehicles. If Carrie were here, she'd be under duress or trying to find a way out. She wouldn't be part of this if she could help it. NASA was not her thing.

Getting home would be. I scanned the environment, looking farther afield. The motel itself was long and thin, with a low-lying roof, and tall palm trees. The area was floodlit with artificial light, but shadows existed under the angular eaves. A movement here. A flash of clothing there. The glint of something as it shifted.

"Come on," Evans muttered under his breath, searching like me, but for what, I couldn't say.

I saw nothing. Just happy people and hopeful faces and beautiful chaos dancing with anticipation. The excitement was contagious, had it been another time. But it wasn't.

It was 1969, but I wasn't meant to be here.

I was out of time.

And so was Carrie.

Evans had said this was an intentional rip, caused by someone who planned to derail Orion. I'd never connected the Apollo Program with NASA's latest missions to Mars. But it had to have started somewhere. And maybe the moon was as good a starting point as any other.

"They're going to kill Armstrong," I blurted.

"Not necessarily," Evans said steadily.

"We have to stop it." I surged forward again, only to have Evans wrap his arms around my body and haul me back into the darkness of shadows.

"Easy," he murmured softly in my ear, hot breath across suddenly sensitive skin. His gentle tone slowed my heart rate.

"We have to stop it," I said more evenly.

"We will. But what it is we're stopping is not yet obvious, don't you think?"

"Neil Armstrong is the first man to walk on the moon…" I started.

"And not the only person here from NASA."

If the time traveller who wanted to derail Orion was targeting this time period, then who they were targeting had to have done something that led NASA down the path to Mars. I struggled to think straight. Fear of what might transpire making it difficult to reason. Fear of what was happening to Carrie making it hard to think.

Who would be here that would tie into Orion?

I'd worry about why they wanted Orion derailed after we stopped whatever was going to happen from happening.

"There," Evans said, his arms around my body loosening. I hadn't realised how right they'd felt until they were gone. "Abe Silverstein."

"Who?"

"Come on, Miss Wylde. He's our man. We need to get to him before they do."

His hand slipped into mine as if he'd done such a thing a thousand times before. His fingers laced with my fingers as he tugged me toward the back of the crowd, circumnavigating the melee, sticking to the shadows.

I spotted the gentleman in question, clearly a NASA official, but the name didn't mean anything. He wore a suit, where suits were not needed. A red tie and glasses. His smile was engaging. I wondered what sort of mind hid behind those kind eyes.

Camera flashes made the whole scene surreal, shadows dancing in the hot air of a Florida beach. I couldn't really believe we were actually here, but just over there, a few short steps away was Neil Armstrong. I'd wanted to walk in his footsteps. I'd never imagined I'd walk beside him.

I almost missed it; I was so busy staring at my idol. Taking in every nuance, every minute detail. Every word he was saying to the reporters.

He was looking forward to launch day.

Yes, they were ready.

He wasn't sure what his first words would be, but he'd think of something.

No, they weren't worried. Good men had gone before and laid the way.

I could have cried for what I was seeing. I could have shouted with joy for the fact that this was happening to me.

But then a gun was pulled; such a modern piece of equipment. Rather like the gun, the KSC security officers had drawn on me. And in one quick move, Evans was flying.

Through the air, towards the group of astronauts and reporters, over the bonnet of a Corvette Stingray.

Shouts sounded out as the sound of the gun firing was muffled by screams of outrage. Off to the side, someone stumbled. For a second I thought it might be Silverstein, but it wasn't. Evans had managed to confuse the shooter enough that he'd misaimed.

I rushed after him, as uniformed police officers swarmed the scene, and hysterical people ricocheted off one another, eager to help Mr Silverstein to his feet. My hands fluttered as I checked to make sure he was unharmed, the sounds and sights of a calamity closing in around me. Orders were given, people started to scatter, and the astronauts were whisked away from the danger under the scrutiny of NASA officials.

"Are you all right?" I asked Abe Silverstein.

"Just a scratch, my dear," he said, dusting himself off.

"I think you should go with the others," I urged. I wasn't sure who this man was to NASA, but Evans had indicated he would be the target. And it damn well looked like he'd been the one the shooter had been firing at, too. Still, he seemed so normal. Could this man have started the path that led to Orion? To Mars? And ultimately to time travel?

"Yes. Perhaps I should," he said, not unkindly. He patted my arm and started after the NASA officials, then spun on his heel and looked back at me. "Will you be all right here? In amongst all of this?"

I looked around at the chaos, no longer promising or alight with anticipation. This chaos was full of fear and doubt. The shooter had disappeared. Police were everywhere. Reporters were shouting for answers. Camera bulbs flashed into the darkness.

Chaos as only true chaos can be.

I swallowed. "I'll be fine," I said softly, hunting for Evans in amongst the disorder.

"Maybe you should come with us," the man suggested. But if there was one thing I'd learned in the past few hours, going where I was *not* supposed to be wasn't a good strategy.

I smiled. "I have a friend here somewhere," I offered.

"If you insist," the kind NASA man replied and started to turn away.

"Mr Silverstein," I called suddenly.

"Yes," he said, not at all surprised that I knew his name.

"What is it you do at NASA?"

His face fell, a look of uncertainty crossed his kind features briefly.

"Why, I created Apollo." He chuckled to himself then. "At least, I gave the project its name."

I somehow thought his involvement was more than just christening the program that launched man to the moon. But whatever it was, it appeared instrumental in the creation of Orion, too. And we'd saved him.

I watched him walk away and then turned back to the crowd around the Stingrays. Suddenly aware that I was on my own in a different time with no discernible way to get back to the module.

"Crap," I muttered, unable to spot Evans.

And then I saw him. Leaning against a police cruiser.

His hands securely fastened behind his back.

In effing handcuffs.

"Double crap," I said, as the sensation of a gun pressing hard against my ribs registered.

And a voice with a slight accent said, "This time you've gone too far, rat."

And all I could do was squeak.

10

AH, CRAP

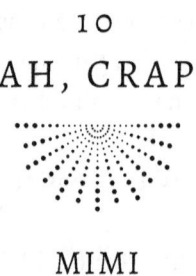

MIMI

I felt a drop of sweat trickle down between my shoulder blades. Followed quickly by another. It was hot, but that was hardly the cause of my perspiring. The gun was real, and I was closer to that particular style of weaponry than I had ever been before.

Even the KSC security guards who'd waved a Glock at me on Launch Pad 39A hadn't come this close with their weapons. But this man, the shooter I presumed, insisted on giving me an up close and personal experience with a firearm.

"You think your organisation can stop this from happening?" he asked harshly, but I was hoping he didn't want an answer to that question because words suddenly failed me.

My eyes frantically searched out the only ally I had in this time. But Evans was still trussed up against a police cruiser being questioned by a very disgruntled looking cop.

And there was no way I wanted Mr Silverstein anywhere near this man.

"How many times must we do this before you meddlesome rats understand?" he snarled in my ear, digging the muzzle of the gun in deeper. And why he kept calling me that particular rodent, I didn't know. Was he aware of my nickname maybe? "Lunik is far superior."

I struggled to make sense of what he was saying, but what with a *real* gun pressed up against my side, and recent events conspiring to force me *out of time*, I really didn't have a hope in hell of understanding.

"I will spare you, Surgeon," the man growled low. "Only so you can deliver a message to Crawford for me." Who the effing hell was Crawford? "I have one of your own, and I will dispose of her accordingly unless all Orion Vehicles are permanently dismantled."

This day had gone from surreal to fantastical in such a short amount of time. I'd broken laws and been quasi-arrested. I'd faced off against hard-nosed federal agents and a rampaging Orion Crew Vehicle. I'd slipped through the fourth dimension to 1969. Been mere feet away from Neil Armstrong. Saved a man's life from a gun wielding psychotic.

Quite frankly, I'd had enough, thank you very much.

I elbowed the shooter in the ribs, stomping down hard on his foot in the process, then spun around and kneed him in the balls.

Or that's, at least, what I tried to do.

I caught a brief glimpse of brown hair and an angular face, a pointed beard, and dark eyes. In another situation - say, one where I wasn't about to be killed - he might have appeared handsome. But the snarl that rent his features, making his fists curl and the butt of the gun come hurtling towards me in lightning quick fashion, dashed that notion pretty spectacularly.

"Oomph," was all I managed, before his fist hit my stomach and the gun crashed into the side of my head.

I'm dead, was my only thought as I crumpled to the hard concrete. *I am so dead.* But death failed to claim me.

Panting, feeling like vomiting again, and now sweating quite profusely, the world spun lazily as hazy images of people moving, and lights flashing and sound warping made the Holiday Inn twirl around me as I struggled to regain focus while on all fours, shaking.

I blinked several times, swallowed copious amounts of saliva, and then came face to foot with someone's leather wing-tipped shoes. For a horrendous moment, I thought they might just belong to the shooter. But maybe my bad luck had finally run out today, because the owner of the shoes reached down and helped me to my feet, words falling off his tongue congenially as though he thought I might comprehend them.

I smiled up at my would-be rescuer, and then promptly face planted. On his broad chest.

"Whoa there, darlin'," he said in a pleasantly American accent. "I've had many a girl fall for my charms, but usually I'm tryin' a little harder than this. Being such a catch and all."

I blinked. His face swam into focus. And blue eyes stared out at me from behind a well-developed beard. Not a pointy one. And he lacked the strange not-accent the shooter had. But the beard did make me think twice about accepting his offer of help. I preferred a small smattering of stubble on my men. Not the full hog.

Hog. I laughed, ridiculously. The bearded American laughed with me.

And then said, "Where's Dr Evans?"

All levity vanished.

"Who are you?" I demanded, the words not quite as coherent as I'd have liked. "And are you with that other guy?" I added, ruining the whole authoritative angle I was going for when I stretched my mouth repeatedly attempting to speak more clearly.

I failed.

But no way was I letting him anywhere near Jack. Or Silverstein. Really, I was sure Jack Evans could look after himself. Abe Silverstein, on the other hand, was the one I wanted to protect.

Right then, however, I was having a little trouble remembering why.

"What other guy, darlin'?" the American asked, bringing me back to my more immediate problems.

"The guy with the gun," I mumbled, glancing down at the American's waist, but if he was wearing a weapon, he was concealing it. A distinct possibility.

"Can you describe the guy with the gun, darlin'?" he asked pleasantly, ignoring my perusal of his nether region.

I lifted my eyes to his face. "He had a gun," was all I could manage.

"Modern or contemporary?"

What?

"Was it something you'd see in 1969 or more likely the future?"

Guns were guns, but even I knew the gun the shooter had held, the one used to fire at Silverstein, was not from this time.

But why would *this* guy even consider that if he wasn't also from the shooter's time?

"Who are you?" The words were crisp and clear and cutting. About effing time.

"Your safety net," he said with a smile.

Strangely, part of me wanted to trust that smile, even as my mind rebelled at the idea of a smile being inherently trustworthy. I was questioning everything about my world order. About the parameters I'd set and the rules I'd lived by. Nothing made sense anymore.

"Look," I said, crossing my arms over my chest, feeling more and more like myself. "I think you'd better just go on your way. I've got nothing to say to you."

He stared at me for a long moment and then scratched his beard, contemplating.

"You have no idea what you've stepped into, do you, darlin'?"

"Don't call me darling."

"*Darlin',*" he stressed. "You're outta time."

Panic settled deep inside my veins, making my heart pump frantically to wash the sensation away. It didn't work. I'd been in a constant state of confusion for too long. Adrenaline coursing through me at an alarming rate. The only break I'd had was when I'd fallen asleep on the Orion. And what the hell was with that? Hyped up on fight-or-flight juice, it should have been impossible for me to relax enough to sleep.

But then, the impossible had become mundane, hadn't it?

I blinked. My eyes landing on Jack Evans over by the police cruiser. His form obscured by the reporters who still crowded around the scene demanding answers. He'd be hauled away soon. And even I knew, in my current devolving mental state, that I needed Jack Evans to get back to the Orion.

I needed him to find Carrie.

I have one of your own, and I will dispose of her accordingly unless all Orion Vehicles are permanently dismantled.

Could the shooter have meant Carrie?

"Listen," the American suddenly said, "we need to find Evans, and Sally indicated he'd be with you."

"Sally?"

"Groves. The Novitiate on your Orion."

He was from Jack's time, I realised, whenever that time happened to be. Closer to my time than 1969, I'd hazard a guess. If not linearly, then at least theoretically. Evans understood the 21st century. Those in 1969 wouldn't have had a clue what my time meant to me.

But I needed to test him.

"Are you a Surgeon, too?"

"Yes. Just like Jack. I'm his *coup de main* when things start to go wrong."

"And things have gone wrong enough to warrant a swift pre-emptive strike?"

He stared at me and then started to laugh. Whether at my military understanding or not, I couldn't say. And then he said, "I'd say so, darlin'. Yeah. 'Bout as wrong as a flight can be. The tear's an Origin Event; it was never gonna go smoothly. But it's continued to unravel. And Orion One has picked up a passenger, setting everything orange back in Dispatch. That's you, by the way, sweetpea. You'd be the passenger in this little equation. And from all indications, the rip is *still* expanding. So, yeah, wrong is one way of putting it.

"FUBAR might be another. And I'm Operation Fix FUBAR. So," he looked down at me, "you with me?"

His entire speech had been delivered in record speed. All the words melding together in one long run of sweetly thick Southern American accent. It suited Florida; I wouldn't have been surprised if he'd originated from around these parts. Which set off all types of chemical warning bells inside my head.

Jack Evans was British. So were Sally Groves and Rafe Hoffman. The man with the gun, who'd shot at Abe Silverstein and tried to deliver a villain-like ultimatum through me, had a slight accent. Not necessarily American, but not British either. In fact, I'd say it was Eastern European if I had to make a guess. Just slightly.

And now this man thought he could convince me he was part of Jack's team. His back-up, so to speak. I wasn't naïve, I knew asking for identification was a waste of time. What would it say? Time Travelling Surgeon, Extraordinaire? But his accent he couldn't hide. Or didn't think to.

And not being British was enough for me.

"He's over there," I said, indicating the reporters' vehicles situated near the front of the Holiday Inn car park. And quite some distance from the police cruiser and where Jack actually was.

"Well then, come on, darlin'. Let's go get Jack, get him back to his Vehicle so he can start stitchin'. And get you back to your time."

I almost said it. I almost fell for the act, completely.

What about my sister?

But this guy, whoever the effing hell he was, wouldn't want to trade my sister for Jack. He'd want what the shooter wanted. Orion shut down so Lunik could fly unhindered.

Oh, I was getting good at sorting this shit out. My mind might have taken a battering, confusion making it difficult to extrapolate hypotheses easily. But I was a scientist. And scientists were damn good at sifting through data.

And all the data pointed to corporate competition. Orion was the British version of time travel. Lunik somebody else's. And if memory served correctly, Lunik was the name given to the Soviet Union Lunar Programme by western media back in the sixties and seventies.

The shooter was Russian. And *coup de main here*...well, I didn't quite know. Maybe a defected US astronaut? Yeah, that sounded about as plausible as time travel. But what else did I have to go on?

Brit accents OK.

Anything else suspect.

"All right," I said brightly, starting in the direction of the reporters' vans.

"You seem to be handling this all pretty darn well, darlin'," the guy announced with a hint of amazement. "Hadn't ever heard of a passenger being picked up on a flight before now, but there's a first time for everythin'. And it ain't such a bad deal. You get to see somethin' you'd never have known existed. And we get to slingshot on your trajectory. Might be, we could crack this OE wide open. Stitch a few rips permanently."

Not much of that made sense, but I had to admit it was nice listening to him talking. Not so bad watching him walking either. The guy was cute. Shame he wasn't part of the good team.

"Just over there, you say, darlin'?" he asked, looking toward the reporters' vans and the obvious lack of Jack Evans amongst them.

"You know," I said, picking up a tripod from a discarded camera off to the side, "you really should stop calling me darling, sweetheart."

And promptly whacked him on the back of the head with it.

He went down like a like a sack of potatoes. Toppling onto the concrete with a sickening *thwack*. I grimaced, almost feeling sorry for him. Then dropped the tripod and ran.

By the time I reached the police cruiser, Jack was sitting inside it. But they'd removed his handcuffs, and, right then, that was all I needed to give me the impetus to act. The police officers were still taking statements from all the people who'd stayed after the shooter had struck. Jack was on his own. No one was near the police car. It was now or never.

Evans had said that the MPCV would appear wherever we needed it. Somehow surfing planes to find us in our hour of need. I had to hope that, whatever method of calling the Vehicle he had, hadn't been taken from him when he'd been arrested. But as they'd removed the cuffs, and just left him in the cruiser, there was a good chance if he had been stripped, the device - if that's what it was - would be in the trunk or something.

I crossed my fingers, held my breath, and ducked low, coming up beside the cruiser's driver's side door. More luck than planning placing me on that side of the vehicle. Americans drove back to front cars. I tested the door handle, found it unlocked, and slipped inside before I could think better of it.

Somehow being out of time, as Jack put it, made breaking laws that much easier.

"What are you doing, Miss Wylde?" Evans asked from the back of the vehicle quietly.

"Rescuing you," I replied.

"By stealing a police car?" Oh, he knew me so well. So quickly.

"Not at all," I argued, for the sake of arguing. "Hold tight now," I added and turned the key.

The cruiser roared to life making several cops in the vicinity turn towards it. It took a second or two for them to realise the woman behind the steering wheel was not in uniform and most definitely not a plain clothed cop.

"This really isn't necessary," Evans murmured.

"You can thank me later," I growled and put the car into drive.

People scattered. Shouts of alarm and anger sounded out. Camera bulbs flashed immortalising this moment for all history. I scowled at that rather disturbing thought, but who would be able to recognise me in an old photo taken decades before my birth?

I snorted. Evans sighed. And we rocketed out of the Holiday Inn car park, sideswiping a reporter's vehicle as I navigated the wrong-side-of-the-road traffic.

"Blood hell," Evans shouted.

"It's OK," I replied, biting my lower lip and gripping the steering wheel grimly.

"No," he said. "It is not at all OK."

I looked up into the rearview mirror, expecting to see his terror at my non-existent driving skills. But it wasn't fear I saw in this amber hued eyes. It was anger.

"That was Bryan Fawkes," he said through gritted teeth.

"Who?" I said looking into the wing mirror and spotting the

bearded American staggering to his feet, big hand rubbing the back of his no doubt bruised head as he wobbled.

Ah, crap.

"Our back up," Evans replied steadily.

Or more pointedly, *coup de main*, I was thinking.

"Ah, crap," I muttered as we took a corner on two wheels.

11

ORANGE

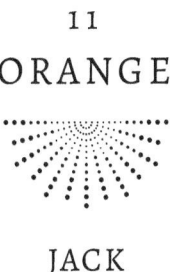

JACK

*B*loody Hell. For Fawkes to be here, Dispatch must have been bathed in orange. And the only thing I could think of that would make Crawford send out a *coup de main* would be the woman sitting in the front of this *stolen* police cruiser.

I watched her from the back seat, horrified and impressed in equal measure. Her misguided rescue attempt involved grand theft auto. This mouse of a woman, who was so far from mousey it wasn't funny. And so far out of her time that she'd set off alarm bells back in mine.

I'd never had to rely on a *coup de main* before. The cute moniker was given to our backup teams in a tongue in cheek effort to minimise the seriousness of a situation that would require a pre-emptive strike to remedy. Causal loops created caustic humour. But if Fawkes was here, then he was here as my *coup de main*.

Never had one of those before on any of my rodeos.

I sighed. We were far enough away now to pull over.

"Stop the vehicle, Miss Wylde. Our ride is here."

She looked up into the rearview mirror, eyes unnaturally wide, face flushed an attractive pink, lips slightly parted as she breathed a little too heavily. God, but she was a compelling creature. More so, I was sure, because of my dreams.

"You can slow down now, Mimi," I added, as she clearly wasn't responding to "Miss Wylde."

"H..he was one of yours?" she asked on a stutter, bringing the cruiser to a stop on the *wrong* side of the roadway.

"Yes. Dr Bryan Fawkes. A RATS Surgeon."

"Rats," she said softly, putting the vehicle, thank fuck, in park. "I thought he was making a joke about my nickname."

"Mouse?" I asked, unsure where she was going with this.

She nodded her head and turned the ignition off, letting the engine tick away quietly.

Everything needed to be pulled from this one. Mimi Wylde did not give up her secrets easily.

"Who was teasing, Miss Wylde?"

"The man with the gun," she replied and promptly exited the vehicle.

Bloody hell. The shooter must have talked to her. Touched her? I banged against the locked rear door frantically, suddenly desperate to check that she was all right, just as the MPCV appeared off to the side, closely followed by a second Vehicle.

Great, reinforcements. Knowing this woman, and God alone knows I was beginning to, she'd clam up.

She opened the rear door for me and stepped back, arms wrapped securely about her stomach, eyes darting toward the two Orions and then back to me. She gnawed on her bottom lip uncertainly.

Rafe appeared in the doorway of Orion One. Eyebrows raised questioningly. Fawkes scowled from the doorway of Orion Two. Mimi squeaked.

I'm not quite sure why, but I snapped.

"Give us a bloody minute, would you?" Rafe's eyes grew bigger. So did Fawkes' scowl. But both retreated to the inside of their Vehicles, and the Orions winked out of sight. Mimi jumped.

I sighed, took a look back down the small country road we'd ended up on, and then leant back against the cruiser. We had time. Fuck, that's all we had. Ours. Hers. Theirs. With an Orion, we could literally make it.

Shame we couldn't seem to catch this one.

"Your presence has upset the time continuum," I began. Her soulful eyes met mine, not leaving. "We already knew the rip was big. An Origin Event. So Bryan would have been put on standby as soon as my crew took flight. I should think, the moment we picked you up, or maybe it was your sister who triggered it, but either way, Dr Fawkes would have been instructed to follow. It doesn't happen often. Most flights are a one module journey. Can't risk more than that.

"But some risks..." I couldn't finish that statement. The risks I referred to had nothing to do with the flight.

I thrust my hands in my pockets and stood up from the cruiser.

"We know now what the cause of the rip in this time is," I advised. "It will take but a moment to stitch it."

"Stitch it?" she asked. I was just relieved she was talking.

"There are three ways to mend Time, Miss Wylde. We can catch it before the rip causes damage. Stitch it if the rip can be contained. Or, worse case scenario, make it from scratch. It was a close run thing, but our intervention with the shooter has enabled us to avoid the last option. But the rip is already too big to leave untended. I'll stitch it, and then we can move on."

Move *back*. I didn't say it, but she heard it. Her eyes narrowing slightly.

I wondered for the umpteenth time since I'd met this woman just what went through her head when she looked like that. Intelligent didn't even cover it.

"And my sister?"

Ah, not so easily mended.

"I don't know where your sister is now, Miss Wylde," I admitted. "But we *will* keep looking."

"And who is we, Dr Evans? You and your Orion teams? Or you and me?"

"You are out of..."

"Time. Yes, I know. So you all keep saying. But that man has my sister. And, from what I can ascertain, his threats are no longer just your problem."

"What threats?" I demanded, taking a step closer. "What did he say to you? Did he harm you? Did he *threaten* you?"

It was irrational, but the anger I felt at that thought was all consuming. I did not want anyone threatening Mimi Wylde.

I forced my ire back down. Forced myself to control my emotions. Losing it now wouldn't help anyone. Least of all Carolyn Wylde.

"What did he say to you, Mimi?"

"What's Lunik?" she said instead of answering.

And I knew then that stitching this time was the least of our worries.

"Bloody fucking hell," I muttered. And then ran a hand through my hair. I shook my head, dislodged one option after the other. And finally settled on a path to take.

Clive Crawford was going to throw a hissy fit.

I stretched my neck and tugged on my shirt sleeve, activating the communicator. Orion One appeared, swiftly followed by Orion Two. Fawkes had linked them. Not unsurprising, but a damn nuisance considering.

The doors opened, and Rafe and Bryan stared out respectively.

"It's Sergei," I said.

"Bloody hell," Rafe spat. "Goddamit," Bryan muttered.

"Who's Sergei?" Mimi asked. "Competition?" she added.

"The worst kind, Miss Wylde." And he has your sister, I didn't say, but her head jerked back in shock anyway, and her eyes met mine. Knowing.

What was with this woman?

It was as if she had a direct line to my thoughts.

"Can we find him?" she asked.

I shook my head.

"He doesn't stick to a particular plane," Rafe offered, receiving a frown from Fawkes while he was at it.

"What's your plan here, Evans?" Fawkes asked. His eyes on Mimi.

I didn't like him even looking at her, let alone suggesting non-verbally that I return her to her time.

I knew what was required of me. I knew what Crawford would

demand. But how could we return Mimi without her sister? It's not like we could make her forget she had a sibling. Neuralyzers weren't actually real. This was.

"We mend the tear," I said, walking towards my Vehicle. "Return home and start again. He'll make a mistake."

Fawkes stepped out of his own Vehicle. I paused on the bottom rung of our ladder. Waiting.

I didn't have to wait long.

"I have my orders, Jack," he said. It was almost an apology.

My head snapped towards him, just as Rafe shouted out a warning. But Fawkes was too quick. Taking the necessary steps required to reach Miss Wylde's side and swapping dimensions to move his Orion closer while he was at it.

By the time I'd jumped down off our ladder, he'd already grabbed hold of Mimi's arm, and was back on board Orion Two, winking out of sight.

"Bloody fucking bollocks!" I yelled, emotions roiling up and consuming.

"Jack," Rafe warned.

But all I could see was orange. Not red. Orange.

My own particular form of hell.

12

YOU ARE NO MOUSE

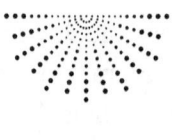

MIMI

*T*he MPCV bounced around as though trapped on a demented trampoline. And I'd thought my last ride was chaotic. I rolled across the dimpled metal floor banging into cabinets, fending off falling items, fighting a repeat of nausea.

"Get a handle on it," the American, Bryan Fawkes, Evans had called him, yelled. "No, not that one! The attitude adjustor. Christ! It's as if we've never flown a module before."

"Easy for you to say, Fawkes," a woman yelled back. "It's as good as a bloody tug lost at sea." She was British, which strangely gave me some measure of comfort. And having ascertained that Fawkes was part of the good team, that thought made little to no sense at all. But there you have it. Rolling around in a tumble dryer of a command module the British accent settled my nerves.

And stomach.

"Shift dimensions then," Fawkes shouted.

"We're dragging something," another voice said. I spotted the speaker as I rolled past him across the floor. Male. Wearing orange.

Effing orange. I was beginning to despise that colour.

"For God's sake," Fawkes yelled. "Someone buckle our passenger in before she breaks her neck or something."

It was the something that did it. What could be worse than a broken neck?

"Touch me, and I *will* hurt you," I snarled at the man who moved to leave his seat at Fawkes' command.

"Snappy, isn't she?" the woman remarked, just as the MPCV took some unknown corner too fast and I face planted into the back of her seat.

Ow.

"Concentrate, Harding," Fawkes snapped back at her. "You're in control of this vessel, act like it."

"We *are* trailing something," the male repeated, having retaken his seat and fastened his seatbelt.

I was a little miffed he'd given up on my safety so easily. I rolled past him and kicked out with my leg.

"Hey!" he cried, and I smirked, right up until an oxygen bottle fell out of a cabinet.

"Goddamnit!" Fawkes shouted, launching himself from his seat, walking sideways, arms outstretched for balance, as the module tipped over precariously, and sweeping up the clattering metal cylinder before it managed to knock me out. "You are way more trouble than you're worth. And you were already worth jack shit, darlin'."

"I sincerely hope you're referring to the O2 bottle," I growled, reaching out and snagging the spare seat, clinging to it for all I was worth. Which, apparently, was jack shit according to the sweet talking Dr Fawkes.

He laughed as he secured the bottle and then crab walked back to his own chair.

"Buckle yourself in, princess. Things are going to get wild."

"I'm already Wylde," I snapped back, hauling myself up unattractively onto the seat and fumbling with the harnesses.

"Does she ever shut up?" the woman, Harding, asked.

"Not since I've met her, no," Fawkes offered, then sent me a wink.

Damn it! I wanted to like the guy. Even when he was irascible. There was just something about him which made me think under different circumstances he might have been all right. What circumstances they could be, I didn't know yet. But hiding behind that grumpy façade he showed the world was undoubtedly someone who understood humour.

The MPCV hit a particularly nasty pothole, then, making me glad I'd managed to buckle myself in at last.

"What exactly are we hitting?" I asked, genuinely intrigued to know the answer. Did Time even have potholes?

And received a sneer from Harding for my efforts.

"Warps in the dimension," the other guy offered, taking pity on me. "When more than one Vehicle uses a particular combination of dimensions to travel to the same plane it can cause conflicts in the stream." He pointed to the orange sine wave on the largest screen beside him. It seemed a little elongated, quite different from the one I'd seen in Evans' Orion.

"Tell her *all* our secrets, why don't ya?" Fawkes muttered, but his heart seemed no longer in it. He sighed. "Drop out, Harding. They're tracing the link. Made their own one by now, no doubt. Nothin' we can do to shake 'em."

"Who?" I asked.

"Your would-be protector." Ah, Evans was hot on our tail. I felt suddenly warm and fuzzy inside.

"And why would I *need* a protector?" I demanded.

"Because you are out of time, idiot!" Harding growled.

Fawkes laughed. He seemed to like to do that a lot. More often at someone, and not with them.

"She's right, you know," he said pleasantly, as the MPCV finally stopped hopping around. "Your presence alone has disrupted Time on so many different planes; it ain't funny."

"And yet you laugh," I pointed out.

"Well, I'm not gonna fuckin' cry about it, am I?" he said, standing up from his seat and walking to the door. "Stay put, darlin'," he said in passing. Then, "If she moves, shoot her."

Harding pulled out a weapon and cocked it.

I raised an eyebrow at her. I'd had my fair share of guns aimed at me recently. The shock had well and truly worn off.

"A bit melodramatic, don't you think?" I said pleasantly. Taking a page out of the Surgeons' books.

"Push me, princess," she snarled, using Fawkes' one-time moniker for me. "I dare you."

"Jess," the other guy warned. "Don't freak her out."

"Why? Are you afraid she might explode, Malcolm?"

"Not her I'm afraid of," he muttered, turning back to his screens and pushing a few buttons. On the largest, the sine wave disappeared, and the outside of the command module flickered to life.

Complete with Jack Evans facing off against Bryan Fawkes.

"Is there any sound?" I asked, eager to hear what was being said about me.

"Push that button, and I will shoot you, Novitiate," Harding growled.

God, she was getting on my nerves. But Malcolm just raised his arms in the air and sat silently.

We watched the screen in mute fascination, the ticking of the MPCV the only soundtrack to what was transpiring outside. But I could guess. In fact, I could almost read their lips they were so agitated.

What the bloody fucking hell are you playing at? Evans was saying.

Saving your ass, jackass, Fawkes replied.

She's my problem! And didn't that just make me feel peachy? Problem, eh? I'd show him...

You're blinded by somethin', Jacko. Don't know what it is. Pretty face. Big tits. Who knows. But you ain't seein' too clearly right now. Let me deal with this.

You're wrong. It's not attraction. It's dimensional. Whatever the fuck that meant.

Really? Fawkes asked, and even though I couldn't hear it, I swore I could see the sarcasm in the lipread words.

Evans ran a hand through his hair, messing it up spectacularly. He scrubbed at the stubble along his jaw and then worried at the scar bisecting it. As though it was a knee-jerk reaction to whatever had caused it storming his mind right in that second.

Jesus, Fawkes muttered, shaking his head. *You dream of her?*

And suddenly, I wished the screen was blank. Harding and Malcolm turned to look down at me, equal looks of dread and shock on their faces. It was Harding who reached for the volume switch, turning it up so loud the speakers crackled, making me flinch.

"The morning of the flight," Evans said softly, but whatever external microphones the MPCV had were pretty effing good.

"Ah, shit, Jack," Fawkes muttered. "And if we take her back to her time?"

Evans shook his head. "I don't know. The dream wasn't...specific like that."

"Then what *did* you see?"

Evans turned away and stared out over a sugarcane field. His right hand tapped impatiently against his upper thigh. His shoulders were rigid.

"I can't let you take her, Bryan," he said eventually. Fawkes, for his part, just rubbed the back of his neck, then clasped both hands behind his nape and stared up at the brightening sky.

Clearly, we were still in Florida, going on the field of sugar before us. But time had changed. Whether that was Time with a capital T or not, I wasn't sure. The MPCV *had* been moving along dimensional planes, so anything was possible.

And reading the multitude of numbers and sine waves and mess of information on the screens in here was beyond me. I was feeling a little tired all of a sudden.

"Crap," I muttered, slumping back against my seat. "Not now." I pleaded with my upper hypothalamus for a reprieve.

"If you take her back to base, Crawford *will* ground you," Fawkes was saying.

"I'm aware of Clive's penchant for rules, Bryan. I made most of them with him."

"If you take her anywhere, he'll put a tag on your file."

"I know."

"The only possible solution is to return with her to her time."

"A possibility. But that would hardly locate her sister."

"Her what now?" Fawkes had gone deathly still. Like statue still. His face set in hard planes. His blue eyes narrowed.

"What sister?" Malcolm asked, staring across the module at me.

"God, please don't tell us there's two of you," Harding spat.

"Shhh," I said, trying to listen to the screen.

"Shh yourself, interloper," Harding snapped. "I'm in command here, not you."

"Sorry, Sergeant Snotty," I said with a sickly sweet smile. "But you're not the boss of me."

Yeah, that was mature. Carrie would have been proud.

"I'm a fully qualified Intern," she growled. "You are nothing but a relic of a previous history."

I blinked at her. "Relic?"

She sneered back. "You are neither RATS approved nor trained. Ergo you are not in any position to make demands. I'm the Intern. Malcolm here is the Novitiate. And as soon as Dr Fawkes returns, he's our Surgeon. You." She sneered again. She liked doing that. "You are out of time."

"What's with you freaks and people being *out of time*? You'd think it was contagious or something."

"Well," Malcolm started, just as the door to the Orion opened.

Damn it! We'd missed the last part of Fawkes' and Evans' conversation. I braced myself for the good Dr Fawkes and his own special brand of humour, only to come face to face with Jack Evans himself.

"Dr Evans," Malcolm said, standing. "Doctor," Harding added but remained immobile after.

Jack nodded his head towards them in greeting, but his eyes soon landed back on me.

"You've been hurt," he said softly. That gentle tone immediately reaching me.

"Just bruised," I replied, rubbing at my elbow and where the cabinet had banged into me. Yeah, like that made any sense at all, but when the module was upside, and inside out, it had sure felt like the thing was attacking me.

Pretty much like Harding really.

I flicked a glance towards her, but couldn't avoid the pull to stare at Evans for long.

"You're with me, Miss Wylde," he announced, almost as if he'd snapped out of something. He stood taller. Looked broader of shoulder. Seemed to take up more space suddenly.

"You're taking her?" Harding demanded.

"She is in my care, Dr Harding," Evans bothered to reply.

"She's out of time, sir," Harding argued.

Evans stopped moving toward me and just stared at the woman.

"Quiet, Jess," Fawkes said from behind Jack's shoulder. "This is complicated."

"What is complicated?" Harding demanded, standing up to her full height, which was surprisingly quite impressive. She must have been close to six feet tall. I hadn't noticed. Her ego had overshadowed everything else about her until that second.

"What could possibly be more complicated than a contemporary out of time?" she demanded. "The rules state…"

"I know exactly what the rules state, Doctor," Evans snapped. "And I'd thank you to remember your place. You *are* still an Intern, are you not?"

Harding looked like she'd swallowed a lemon.

"Yes, sir," she eventually offered.

"Good. Then you'll allow your *Surgeon* to guide you in this matter."

Harding looked toward Fawkes. He wore the glare quite well, considering.

"She's with him," Fawkes said, backing Evans up on the matter. "For now, anyway," he added, ruining the united front he'd had going.

"Gee," I said. "It's almost like I'm a possession. Don't I get a say?"

Evans swung his glowering face back towards me. It didn't soften in the slightest. I swallowed thickly.

"Take your pick, Miss Wylde," he said, voice low and threatening. "Me or Dr Harding? Which is it?"

Well, when he put it like that. I nodded and took a step toward his side.

"Thought you might choose wisely," Evans muttered.

Then slipped his hand into mine and tugged me outside.

The motion, fingers laced, had felt so normal to me that I hadn't thought anything of it. Until I heard Fawkes mutter, "Goddamnit, Jack. At least try to deny it."

Evans dropped my hand as though it had scolded him. And suddenly I felt as cold as ice.

We both turned slowly to look at Orion Two, thankful that it was only Fawkes who stood in the door and watched us.

And then I remembered the screens were still on inside the module. I let a slow breath of air out and waved. I might have flipped Harding the bird at the last minute, can't be sure. I was distracted by Fawkes laughing.

"You'll deal with the stitch?" Evans was asking.

"On it," Fawkes replied. "Always cleaning up after your ass, Jacko."

"Much appreciated, Bryan."

Fawkes chuckled, then let his eyes land on me.

"Sort this out, Jack. Sort it out, or Crawford will sort it out for you. And you won't much like his method or style."

"I'm well aware of Clive's proclivities, Dr Fawkes."

Fawkes shook his head and started to turn back into his own module.

"Not when you're flying blind," he muttered, and then the MPCV winked out of sight.

Silence stretched for a long moment. If our Orion was near, it was still hiding. On a different plane. A different combination of dimensions. Whatever. It boggled the mind. But more pressing matters held my attention.

"What does he mean 'flying blind'?" I asked.

"Never you mind, Miss Wylde."

"Oh, but I do, Doctor."

He smiled to himself, half watching me behind shadowed eyes.

"You are more trouble than you're worth, you know," he murmured.

"Oh, don't you start. I've already had the shakedown by Harding. That woman didn't pull any punches."

"Jessica Harding is a very skilled Intern. She wouldn't have lied."

"But you will? Is that how it works? Make Surgeon, and you not only mend Time, but you can lie about it? Where's my sister?" I demanded. "Who is Sergei?"

Evans stared at me for a long moment and then tugged on the sleeve of his shirt. Once.

The MPCV blinked into sight.

"Fuck me!" I squeaked, staring at the imposing structure.

"You are no mouse," Evans murmured, walking past me and up the ladder.

"And you, Doctor, didn't answer my question," I muttered, following behind.

I was beginning to see that was his style. Harding blustered. Fawkes joked. Hoffman smiled. But Jack Evans evaded.

Just what the effing hell was he hiding?

13

WELL, TWO COULD PLAY
THAT GAME

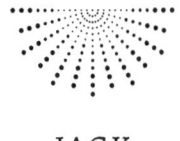

JACK

She was too clever for her own good. Distracting her worked. Dodging her didn't. Mimi Wylde needed something else to focus on. Otherwise, she was like a dog with a bone.

Or a scientist with a hypothesis to prove.

"We could retrace our steps," Groves was offering. "Try to pick up a shadow to follow."

"Orion Two will be back there," Rafe said. "Crossing paths with Harding right now wouldn't be wise."

"I'm sure Dr Fawkes has her in hand," Groves argued.

"As in hand as a snake charmer and his rattler."

"She can't be that bad," Groves offered.

"Sally, she's a fucking viper."

"That's enough," I murmured, searching sinusoids in an effort to locate Sergei. I'd told Mimi I was watching the rip, making sure Bryan stitched it correctly.

I was certain she'd seen right through me.

"Rafe," the woman in question asked now from behind me. I refused to turn around and stare. I'd thought she was dosing, subject to time travel stupor. The fact that she'd been awake and watching made the hairs stand up on the back of my neck. I worked hard not to rub there.

"Yeah, Mouse?" Hoffman replied. I did look at him, then. He purposefully ignored me.

"What is Sergei trying to do exactly?"

I'd laid the ground rules. I'd made it perfectly clear that Sergei should not be discussed with our passenger. I tilted my head and held Rafe's stare.

"What any plonker with a module is wont to do, kid," Rafe muttered. "Change Time for profit."

"So he's wanting to sabotage Orion, making Lunik the only way to time travel?"

"Pretty much," Rafe said, raising his eyebrows at me when I started to growl.

"Thanks, Rafe," Mimi said pleasantly. "At least someone here isn't lying."

"And how can you be so sure of that, Miss Wylde?" I asked, turning to face her at last.

Not a hardship. But I fought the urge, all the same.

"Dr Hoffman has no reason to lie to me," she pointed out. "I didn't appear in *his* dream."

Oh, for fuck's sake!

"You have no idea what you're talking about," I ground out.

"Then enlighten me?"

"Not in this lifetime, Miss Wylde."

"Then I'll find out the answers on my own."

"Try."

"Oh, watch me."

How could I not? She was on fire.

"Sally," Mimi asked then.

"Oh, no you don't, Mouse," Groves rushed to say. "I'm a Novitiate. Dr Evans only has to scowl in my direction to get me fired."

"I'm not that bad, Miss Groves," I muttered.

"I'm sorry, sir," Groves said quietly. "But you are a little frightening."

Rafe snorted. Mimi just smiled.

"And why is it I can't scare you, Miss Wylde?" I asked.

"I don't care if I get fired," she said with a smile.

More's the pity. Maybe I should threaten her with something else. Spanking?

I cleared my throat and returned my attention to the sinusoids. Nothing. Not so much as a peep out of Sergei. What the bloody hell was he up to?

"We're going to need some down time soon, Jack," Rafe murmured. "Maybe some food and rest will make things clearer."

"Do you guys sleep in here too?" Mimi asked. "Or do you drop out of a dimension onto a plane for a while?"

"Hey, you're getting pretty good at the lingo," Rafe said, amusement coating each word. "But nah, we just take turns sleeping, while someone flies."

"Why?"

I turned back to look at her. It fascinated me how her mind worked sometimes.

"Why not pick a time and just use it. Grab some fresh air while you're at it."

"It does stink in here," Groves muttered.

"Sorry. The nausea," Mimi supplied.

"Oh, no!" Groves rushed to say. "Boy stink. Not, well, you know, *that*."

Mimi burst out laughing. It was mesmerising.

"Yeah, boy stink has a distinctive note," she said between laughter.

I realised Rafe was watching me. Again. I turned my gaze reluctantly away from Miss Wylde and met his eyes. I could see the question there. The same one Fawkes had asked me when I'd admitted to dreaming about Mimi Wylde.

There was no bloody way I'd tell either of them what had transpired in that dreamscape. Not a bloody fucking chance.

Rafe smirked. Maybe I didn't have to say a word for either of those two to work it out.

"Perhaps we *should* drop out of space," I said suddenly. "If we can't pick anything up whilst surfing the waves, then maybe we will if we're more stationary."

"Good point," Rafe agreed. "How about somewhere warm, secluded, and with a beach."

Groves perked up. I just offered a jaded smile.

But it was Mimi who said, "Why not somewhere further back in time where Abe Silverstein will be?"

I have no idea why this woman was picked up by our Orion. Why her sister was picked up by a Lunik. I couldn't work out what was different about these two females that would cause such an event to occur. Granted it was an Origin Event, and almost anything is possible with them. But why her? Why her sister? Why now?

One thing I did know, though, was that Mimi Wylde was highly intelligent. She'd not only adjusted to time travel in lightning fast speed, but she'd also started thinking like a Surgeon while she was at it. It didn't fail to register how much of an addition she would make to the RATS team. How easily she would fit in back at the Academy.

"Valid point, Miss Wylde," I said slowly, watching her preen under my praise and desperately wanting to offer her more. "Perhaps when he started working on Gemini?"

"Yes," she said enthusiastically. "The early sixties. Mercury led to Gemini which led to Apollo. Which clearly led this Sergei dude to Orion."

Time to distract.

"We'll make a RATS Surgeon of you yet, Miss Wylde."

Hook, line and sinker.

"What *does* RATS actually mean?" she immediately asked. I smiled to myself, turned back to my screens and started entering coordinates, as Groves and Hoffman picked up the slack and ran with it.

We made a well-oiled machine.

"Royal Academy of Time Surgeons," Rafe was saying. "We're the good guys!"

"And Sergei?" the damn woman asked. Dog with a bloody fucking bone. "Where does he hail from? The former Union of Soviet Socialist Republics Academy of Time Travel?"

Too bloody intelligent by far.

"Got it!" I said, interrupting further discussion. I'd never declared "got it" before in my life. Rafe hid a smile. Groves blatantly stared at me. "The coordinates, Miss Groves," I said, handing them to her. "Perhaps you'll do the honours and check them for me."

"Of course, sir. But shouldn't Dr Hoffman be the one?"

"Oh, he can watch over your shoulder. It's time we made an Intern of you."

"Oh," Groves said, smiling uncertainly.

"Why don't you show Miss Wylde how it's done," I suggested.

"OK," Groves said, as Mimi muttered, "Coward," under her breath.

I stared at her. She held my gaze resolutely. This woman was going to be the death of me.

"Can't you just leave it?" I asked. God alone knows why that spilt out. She frustrated me. That had to be it.

It had nothing to do with the dream.

"Can't you be honest for once?" Mimi threw back in her lightning-fast fashion.

"You might as well tell her, Jack," Rafe offered with a shrug of his shoulders. "You're practically teaching the woman to fly an MPCV."

He was right. This was getting out of hand. But she needed to know the consequences. There were many.

"Check the coordinates with Groves," I muttered, dismissing my team and turning my attention to Miss Wylde.

"Well?" she said in challenge. Definitely not mousey.

I smiled. It might have shown a hint of teeth.

"You are out of time, Miss Wylde," I started.

Only to have the bloody woman fly right at me.

"Oomph," was all I managed as all air was knocked from my body. Her fists came down in surprisingly hard pummels, rapidly alternating with each growled word as she belted the living daylights out of me.

"What...is it...with...you lot...and...me...bloody...effing...being... out of...time!"

"Oomph," was all I was momentarily capable of right then, it seemed.

"I am…sick…and…tired…of being…told…that!"

I grabbed her wrists and flipped her over, both of us landing hard on the floor of the module. Her harder than me, but then she'd also cushioned my fall splendidly.

"Oomph," she muttered in return, making me smile. There was definitely teeth showing.

"Are you done?" I asked, breathlessly.

"No!" she snarled back.

"I was merely pointing out a salient fact," I growled in return.

"Get off me!"

"Not if you plan on hitting me again."

"I won't."

"I don't believe you."

"Arghh!" she growled trying to head butt me.

"Where the bloody fucking hell has Miss Wylde gone?" I demanded, struggling to contain the woman beneath me. It didn't help that every time she moved I fell farther into all manner of unspeakable places. Felt every single press of her skin against every single part of me.

Just like my dream.

"Damn it, woman!" I yelled.

And then she kissed me.

I'd been bamboozled by her intelligence. I'd overlooked entirely the fact that coupled with her lightning fast reflexes, her surprising ability to adjust to any situation with exemplary talent and success made her far more lethal than she'd at first appeared.

Machiavellian even.

Well, two could play that game.

I kissed her bloody well back.

14
I WAS THE OE

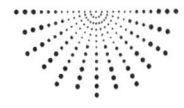

MIMI

*H*e kissed angrily. I liked it. But it was nothing like my dream. Then he'd kissed me languidly like he'd kissed me a thousand times before and planned to kiss me a thousand more.

Now he kissed me almost hungrily, desperately, wildly. As if he was trying to make a point. To me? Or him? I didn't know. Either way, it was a point well made. His kiss ruled my body.

His kiss left me slightly insane.

I wanted more; my hands frantic, my tongue desperate, I was sure I was moaning. He wrapped a fist up in the strands of my hair and tugged. Hard. As if to say, not here. Not in this. I kiss, you get kissed. End of bloody story, Miss Wylde.

I bit his lip. He growled, pulled me closer, kissed me harder. Ruined me for other boys.

And then someone said, "Shouldn't we stop them?"

No! This was *my* dream.

"Nah," someone else said. "They'll run out of steam sooner or later. Just ignore them." I liked that plan. Downright genius in fact. "Besides, it could get entertaining."

"There is something seriously wrong with you, Dr Hoffman."

"Why thank you, Miss Groves. I do try."

"No, seriously. I think we should stop them."

"Oh, all right."

I made a sound I'm not proud of, something between a mouse squeaking and a cat hissing. But I challenge anyone to do better when doused with a bucket of cold water.

"Bloody fucking hell!" Evans shouted, rising out of the water like a wrathful sea god. And then he looked around. Spotted me on the floor of the module, equally as wet and dishevelled, and swallowed.

"Welcome back," Hoffman greeted. "And congratulations. You've now trained our Novitiate in all aspects of prophetic dreamscape realisation. I'd give her a solid A+ on problem-solving. And a C- on letting things play out."

"Fuck," I thought I heard Evans mutter. He didn't look at me. He didn't look at much, really. But then he lifted a slightly shaking hand to his lips, let it hover for a suspended moment, before reaching for his scar.

Right then. Evasive Evans was back. Good to know.

"The coordinates?" he asked, just as Groves handed me a towel. I started angrily drying my hair, the hand movements reminding me of Jack's equally hard kiss. Wasn't going to forget that anytime soon.

"All fired up and ready to go," Rafe answered.

"Good. Engage, then."

As if none of it had happened.

I stood up stiffly from the cold floor and crossed to the command chair. Evans stiffened. I scowled. And dumped the now wet towel on his lap.

That should do it.

A few seconds later he was up and hiding in the bathroom doing whatever it was he did when he evaded.

"Well, that wasn't at all awkward."

"Dr Hoffman! Really."

"You know, Groves. I think I liked you better when you were silent."

"Oh," she gasped. "You don't mean that."

He smiled. "Not in the slightest." And then he turned to me.

It was always going to happen, sooner or later. But I would have preferred becoming the centre of attention much, much later.

"So, seen any good movies lately?" Hoffman asked. Groves stifled a giggle and studiously returned her attention to her screen. I shook my head.

Hoffman watched me for a while and then crossed his arms over his chest and kept staring.

"The better question would be," he said eventually, "have you had any good dreams lately?"

I knew that was a question better left unanswered.

"I don't know what you mean," I said, mirroring his stance; arms crossed over chest lightly.

"There's a lot you don't know about time travel, Mouse," Hoffman said. "A lot."

"And you're not going to enlighten her," Evans interrupted from the bathroom.

He was washed and dressed, this time in a cardigan and tie, a combination I hadn't seen in anything other than old photos. And then I realised what he was wearing; clothing appropriate to the early sixties. Clothing appropriate for our next trip. Back in time.

It would have been easy to get distracted and demand what clothing I should be wearing, but I was a much more tenacious scientist than that.

"And why can't I be enlightened?" I demanded Evans.

He flicked me a look that said more than words could ever convey. I saw a conversation's worth of sentences in that one intense gaze. Are we to do this again, Miss Wylde? Will you attack? It didn't go so well the first time I tried to explain.

OK, he had a point. And that was the last time I would bring out Hyde, I decided. I swear. But he didn't exactly fight me off with a stick, did he?

I cocked my hip. Tightened my crossed arms over my chest. And raised my eyebrows at him.

"Try me."

His lips twitched, but he fought the smile valiantly. Crossing to his command chair, he checked the sine wave on the screen and took a seat. Only then turning his attention back to me. He played games, I realised. Not the nasty kind. I wasn't even sure if he was aware he did it. In his evasion, he laid traps.

I was never very good at avoiding obstacles.

"Or are you a coward, Dr Evans?"

Rafe snorted. Groves gasped. And I thought perhaps I'd gone too far this time.

Evans blinked once. Twice. And then shook his head, jaw firming.

"Why you?" he muttered.

"Maybe fate decided you needed a challenge, Jack," Hoffman offered helpfully.

"That'll be enough of that, thank you, Dr Hoffman."

Suitably chastised, Rafe returned his attention to his screen. There was nothing on there of interest, so it was obvious he was just humouring Evans more than anything.

"The more you learn of our time, the harder it is to get you back to yours."

It was a simple statement that made no scientific sense at all. But I didn't take Jack Evans as a jokester.

"That's ridiculous," I mumbled.

"Travelling through Time carries risks, Miss Wylde. Not just physically, but temporally. The longer you are out of time, the farther away you travel. Not linearly. We're still only half a century past yours in terms of history. It's not the accumulative years, you see. It's the number of loops you bisect. And you have bisected two at once. Minimising your knowledge will ease your return."

"I don't believe you." Such a childish thing to say. But I couldn't accept returning to my time would be so difficult. We'd already travelled to 1969 and 1961 respectively, and none of the RATS team looked remotely worried about getting back to their time.

"Were you this argumentative with your professors?" Evans asked.

"Always."

He laughed. It surprised him, I think. It certainly surprised me. I'd heard him laugh once already, but I was beginning to think each time I did would be as if a precious gift received.

Evans sighed, the laughter subsiding much too quickly.

"The less you learn, the easier your return will be."

Ever the scientist questioning things, I said, "This still doesn't make any sense at all."

Hoffman turned around in his seat, letting us know he hadn't missed a thing staring at nothing.

"He's right, Mouse. It's a proven fact. But he's not telling you everything."

"Is there a reason why you continue to defy me, Dr Hoffman?" Evans barked.

"She won't understand unless you tell her the truth."

"The whole point of keeping her in the dark is so she'll return to her time unscathed."

"At this rate, it's already too late, and you know it."

Silence.

"What does he mean?" I asked Evans. He didn't reply. "Sally?"

"Please don't, Mouse," she whispered.

"Why is it so hard for any of you to tell me what's going on?" I demanded. "I'm here. I'm not going anywhere until I find my sister. You can't get rid of me, so you might as well tell me. What does Hoffman mean?"

"You're an Origin Event," Evans said softly. Gently. That tone.

"Unpredictable, I know," I offered.

He smiled. Amused but not. There was too much sadness.

"Origin Events have to be corrected."

"And we will correct this one," I said. "Find Carrie. Go home."

"Sometimes how they are corrected is...unpredictable."

"You're talking in circles."

"The bane of a Surgeon's life," Hoffman quipped. "Causal loops? Temporal paradoxes? All one big bloody circle."

"Yes, thank you, Doctor," Evans said. "We get the picture."

I hated to admit it, but it had to be said. "I still don't understand."

Evans sighed. It sounded weighty. "Origin Events are unpredictable, yes, but why they are is quite well known. More often than not they're a temporal paradox. Usually, an ever evolving one until the loop is broken and the OE fixed."

He was losing me again. Not hard, considering the subject matter. But still...I needed to comprehend this. Something told me, it would be vital in finding Carrie.

"Explain," I said. Evans leant forward in his seat, resting his elbows on his knees, eyes glued to mine, seeing everything.

"A self-perpetuating loop. Event two causes event one, which in turn causes event two, which causes event one again, and so on and so forth. But an Origin Event is bigger, stronger, wider reaching. Event two causes event one, which causes event three, which causes event four, which causes event two, which causes event one. But herein lies the rub, event three and event four are undecided. They aren't set in stone, even though, technically, because this is a causal loop we're talking about, they've already transpired. In an Origin Event, they can be changed."

"They will happen. But how they happen is open to influence. Such as an Origin Event learning too much."

"Such as me knowing about event three and four even existing," I finished for him.

He sat back in his seat and grimaced. "Yes."

"So now what happens?"

"I don't know. Event three and four are still unwritten. If we can keep it that way, we may have a chance of correcting this loop."

"And returning me to my time."

"Yes."

I didn't say what I was thinking. I didn't voice the hurtful words on my tongue.

There was nothing for me in my time without Carrie. Mum and Dad were gone. My Ph.D in tatters. I'm not even sure I could pick up my thesis now and believe in what I had been trying to prove with it. So much had changed. Least of all my knowledge of time travel.

It exists. It actually effing exists.

How did I go back to talking about quantifiable hypotheses when non-quantifiable ones existed?

I couldn't. Event three had already happened.

I was tied up in this inextricably. I was as involved as RATS. As committed as Sergei and his Lunik team of mercenaries. He had Carrie. The moment he'd threatened her life, event three happened.

I looked up from where I'd been staring at the metal dimples on the floor and met Jack's eyes. A whisky so rich I could almost taste it.

"What is it?" he asked. He could read me so well. "What's put that look on your face, Miss Wylde?" I could have sworn he felt my pain, as well.

I smiled. If you can call a twist of the lips filled with such heart-rending agony a smile.

But I didn't say the words. Words failed me.

"Mimi?"

I shook my head. I was just so effing tired.

"It takes it out of you," he said softly. "The first few times are hell on the upper hypothalamus. The part of the brain that stimulates wakefulness and sleep. It throws you out of kilter."

I was thinking, perhaps, it was more than that. Maybe a mix of exhaustion and knowledge. The knowledge I wouldn't be going home.

It was almost no choice at all to embrace it. But still some part of the mind rebels. Being out of time went against all known parameters. Being out of time felt wrong.

But going back would feel worse.

"When we find Carrie and fix this loop, what will happen?" I asked.

"We'll get you both home."

"And if the Origin Event doesn't allow it."

"That won't happen." It was a promise.

One he couldn't keep.

And that knowledge was perhaps what made it easier. At some point in the last few seconds, I'd made my choice and accepted it.

"He says he'll kill her if you don't destroy the Orions."

The silence was almost deafening; it seemed so complete.

And then Evans burst out of the bubble in spectacular fashion.

"What the bloody fuck do you mean? He did threaten you, didn't he? Bloody fucking bollocks, Mimi. Why didn't you say something?"

"Because knowledge changes everything."

He stopped pacing and stared down at me, his fists slowly unclenching.

"Event three."

"Bloody hell," Rafe muttered.

"Oh, no," Sally added. "It's too late."

"It is not too late!" Evans growled. "This is still doable. The loop has expanded, granted. But we can contain this."

"You mean me," I said.

"Yes. No. That's not what I fucking well mean."

"Jack," Hoffman warned.

"Shut up, Rafe. I just need to think."

"He's here."

Evans swung around to look at the sine wave on the screen. I was sure it hadn't been orange before, but a pinkish colour. Now it was bright International Orange, glowing softly.

"Bollocks," Evans muttered. "Did we cause this by coming here?"

"This is the most unpredictable OE I've ever seen, Jack. There's no way of telling what is causing what right now. But us being here has to be for a reason."

"To get Carrie."

Rafe looked across the Vehicle to me. I saw such a depth of pity there; I couldn't breathe.

"We'll get her," Evans murmured. Another promise I knew he couldn't keep. He met Rafe's eyes and shrugged a shoulder. "It seems to be the only constant. Carolyn Wylde. We get her; we might just save the OE."

Three sets of eyes shifted to me. Yeah, I got it. I was the OE.

15

IN A MANNER OF SPEAKING

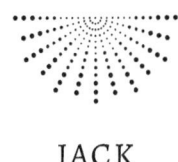

JACK

The longer I knew her, the harder it was to breathe. As if what I'd ridiculously called breathing before Mimi Wylde visited my dreams was no longer working. As if I needed to learn how to do it all over again.

As if the mere thought of returning her, losing her, made breathing impossible.

The only time I'd felt like oxygen was reaching my lungs was when her lips had been pressed against my own. When her breath had sustained me.

I couldn't breathe air anymore. I needed to breathe Mimi.

Oh, this was a disaster. A bloody fucking nightmare. Not a dream.

She was an Origin Event. And every single Origin Event I'd ever encountered had required all parts to be returned to their original plane. The original combination of dimensions. Stitched. Remade. It didn't matter how as long as all components were back where they were meant to be.

If I returned Mimi to where she needed to be, there was a distinct possibility that I'd suffocate without her.

I wanted to laugh in the face of that thought. I wanted to tell it to bloody well fuck off. But then I'd try to breathe, and all I felt was an ache in my chest so deep, so debilitating, that I realised I was suffocating.

Without Mimi.

But she was still bloody here! Right here inside the MPCV. Right inside my dreams.

I needed to rest and to eat. I needed to think. But an orange sinusoid meant only one thing. Time was unravelling. The original rip tearing apart this plane as much as it had done 1969. Sergei had either followed us here, or we were as much a part of the temporal paradox as Carolyn Wylde.

Egg meet chicken. Chicken meet egg.

I slammed my fist down on the dashboard of the module, making Groves startle and Rafe swear out loud. Thankfully Mimi was in the bathroom. Hence the reason why I couldn't breathe.

"You all right, Jack?" Rafe asked solicitously.

"Never better," I ground out. "What do we know about Silverstein in this time?"

My Intern jumped on the question, needing as much of a distraction as me.

"By 1961 he was Associate Director of the Lewis Laboratory, as it was known back then, at NASA," Rafe said, reading off his tablet screen. "He'd had an influential hand in the eventual success of the Mercury Project, well on the way to establishing the technical basis for Apollo."

"No mention of Orion probabilities?"

"None, but that's not to say he hadn't already started research into the possibility."

"If killed now, though, it would solve Lunik's problems."

Rafe leant back in his chair and stared at the ceiling. Not much to see there other than exposed pipes and wires, a few electrical circuits and bypass switches. But he studied it all with a singular focus.

"It doesn't make sense, Jack," he finally offered.

"What part?" I asked. "Picking up passengers on a massive OE? Or going to 1969 first?"

Rafe's head came down, and he stared at me, finger out, pointing.

"Exactly. Why try to eliminate Silverstein in 1969 when it's more than likely he'd already started research on Orion probabilities? Why not bypass that time and head straight for now? A known plane where Silverstein will be, well before Orion was made public knowledge. We've found evidence of Orion in the early seventies. By 1969 Silverstein would have been discussing its possibility around NASA. Taking him out then wouldn't have destroyed Orion. Just delayed it."

"Maybe a delay was all Lunik was after," Groves offered.

"Or maybe 1969 was a mistake," I countered. "Driven there by the anomaly of the Origin Event. The two Miss Wyldes."

"Or maybe," Rafe said voice heavy, "his prime objective is not destruction but knowledge. Maybe Lunik is its own causal loop. Maybe Lunik can't exist without Orion. He needs to secure that knowledge in some way, before destroying Orion for good."

Bloody hell. He had a point. And as the bathroom door opened and Mimi walked out in clothing circa 1960, I realised how Sergei was going to do it.

"He's not here to kill him," I said, my eyes inexorably drawn to Miss Wylde. "That's why he missed in '69."

"He meant to. To distract you," Rafe muttered.

"And get his hands on Miss Wylde."

"What?" she whispered, as Rafe said, "He couldn't have planned this. No one could have planned this. There's no way to predict an Origin Event, let alone a passenger being picked up on one."

"I'm not sure how he did it," I said. "But his motives may not be as straightforward as we've been led to believe."

"He was always a bloody tricky bastard," Rafe muttered.

"What's going on?" Mimi asked.

How to assuage her fears and somehow keep her knowledge from expanding?

Did I even want her to have the chance to return home? Could I be so selfish as to sabotage her chances?

Was that what I had subconsciously been doing?

I cleared my throat. Rubbed my jaw distractedly. Then sighed.

Nothing I did now would alter that dream. It had happened. I'd seen it. Her mere presence confirmed it was real.

At some stage in the future, I would sleep with this woman as though I'd slept with her a hundred times before. As though I planned to sleep with her a hundred more. It would be extraordinary but familiar. It would be the best fucking sex of my life but only because I knew exactly how to turn her on, how to make her moan, how to tease a scream of ecstasy from between those luscious lips.

I would know her intimately. And she would know me.

It was a done deal. Only Time needed to catch on.

That didn't mean telling her she would never go home again was easy. It didn't mean involving her more in our troubles was at all acceptable to me.

Besides sleeping with her in my dream, one other thing had been more than obvious to me.

I wanted to protect her. Like I have never wanted to protect a soul before in my life. Her mere safety and wellbeing had been paramount to me. The sense of how important, how essential, she was to my own happiness inescapable.

Mimi Wylde was the air that I breathed.

The caveat here should have been "in my dreams."

But I think I'd established that was already bollocks.

"Silverstein will be at the Lewis Laboratory," I said. "You probably know it as the Lewis Research Center."

"OK," she said slowly. Watching me intently. Seeing the lie behind the truth, it seemed.

"We're not entirely sure what the Lunik Vehicle is here for," I added, feeling like the worst kind of future lover for pulling her deeper into this thing, "other than to draw us into some sort of confrontation."

"You're dismissing Silverstein as a target?" she asked, so astutely.

I rubbed a hand over my face. "It's not as straightforward as that. He's still the drawcard, but for what, we don't yet know."

"So our plan?"

Was Mimi something Sergei would need? Or was it just me? He'd used her as a messenger. He'd lured or followed us here to see his message received. He already had Carolyn Wylde. Gaining Mimi wouldn't leverage him more than he'd already achieved. But if Carolyn had divulged anything, he'd know that Mimi was an OE.

Bloody fucking hell...Did I take her? Or Not?

"Miss Groves and I will investigate this time," I announced, seeing the shock register on Mimi's features. *Feeling* it. "It's best if you remain out of sight, Miss Wylde," I added. Digging the knife in deeper. *Feeling* it.

"Carrie doesn't know you," she argued. So simple. Not so easy.

"But Sergei does know you."

"It might be wise to hang back, Mouse," Rafe offered. I'd thank him later. "Let Jack and Sally check out the lay of the land, and then you and I can tag-team. Go in afterwards and seal the deal."

I threw a threatening look toward my Intern. He just smiled winningly back.

When I returned my gaze to Mimi, she was watching me.

"I'm going with you," she said, "because Carrie is *my* sister. Because *I'm* the OE. Because whatever the effing hell is going on involves *me*. I don't know why we're here. I don't know why this has happened, but I am not abandoning my sister. I won't. Not now. Not after we've lost everything. I can't. Don't ask me."

She took a deep, shattering breath in. My hand lifted, reaching for her. I forced it back down. My heart ached, but she was wrong. It wouldn't be safe.

I couldn't let her. Then how would I breathe?

"Carrie is the second half of me," she added, not losing steam. "Not just my sister. Not just my twin. Carrie's me, in reverse. Or mirrored. I don't know. She shares my genes." She laughed; a half sob, half chuckle. "Did you know we're identical? Monozygotic. So don't you dare..."

"What did you just say?" I asked.

"Huh?" Mimi managed, cut off mid-rant.

"Bloody hell," Rafe muttered.

"What?" Mimi asked.

"Your sister shares the same genetic makeup as you. Genetically nearly identical. Not a mirror, Miss Wylde, but a replica. And a massive Origin Event just happens to suck not one but two contemporaries out of their time, into a space-time nebula. A never before seen event, but one we now know is linked to you specifically. As if, let's say, dialled into your DNA."

I let a long breath escape me.

If I couldn't breathe without her, then...

"Do you understand what this means?" I asked softly.

"No," she whispered, but I think she did.

Too bloody clever by far, Miss Wylde.

"Ah, bloody hell," Rafe muttered.

"No," Mimi repeated. "No."

"We're caught in two causal loops," I said. "Not bisecting. But parallel. One nearly identical to the other."

"I don't understand," Miss Groves murmured. "Does that mean, whatever happens in this one will happen in the other?"

My eyes didn't leave Mimi's. I saw the realisation there. I saw the fear.

I smiled softly and gentled my tone. From this there was no protection, only treading with care.

"Yes," I said, my heart aching.

Hers, though, was clearly breaking.

"In a manner of speaking. Yes."

16

IT JUST MADE IT MORE REAL

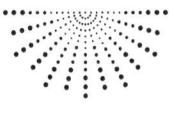

MIMI

I was losing her. I could feel it. As if part of me was being torn off, ripped away. And no amount of stitching would repair it. No RATS Surgeon could prevent this path in history. It was written on my very soul. Imprinted in my DNA.

I'd lose Carrie like I lost our parents.

"Tell me about him," I said into the heavy silence. The only sound that of waves.

We'd left 1961, attempting to draw Sergei away from Abe Silverstein. We'd not gone far; in both Time and space. It was too great a risk; should we ever solve this and get both Carrie and me back to our time, we needed there to be as few bisections as possible. We needed to get us home unscathed.

So we'd stayed close. 1962. Miami. South Beach during the Cuban Missile Crisis. Somewhere out there were boatloads of refugees. I felt a kinship with them.

They were out of time, too. Just like me.

Jack sifted the sand through his fingers, as he stared out into the Atlantic Sea.

"His full name is Sergei Anton Ivanov. He's an ex-Russian cosmonaut. Very astute. Very enigmatic. He spent the better part of the start of the century promoting international relations through cooperative exchanges on the International Space Station."

"Which century?"

He smiled. Let the sand fall from his fingers. And said, "You're very clever, you know? Too clever."

"You won't tell me?" I'd suspected as much.

"I'm rather biased when it comes to you."

I turned my head, resting it down on my bent knees, and watched him.

"I want to protect you," he explained. "Desperately. Keeping things from you is a means to accomplish just that. You already know too much. Getting you back in one piece is quickly becoming an impossibility."

"What if I don't want to return?"

"Don't you? What about your sister?"

I looked back out to sea.

"I can't feel her," I admitted. "In here." I tapped the centre of my chest. "I've always been able to feel her. Know when she's happy or when she's sad. Know when she needs me. Or when I'm driving her crazy with how anal I am."

Jack snorted. "I can't imagine that sort of connection to someone."

"You don't have a brother? Sister? Cat?"

He laughed, that brilliant laugh. The one that lifts you up along with it.

"No cat. No sibling either."

"Carrie's more than a sibling."

"I know."

"I'm losing her, Jack."

"You don't know that. Nothing's set in stone. After all, this is an Origin Event."

Which scared me. Because I was sure, it scared him too.

"So, he was a cosmonaut," I said, changing the subject most poorly. Jack let me.

"Yes. Admired. Respected. Trusted. Do you want to know?"

"Know what?"

"What century."

It meant more than the words. I knew. He was letting me choose my fate. Not dictating it. Say no, and trust I will get home safely.

Say yes, and change my path. Completely.

Carrie would say I was being adventurous.

I would have called it reckless.

What if I do this, choose this, am I choosing it also for Carrie? Getting home, getting her home, should have been all that mattered.

But I know Carrie, as well as, if not better than myself.

Pick adventure, Mouse, she'd say. *Live life, don't mourn it.*

"No," I said eventually. "Not yet. Maybe one day." It wasn't necessary for understanding Sergei Ivanov. It wasn't necessary in order to save Carrie.

It was one more tether to my twin I couldn't risk cutting.

Even if part of me wanted to. Wanted to stay.

"I understand," Jack said, softly. I thought my heart might break.

I'm not sure why. But the softness of his tone felt sad as if he was letting something precious walk away. He started sifting the sand through his fingers again. The rhythmic action somehow settling my heartbeat.

"Something happened," he said. "We don't know for sure what. But he returned from a routine flight to the ISS in an Orion. Nothing immediately set off any alarms. But the Orion vanished over the Pacific Ocean. And didn't reappear until sixty years later.

"By then RATS had been established. Not in its present form, of course, but close enough."

"And the Lunik he uses?"

Jack patted the sand flat at his side.

"Unsurprisingly, much like an Orion."

"He stole the technology."

"The technology didn't exist when he hitched a ride on that Orion. But by the time he landed, we'd been surfing sine waves for a decade."

"Temporal paradox," I said.

"A bloody big one, Miss Wylde."

I started sifting the sand through my fingers.

"Why is Cape Canaveral an Origin Event?" I eventually asked. The sand was hypnotic. The heat unbearably relaxing.

The company...

"The Orion was made there," Jack said. "You're making it hard to respect your wishes, Miss Wylde," he added.

"What wishes?" I asked, pausing in my sand sifting.

"To go back."

Ah. I was asking dangerous questions. The more I knew, the harder it would be to return to my time.

I could have argued that. He was making it too easy to stay.

We both stared out at the ocean in silence.

I didn't feel alone anymore. Carrie was missing, but somehow I was still OK.

"Why hasn't he arrived here yet?" I asked. We'd been in 1962 on Miami Beach for hours. The sun was cresting the horizon, a faint orange and red glow seeping into the sky. We'd eaten, even slept a little. Dreamed.

And still, no Ivanov or orange sine wave to indicate the rip was extending to here.

"It appears he has some control," Jack murmured, watching the sun's light-show. "Possibly not enough to dictate where we choose to go but to choose whether to confront us there. 1962 Miami apparently doesn't suit."

"So what? We wait?"

Jack squashed a handful of sand in his palm, as though squeezing it tightly enough would elicit an answer. He was a tactile person, I realised. Very vocal when angered. Never still when undecided. Right now, he knew barely more than me; a novice at this time travelling thing.

I wondered how his day had started. I wondered if he'd ever imagined I could have crashed into it so spectacularly.

"If he won't come to us, then we will have to go to him," he finally said. The sand fell from his fingers, and he shifted to stand. Turning around, he extended his hand out to me and waited patiently for me to accept.

I looked up at him, the hint of sunlight behind his shadowed form made him appear wreathed in a golden glow. What was this man to me? An anchor in an otherwise storm-tossed sea?

Or more?

I took his hand and let him pull me up from the sand. When I was close, close enough to see him inhale deeply, I asked, "Will you tell me what the dreams mean?"

He stilled, his hand still clasping mine, a look of bewilderment crossing his features briefly. And then he shook his head and smiled.

"You have a way of catching me off guard, Miss Wylde. I wonder if it is intentional or not."

I smirked.

"I had rather planned the timing of that one."

"Ah, I see. I shall endeavour to remain focused in the future."

"Will there be a future?" For us, I didn't say.

"There is always a future, Mimi. Our part in it, though, is not yet written."

"Unless we're part of a temporal paradox," I argued. "Then we wouldn't even know that our future has already happened."

"Do you always argue every point made?"

"Of course. I'm a scientist."

I walked past him and up the ladder to the Orion, brushing my hand over the external casing lovingly. I'd seen a mock-up of the Orion MPCV at the Kennedy Space Center. A mushroomed cone in white, with a black tip and bronze base. Half again as big as the Apollo capsule. Standing beside it, it had dwarfed Carrie and me.

I still couldn't believe I'd been inside one. But whether this Orion matched those being made in my time, I couldn't say. There had certainly not been a colourful nebula surrounding it, or a thousand twinkling stars direct from space.

I swallowed thickly as I entered through the door, remembering that day with Carrie vividly. She'd seen the nebula. That's what had drawn her towards the Lunik. Just like I'd been drawn towards an Orion.

I turned when Jack entered the Vehicle and asked, "Ivanov's Lunik. Why do you call it that when it's an Orion MPCV?"

Jack raised an eyebrow at me, then took his seat in the command chair.

"There are differences," he said. "They're subtle, but they exist. It is not the same Vehicle."

"But they look alike." Evans had said as much earlier.

"You saw it?" Rafe asked from his own seat. He'd been snoozing when we'd entered but was wide awake now.

I shook my head. "When Carrie..." I couldn't finish the sentence.

I looked around the module we were in and tried to picture my sister in one similar. Had she awoken on the dimpled metal floor? Had the stars blinded her? Did the nebula make her ill, too? Or had she not embarrassed herself like me?

And the one question I so desperately wanted to be answered, but was too scared to ask.

Had she been treated as well as I had?

He was clearly mad. This Sergei Anton Ivanov. Power hungry and insane. How would a man like that treat my sister? I doubted he'd sit on a beach at sunrise and talk softly.

I suddenly felt like crying. It was all too much to bear. Carrie was with a psychopath. Who had an endgame. Who would kill her if we didn't do what he demanded.

"It's all right," Jack's gentle tone said from beside me. "We'll figure it out." I stifled a sob. "Shhh," he whispered.

And then his arms were around me, and the MPCV vanished, and Hoffman and Groves ceased to exist. Just this man and his soft words and gentle tone, and his strong arms and steady heartbeat.

Just the familiar scent of his cologne.

I shouldn't have sought comfort in that. I shouldn't have recognised it. It shouldn't have meant what it did to me.

Home.

I pushed away and stumbled to my chair, frantically trying to secure my seatbelt.

"Here," Groves said carefully. "Right. Left. Under. Over. There's a pattern." Her hands took over the action of belting me in, like a mother tending her child.

"I gather we're flying?" Rafe asked quietly.

"He's not here," Jack replied.

"No orange," Rafe agreed. "But any idea where he is? Flying blindly isn't my style."

I knew Jack was watching me; I could feel the intensity of those amber and whisky eyes. I didn't look up. Just watched Groves fasten the seatbelt, meeting her eyes once she'd done it. If Sally knew what I was doing, evading, she didn't call me out.

"Ordinarily," Jack was saying, "I'd recommend we do this on our own. Risking one MPCV is enough."

"You want to send a probe?"

"Do we still have the link attached to Orion Two?"

"It's there, but I haven't tested it," Rafe advised. "Last time we saw Harding, she was fit to spit nails."

"It's not Harding I want at our side," Jack argued.

"Well," Rafe said, inputting a command into the computer, "if there's ever a gunslinging, gator wrestling redneck you want at your back, it'd be Fawkes."

"Anything?" Jack asked.

"Huh," Rafe muttered. "They're still in 1969."

"Shouldn't they have repaired that rip by now?" Groves asked.

"Yes," Jack murmured.

The Vehicle became very quiet.

"Shall I send a probe?" Hoffman finally asked.

"What colour's the sinusoid for their time?" Jack asked. Rafe entered a few commands, and the main screen changed, flickering from our pale blue sine wave to a bright International Orange.

"Bloody fucking bollocks," Jack swore. "He's still there."

"Then what's happened to Orion Two?" Sally asked, her voice several octaves higher.

Her panic incited mine. I didn't even like Dr Fawkes that much. And Harding, well, I told myself I had no feelings whatsoever about *that* woman. Still, Groves seemed beside herself with worry. It rubbed off on me, making my breaths hitch and my heartbeat go wild.

Jack flicked a look over his shoulder and frowned, then he turned back to the dashboard and announced, "Only one way to find out."

His hand came down on a button. I hadn't seen it before, but it had a little plastic cover over it, as though to prevent inadvertently hitting it. The cover was already up, and Jack's hand found no resistance.

"Bloody hell!" Rafe yelled. "Next time warn us!"

Jack's eyes met mine and then did a quick scan of my seatbelt; making sure it was buckled?

"Hold on," Rafe shouted. "This could get a little wild."

Sally yelped, and everyone leant forward grabbing hold of the dashboard or whatever they could to secure themselves. My head flicked from side to side, trying to find something for me to grip. But my seat was off on its own, as if an afterthought. There was nothing for me to hold onto other than myself.

I gripped the harness tightly, closed my eyes as the Vehicle filled up with that nebulous cloud. But still, I could see them. Stars. So many. So bright. Almost as if I could reach out and touch them. With my eyes closed, I extended one arm, fingers stretched, reaching for the impossible.

The metal of the ship screeched.

A whooshing noise surrounded us and then became a roar.

My body jolted. First one way, then another. And then I got flung back in my seat as if the weight of God knows how many tonnes was pressed down on my chest and body.

I lost consciousness then, as the silence of space engulfed us. Images of Carrie swam before my eyes. Interspersed with Jack Evans and Sergei. When I woke up the Vehicle was quiet, a soft ticking of its engines the only sound I could make out. I stretched. Felt the harness dig into me. And then blinked the fog from my eyes.

Groves was still out, head lolling to the side. It didn't look comfortable. Hoffman was waking up slowly; the first words uttered not fit for young ears. And Jack was at my side.

"Sorry," he murmured, releasing the seatbelt buckle. "A return trip is usually only used in extreme situations."

"Uh-huh," I managed.

He looked over his shoulder at a still unconscious Groves and a now irate Hoffman.

"You did well," he whispered. "Groves probably won't wake up for another few minutes, and it took Rafe several months to manage a return to consciousness upon landing the first time he did this."

"Why, the bloody fucking hell, would you use a Return?" Hoffman muttered. "I could have entered in the coordinates manually."

"A swift flight seemed pertinent," Jack said, standing to full height. But not before his hand squeezed mine. And then vanished.

He'd panicked, I realised. When he'd seen me panicking. A notion that didn't fit.

What the hell was happening to us? I doubted Jack Evans had ever truly panicked before now. Exploded, yes. Acted on instinct without prior thought, no.

I needed to know what those dreams meant. This was all linked to it somehow. I didn't know how that was possible, but it was. I was sure of it. I'd had two of them now. Last night's dream as real as the first. Jack. Me. Skin on skin. A desire I'd never experienced before in my life.

It made me feel things. Think things. I wouldn't have contemplated otherwise.

But knowing could be that one thing too much. The one thing that cut the tether. The one thing Jack was afraid of. That I was afraid of too.

It was all mixed up. My emotions. This situation. Carrie.

I was losing her, and still, I denied it.

"Well, that sucked," Hoffman exclaimed, rising from his chair and crossing to Groves. He began checking her vitals.

"We're here now," Jack said steadily. "And somewhere out there is Orion Two as well."

"Somewhere out there is the Surgeon I used to know," Hoffman growled.

"They could be in trouble," Jack persisted, ignoring Rafe's ire.

"And we're not?" Hoffman demanded.

Jack gave him a look that would have cowered a lesser man. Hoffman just grunted and gently slapped Groves on the cheek. Making the young woman startle awake, shouting, "Bryan!"

Hoffman pulled back and slowly smiled.

"Well, that explains that," he said.

"What?" Groves squeaked back.

"Why *Bryan* Fawkes palmed you off on us, Miss Groves," Jack replied with a sardonic smile.

"Had any dreams lately?" Rafe asked with a wink.

Sally's eyes darted everywhere but at her teammates. Then settled on me.

Looks like I wasn't the only one. But somehow the knowledge didn't make it better.

It just made it more real.

17

JUST WHAT THE BLOODY HELL
WAS SERGEI PLAYING AT?

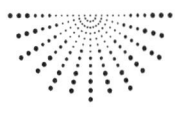

JACK

*T*he streets were deserted this early. A golden glow making everything look surreal. My guard was up. My attention divided, but on point. Every nerve in my body on fire. If Sergei was here, he wasn't showing himself.

We strolled along North Atlantic Ave, past the Holiday Inn and Ramon's. The sound of waves breaking on the shore drifted through the lush palm trees. The odd purr of a Chevy or Cadillac as it started interrupted the hypnotic flow. A bright sign ahead announced an upcoming visit by Barbara Eden. I knew the instant it caught Mimi's eye.

"I used to watch *I Dream Of Jeannie*," she said quietly. No doubt in deference to the silent morning surrounding us. "Carrie and I dressed up as Jeannie and Major Nelson for a party once. She won the coin toss and got to wear a NASA uniform."

To Mimi that would have been a win. I didn't dare tell her I would have much preferred her in Jeannie's outfit.

"Where is he?" Groves growled under her breath. It was hard to tell if she meant Sergei or Bryan. Both elicited suitably volatile emotions.

"Easy, Miss Groves," I murmured. "The Orion is close. Therefore the Lunik will be as well."

"He's playing us, you know," Mimi said softly. "It's like walking into a trap."

"In the jungle," Groves added. "Bloody hole dug in the soil and covered with leaves."

I blinked down at the woman. She hadn't seemed the imaginative type. But then, a day or so with Mimi Wylde at your side did make a person start to dream.

I stifled a snort. The dreams began well before Mimi arrived.

"You said he'd come to us," Mimi murmured. "Where's a good place to be?"

I glanced around the street we were on and spotted a diner. Public. Visible. And gave us a reason to be out and about this early. Cocoa Beach was not known for its early starters. A few people would be walking their dogs on the beach itself, but Rafe and I had decided that was too secluded. Everything we did on this flight was foreign. Every rule we broke seemed to make it harder to believe we'd mend this tear.

The rip had already been large; now it was nearing catastrophic.

"In there," I said, nodding towards Wolfie's.

I crossed the street, checking in my periphery if we were being followed. Misses Groves and Wylde followed, neither looking particularly fashionable. They'd had to share the outfit for this era, stealing from the early sixties and seventies to hash together something that would make them both appropriately attired.

Thankfully fashion was minimal in 1969 and getting shorter by the minute. Rafe had remained with the Orion. Not necessary, but a precaution we thought wise considering our opponent. I was sure Miss Groves was also wearing part of his allotted outfit as well. The woman was proving quite adaptable.

The door's bell dinged merrily as we entered. I glanced around, but Sergei wasn't in sight. Neither, unfortunately, was Bryan Fawkes. Worry dug itself deeper inside. I escorted the ladies to a table and ordered us all coffees as soon as the waitress arrived. She didn't blink once at my accent; that's why I hadn't bothered to hide it. British tourists were not an unknown commodity at Cocoa Beach in 1969.

Kiwis, on the other hand, might well be.

When the waitress departed, I said quietly, "Best if you don't talk, Miss Wylde."

"Why not?" she asked. Of course, she did.

I smiled. "You are neither British nor American. You stand out."

"Perhaps that's a good thing," she argued.

"Why on Earth would that be good?" I demanded.

"An anomaly would attract attention," she explained as if to a child. "Don't we want to be noticed?"

I hadn't looked at it like that. Everything we did when we travelled via Orion was done incognito. If history were changed by our presence, we'd be mending rips night and day. Ours adding to the already plentiful that occurred naturally. Not even considering the rips caused by the presence of those who flew with Sergei.

So staying under the radar, as some of the Surgeons liked to call it, was imperative.

But nothing about this particular flight was normal.

"Perhaps you are right," I conceded. "Although how your accent could garner us the attention we're after is beyond me, right now."

The waitress returned, and Mimi smiled up at her.

"Thank you," she said, most enthusiastically I thought. "Have you worked here long?"

Bloody hell, but when she decided something, she ran with it freely.

Groves took a sip of her coffee and had the audacity to smirk at me over the rim. I raised an eyebrow, as the waitress answered.

"Three months this Friday."

"Oh, how exciting!" Mimi exclaimed. "So near the rockets. Have you seen any?"

"There was a launch in May. Apollo 10."

"Of course. Stafford, Young and Cernan. How wonderful," Mimi offered with a beaming smile.

"Where're you from, anyway?" The waitress asked, leaning against the bench seat, accepting the offer of conversation readily. There weren't too many people in here this early.

"New Zealand," Mimi replied. "Have you heard of it?"

I watched on in utter amazement as the waitress's eyes widened and she started pointing a finger at Mimi wildly.

"Oh, I thought I'd heard your accent before."

Bloody hell.

"Actually, you look a lot like her."

Mimi's face paled. Groves leant forward. I was too stunned to make a sound.

"Like who?" Miss Groves asked.

"Like the gal who was in here earlier. It's not you, is it?" she asked, looking back at Mimi.

Mimi shook her head from side to side.

"Did she say where she was staying?" Groves asked, as I leant over and slipped my hand into Mimi's.

She didn't squeeze back.

"Oh, no. Nothing like that. But the gentleman with her, he did say they'd be taking a look at the pier today. You know, you might just catch them. They wanted some pictures to take home of the sunrise. Be rather funny to come face to face with your doppelgänger."

"Yes," Groves said, downing her coffee in record style and handing the woman a bill. "Splendid idea. Thank you."

Groves pushed out of the bench seat and bustled the waitress off with a smile, and then leant down over Mimi.

"Now or never, Mouse," she whispered, grabbing Mimi's free hand and tugging her upright.

I followed, not sure what to say or do, completely astounded at Mimi's successful tactics.

Utterly devastated at her current mood.

"She's right, Miss Wylde," I said, finally finding my voice. "Time is of the essence."

Literally.

We tore out of the diner and headed toward the beach proper. My hand in Mimi's left one. Groves' in Mimi's right.

"Don't flake out on me now, Miss Wylde," I urged. "Your sister needs you."

It was a low blow, but she was spiralling. I'd seen it before in new Novitiates. Hell, Groves had probably done it on her first few flights. But Mimi didn't have the luxury of easing into this gently. There were things I could protect her from, but not this. Not the reality of time travel when lives were at stake and the threat was real.

Carolyn Wylde was the key to fixing this mess. Mending a rip that had gone, well, quite wild.

The Canaveral Pier rose out of the ground like a huge leviathan before us. Cutting a swathe through crystal clear waters, unheeding of the waves that crashed into its underside. A plethora of signs told us this was Cocoa Good Vibrations Beach and to get our gear from Ron Jon's Surfing Shop. Another sign brightly declared, "Good Luck, Astronauts."

I thought that rather portent but chose not to comment. My attention split on our surroundings and Miss Wylde. That's why I missed it. That's why she was there one minute and gone the next. Mimi's outstretched hand the only indication she'd been there, to begin with.

That and her strangled shout of "Sally!"

Miss Groves flickered in a cloud of red and blue and yellow and then disappeared in a burst of starlight. A Lunik shot past, the sound of it surfing the sine wave this close to us deafening.

I pulled Mimi down to the boards of the pier and shielded her with my body. Silence descended. That of space and shock intertwined. And then the roar of waves as they crescendoed, crashing into the underside of the pier beneath our cheeks.

"No!" Mimi whispered.

Bloody fucking bollocks! I wanted to shout.

And then a small voice said, "Mouse?"

And Mimi was up out of my grasp and running along the pier at an alarming pace, arms outstretched, a cry of elation on her lips before I could stop her.

"Miss Wylde!" I yelled, and realised much too late that it should have been, "Misses Wylde."

Just what the bloody hell was Sergei playing at?

18

FORGIVE AN OLD MAN HIS QUIRKS?

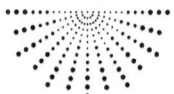

MIMI

*I*t was her. Really her. I held my sister in my arms.

Tears streamed down my cheeks, as we jumped up and down, clinging to each other, laughing. Dear God, I'd found her. I'd got her back. I was never letting her go again.

"I have to tell you something," she said.

"Oh, boy! Have I got so much to tell you," I threw back.

"No really," she said. "There's not much time."

"Damn, sister. We can *make* time!"

Carrie laughed. It was achingly familiar, so full of sunshine. She punched me playfully on the upper arm.

"You're such a goof! What have you done with my sister? Mouse! Mousey! Where are you?" she shouted at full volume.

"Carolyn Wylde, I have missed you."

She threw herself into my arms again and hugged me tightly. For a moment I felt scared. I don't know why. Carrie's hugged me before. Many times.

But not like this. Not as if saying goodbye.

"Caz?" I whispered, using the name I gave her when just a child.

She clung tighter.

"You know I love you, don't you, Mouse?" she said gruffly.

"Of course."

"You know I'd do anything for you."

"The feeling's mutual, squirt."

She sniffed, pulled back and looked at me. So much love staring back I just sighed.

"We have to go home," I finally said and her face shuttered.

"Home," she repeated, her voice was flat. "I'm not sure where home is anymore. It's all a lie."

I frowned. She wasn't making sense.

Then I heard a footfall behind me.

"Carrie, I want you to meet someone." I turned and caught Jack's eye. He didn't look happy. In fact, I was sure that was his weapon drawn down by his thigh.

Carrie took a step backwards, towards the end of the pier, causing me to swing my gaze back to her abruptly.

"You can't trust him, Mouse," she said quickly. "Don't believe a word he says."

"Carrie," I chastised. "This is Dr Jack Evans."

"I know who he is, better than you, clearly. I know who he works for."

"What are you talking about?" My head swung between them both, but Jack wasn't giving anything away, and Carrie was just scaring me.

"Go home, Mouse," she said. "I've got this."

"Carrie."

"For once in your life let me be the responsible one. Let me take care of you."

"You've always taken care of me," I argued. Lately, it had been Carrie who'd pulled me through.

"Not like this. Not like you used to."

"Carrie, you're not making any sense at all."

Her eyes drifted off me and settled on Jack.

"A show of good faith," she said. "A reminder that Lunik is far superior."

Holy effing hell, what the...?

"The message?" Jack asked. Did he get this? Did he know what was wrong with my sister?

"You have one week," Carrie said. I started to hyperventilate. "If RATS isn't disbanded by then, the next one we'll keep."

"Carrie," I said, my voice pleading.

"I love you, Mouse. Remember."

"Carolyn Wylde, you stop this, right now."

She just smiled. "Thatta girl, Mouse," she whispered with stars in her eyes.

No, not in her eyes, but everywhere, as a nebula-like cloud billowed behind.

"Carrie!" I yelled, taking a step towards the maelstrom.

"Go home, Mouse. For fuck's sake, just go home! Please!"

It was the please that stopped me, not the bands of steel wrapped 'round my chest. Not Jack yelling in my ear to "Don't go!" But Carrie. Pleading with me to stay. To let her go.

And go home myself.

"No!" I screamed. I wouldn't lose her. Not now. Not again. Not by choice.

"She's gone," Jack said softly, the silence of space evaporating on each word. "She's picked her side. She's chosen."

I pushed out of his embrace and ran to the end of the pier, only to trip over someone who hadn't been there.

"Oomph!" Sally Groves moaned beneath me. "You weigh a tonne."

"Sally," I said, stunned. "Where is she?" I demanded, gripping her shoulders tightly.

I hadn't realised I was shaking her, practically shouting in her face, spraying her, no doubt, with spittle.

"Easy," Jack said off to the side, reaching for me. I scrambled back, away from them both, and held up my arms to protect me.

But nothing could protect me from this. From the empty hollowness inside. From the ache of truth registering. From the shock and loss all over again.

"No," I said, my head shaking. "I want her back."

Sally flicked her gaze from me to Jack, and back again. I watched her take everything in.

"Why did he return *her* and not Carrie?" I shouted, pointing an accusing finger at Groves.

"I don't know," Jack said carefully.

"Yes, you do!" I shouted. "You just won't tell me. You want me to go home too. But I won't. Not without Carrie. You can't make me!" God, I sounded like a child.

"Mouse," he said as if that would reach me.

It only made me turn into Hyde.

"No!" I growled and turned away, realising I was at the edge of the pier and had nowhere to hide.

I started to panic.

"Call the ship, Miss Groves," I heard Jack say. Then, "Mimi, don't run."

I couldn't run. I had nowhere to go.

"Jack," I said, gripping the pier railing and sobbing.

"I know," he whispered in my ear. "Sweetheart, I know."

I collapsed against him, my fists raining down on his chest, my tears wetting his shirt collar, my voice rasping into his neck. He let me. He didn't fight back or try to contain me. He let my temper reign, and he took it all.

Each weakening pummel of my fist. Every single drop of tears. And when I was done, he picked me up and carried me into the module, sitting down in my seat with me curled up on his lap.

"Home, Dr Hoffman," I heard him instruct.

"Yes, sir," Rafe replied quietly.

But I'd only registered the one word.

"Not home," I pleaded, fighting exhaustion.

"No," Jack murmured, his hot breath in my hair. "Not your home. Trust me," he added, but all I could hear were my sister's words.

You can't trust him, Mouse. You can't believe a word that he says.

It wasn't surprising that my dreams were fragmented. That they messed with my mind. Jack. Carrie. Carrie. Jack. I felt lost in the ones with my sister. I hated how safe I felt in Jack's bed. I fought them. I screamed inside my head. I railed against my mind.

Maybe it was all a dream. Maybe I was catatonic, having suffered a breakdown at the knowledge of my parents' deaths. Maybe Carrie was at my bedside, crying. Willing me to come back.

Go home, Mouse. For fuck's sake, just go home.

Don't go!

Please!

I woke up in a bed. No dimpled metal floor. No exposed wires or plumbing. No dashboard. No moulded seats with full body harnesses. No smell of electrical wiring burning.

No Orion.

I knew before I fully woke, that this was not a good thing.

The embroidered coat of arms on the pillow slip amplified that feeling. The words carefully stitched beneath added weight.

Royal Academy of Time Surgeons.

He'd brought me home.

To his time, not mine.

Oh, eff me. If I was out of time before, what was I now?

And where was Carrie? Parallel to me? Or was that all a lie, a wild suggestion, to keep me in the dark about more nefarious things? Like why Carrie thought she was saving me.

Go home, Mouse.

I'm not sure I knew where that was.

Neither did Carrie.

I frowned, threw back the covers, and climbed down from the bed. I glanced around the room, but nothing suggested it belonged to Jack Evans. The bed, though, was familiar. Big, wide, and luxurious. If this was a guest-room, then why had it featured in my dreams already?

I was still dressed in a 1969 era mini skirt and bold print blouse, so I splashed some water on my face at the basin in the corner, brushed fingers through my tangled hair, and reached for the door. I half expected it to be locked, but it wasn't. I peered around the door jam into a gloomy hall. Nothing jumped out at me.

Brushing myself down I started to walk. I guess I was following my stomach; the smell of something delicious meeting my nose. I sniffed the air before me, noting the number of closed doors along the way but not a single soul, and finally came out in what had to be a cafeteria.

Locating exactly where all the people had been.

Thirty odd pairs of eyes all turned toward me. The sound of cutlery clanking and glasses clinking ceased. Along with all conversation. If I hadn't already heard the vacuum of space, I would have likened it to here.

No one said anything. Then an older man, perhaps late sixties, walked out from the centre of the room, leaning heavily on a walking stick. Everyone watched his progress towards me. The utter absence of sound, not even whispers, made the entire episode surreal.

The man stopped before me and inclined his head, his bushy old-man eyebrows arching.

"You would be Miss Wylde."

I nodded. It didn't seem wise to talk.

No one else was. And where was Jack? Or Sally and Rafe? Had they just left me here and gone back to look for Fawkes' team? Hell, I might have even welcomed a sneer from Harding.

I suddenly felt very alone.

"Well," the man said, "this is a first."

I nodded again. I don't know why. And then the silence stretched between us.

My eyes reluctantly returned from their desperate darting around the room, from trying to ascertain threats and potential exits. To land on the man before me. Who seemed to be waiting for something. Waiting and watching, eyes searching my features, expecting to see something. But what, I did not know.

The longer he stood there and waited, the more uneasy I got.

I shook my head slowly. This place freaked me out. This man...

He just smiled.

"Never mind me, Miss Wylde. Forgive an old man his quirks?" he asked, genially.

I went to nod my head when Jack's voice suddenly sounded out from across the room.

"Clive!"

And then he was striding towards us, Rafe and Sally hanging back at the door, as I took one step, and then another, unable to stop my feet from taking me to safety.

When Jack's hand slipped into mine, I finally felt at peace.

And then the room erupted.

19

BLOODY FUCKING BOLLOCKS!

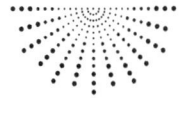

JACK

I dropped her hand before it could brand me. Too late. I'd been branded in other ways by Mimi Wylde. There seemed to be a part of me that was inextricably drawn to her. Unable to stop myself from reaching for her. Touching her. Even if that touch was merely through holding hands.

I cursed the dream's existence mentally and assessed the level of disquiet in the room.

"What the bloody hell is a contemporary doing in our time?" someone shouted.

"This is it, isn't it?" someone else asked, voice elevated to an unnaturally sounding high. "This is how it happens."

"She has to go back!"

"What are you going to do, Dr Crawford?"

"Dr Evans, what were you thinking?"

"SILENCE!" Crawford yelled at the top of his very capable voice. "Remember you are Surgeons! Trained at the most prestigious Academy in the world. Remember yourselves, Doctors! RATS is better than this."

He turned to look at me, that affable façade he'd been wearing long evaporated. Now stood the Chief Surgeon of the Academy. Clive had poured his heart and soul into this venture. Into a controversial undertaking that had threatened his good name. He'd risked everything for RATS. He'd laid himself bare before the King.

Thankfully, the King had understood science and backed him. But that did not mean Parliament did. Nor the general public. Crawford walked a fine line between success and failure. And now I'd done this.

"We need to talk, Clive," I said.

"Damn right we do, son." He spun on his heel, surprisingly agile and ambulatory, proving yet again how he used his injury as a weapon, and marched from the room. Daring anyone to halt his progress with a fierce glare.

Bryan had warned me. Bringing Mimi here had been an awful risk. To the Academy. To Clive. To me. But most of all to her. I looked down at her, standing so silently beside me. Here stood the mouse.

Bloody fucking bollocks!

"Come on," I said softly. "I'm not letting you out of my sight."

God alone knew what the Surgeons would do to her if I left her to fend for herself in the cafeteria. This needed to be sorted, and until Clive was onboard, Mimi would be glued to my side.

My eyes met Rafe's as we walked from the room. His look said it all. He thought I was headed to the executioner. He thought I'd well and truly done myself in.

Silence descended as we traversed the gloomy hallways. The building living up to its nickname: Shadowship. For a relatively modern premise, RATS' home base was definitely on the dark side. The Royal Academy of Time Surgeons was a proud establishment set on twenty acres of lush real estate in Greenwich; the site formerly known as the Old Royal Naval College. If our funding ever got cut, we could make money selling off acreage. That's if anyone was game enough to build so close to us.

RATS had a name for the unusual, and that was before you considered we travelled through Time.

Clive slammed into his office, bypassing his secretary by using his private access. I held the door open for Mimi to precede me, and followed them both in.

"Sit," Clive ordered. Mimi sat as if pulled down by strings.

I sighed.

"You think this amusing, Jack?" Clive asked.

"Not at all," I replied, taking the seat beside Mimi, opposite Clive's desk. "I think you'll understand why I did this once I have a chance to explain."

"Allow me to vent before we get there," Clive said acerbically. "What the bloody hell? Not only is she *here*, but you let her wander around a classified facility freely! You allow her to bear witness to the operations of an MPCV." Rafe had been talking. "You take her to not just one time, but several. Bloody hell, Jack, you allowed her to come in contact with Lunik!"

"All quite explanatory."

"Damn your explanations, Jack! How the bloody hell will I explain this to the King?"

I raised an eyebrow. "Must you?"

Clive scoffed. "He's the only thing between us and closure, as you well know. I keep him abreast of operations. A Monarch in the dark is a very dangerous thing."

"An uneducated person involved so intricately in our business is a very dangerous thing," I countered.

"You want to argue this now? With *her* sitting right here in my office!"

"You always play the political card, Clive. When you know damn well without us, the entire world would be fucked."

"And you think holding it over a barrel will keep us open? Pay attention, son! We are borderline closed already."

I stilled.

"Have I missed something?"

"You've missed a whole bloody lot. Chasing after a bit of skirt, traipsing through the timeline tearing rips the size of Australia in it. While you've been satisfying an itch, Lunik has gained ground in our time." Clive sighed and finally sat back in his seat. I realised he looked drawn, tired. Exhausted even. Beaten down and barely able to get back up. "He had an audience with the Prime Minister."

"He was in 1969," I pointed out.

"Did you see him?"

I froze. Oh, fuck. My head turned slowly to look at Mimi. Who was curled in on herself in her oversized armchair. Her eyes widened slightly with both of our attention on her. I was sure she was hoping to blend into the chintz or something.

"Yes?" she squeaked.

"The man who threatened you. What did he look like exactly?"

"He..he had short brown hair. A b..beard. It was pointed. Um… dark eyes and an angular looking face."

I hated this. I hated that she'd become her nickname. I hated that the fire I knew existed inside her had been snuffed out in the presence of Clive Crawford and RATS. Mimi Wylde was an inordinately intelligent and capable woman. She could hold her own with these people if she weren't so bloody fucking scared right now.

I wanted to reassure her. I wanted desperately to reach out and comfort her through touch.

My eyes caught Clive's.

I did nothing.

"Certainly sounds like Sergei," Clive muttered.

"He could have returned," I offered.

"And then what? Bounced around Time dogging your footsteps? That is what happened, isn't it, Jack? That's what Hoffman and Groves supplied."

"So, you've debriefed them already?"

"Of course I bloody well have! I'm not incompetent!"

"I didn't say you were, Clive."

"Then what are you saying exactly?"

I held his fierce glare.

"Riled," I offered.

"Damn straight I am."

"You bluster when you're riled," I pointed out.

"What the bloody hell would you have me do right now?"

"Think, Clive. For fuck's sake, think! Would I have brought her back here, knowing the consequences, if I hadn't deemed it absolutely necessary?" I didn't wait for a reply. "Orion Two is missing. Sergei, or whoever was operating that Lunik, picked up Groves as if she was a piece of luggage, and then dropped her off again to prove a bloody point. He has capabilities we aren't even aware of. I'd assumed picking up Miss Wylde ourselves had been an anomaly. But Sergei's moves since have proved that perhaps it is not. Perhaps it is something that we've overlooked, and Sergei hasn't.

"Can you conceive what he could do with such technology? What he's already done with Lunik and his original Orion is bad enough. But with added abilities such as this? I fear he's gone too far, Clive. This time, we will *all* pay for his actions. This time, there won't be a rip to repair, Time will simply not be there."

Clive's jaw flexed, but he said nothing.

"Fawkes," I said, running a hand through my hair and then scratching at my stubble. I worried at the scar, remembering. Grounding myself again. "He's a damn fine Surgeon, Clive. If he can get back on his own, then he will. But if Sergei has him, the Russian would have crowed, and he didn't. The message was quite clear. 'The next one, we'll keep.' They don't have Orion Two. Returning Miss Groves had been the message. Keeping Orion Two would have been a greater one, a threat held over our heads. Instead, Sergei has gone for a show. A performance. *Look at what I can do*. Not what I have done."

"Perhaps," Clive conceded. I went in for the kill.

"Something happened with that Origin Event tear. Something that involves the two Misses Wyldes. The loop wasn't bisecting, Clive. It was parallel. Have you ever heard of that before?

"No," he murmured. "There's a lot we still don't know about time travel."

"And yet, here we have," I waved a hand toward Miss Wylde, "a key to it all. Right in our hands. Ripe for the picking."

"Excuse me?" Mimi said, suddenly coming alive. I'd almost forgotten she was cognisant. Actually, I'd partially thought she wasn't. My bad. "Ripe for the picking?"

"We'll get to you in a moment, Miss Wylde," Clive said dismissively. "Jack, you..."

Mimi stood up from her chair.

"No," she said, quite steadily. "You'll address me as if I am in the room. You'll include me in your conversation, gentlemen. And you'll remember, Doctors, that I hold a Master of Science. That I *am* quite capable of understanding every word you say. That *if* I am the 'key' to your problems, you better ask nicely, because this mouse has teeth. On occasion," she added and promptly sat down again.

I tried hard, but for the life of me, I couldn't contain the smile.

Thatta girl. I stilled. Her sister had said the same.

"My apologies, Miss Wylde," Clive immediately offered. Behind that gruff façade was a gentleman. "But you can't possibly understand all that we say."

Mimi sat up straighter in her chair. "I know you're the Chief Surgeon for the Royal Academy of Time Surgeons. I know Sergei Anton Ivanov stole the Orion technology back at the beginning of the century. My guess, that century was the twenty-second." I closed my eyes as she continued. "I know you have a team missing. I *know* them, so don't think I don't feel your fears. I also know this lunatic, this ex-cosmonaut, has *my* sister. That somehow he has brainwashed her or coerced her into delivering his messages. I also know he wasn't lying when he said he'd kill her if you didn't destroy your Orions.

"The way I see it, Doctor, I know about as much as you do. In fact, I might know a bit more. Because *I* know my sister. And you do not."

My eyes snapped open, and I looked at her. She was fierce Mimi again. Try as I might, I think I was falling for her. I struggled to disassociate my feelings from those of the dream.

I no longer could.

"You are not RATS approved," Clive pointed out.

"Then make me," Mimi argued.

"It's not that easy, Miss Wylde."

"It's extremely easy. You're the Chief Surgeon, are you not?"

"I must answer to certain committees."

"But they listen to your guidance?"

"Yes, but..."

"Then guide them."

"I'm not sure I wish to in this," Clive blustered.

"Do you want to find them, Dr Crawford?"

"Find who?" I almost laughed. She was talking him in circles; he could hardly keep up.

"Orion Two."

"Oh, yes, of course!"

"Then approve me."

"Why?" I sat forward in my seat. Where was she going with this?

"Because, like I said, I know my sister."

"And?" both Clive and I said.

Mimi's eyes darted from one of us to the other and back again. Settling on Clive for some reason. She swallowed. Only slightly. Clive might have missed it. But I notice every single detail about Mimi Wylde.

"*And*...to keep me safe, she'll come out of hiding."

"Now wait just a minute," I said as Clive asked, "And this will help find Orion Two, how?"

Mimi chose to answer Clive's question. Of course, she did.

"Because they were linked to Orion One when Carrie confronted us on that pier. In another combination of dimensions, of course," she added, impressing us both with her understanding of what had happened. "But linked all the same. Somehow they're stuck, but the only way to find them is to have *both* Orion One and the Lunik present. Recreate whatever has happened to make them go dark.

"So, we use Orion One to lure them out, while we use *me* to lure out Carrie. I face Carrie; you work on the combinations of dimensions to find Orion Two while I distract. Once Orion Two gets secured, Carrie gets captured." She paused, no doubt for effect. It worked. Clive and I waited silently. "And then Sergei has something real to feel threatened by," she finally added.

"Why would he feel threatened?" I asked, kicking myself for continuing this ludicrous conversation.

"It's like you said, Jack. A parallel loop. We take Carrie; the opposite happens to Lunik. And I'm far more dangerous than my sister."

Clive perked up. I stood up. So did Mimi.

"Not on my bloody watch, Miss Wylde," I growled.

"Sit down, Jack," Clive muttered. "That's an order." I spun and stared down at my old friend.

"You can't mean that," I whispered.

"Jack. Sit." I sat, only because he was still my boss.

Clive looked toward Mimi, who was still standing. She abruptly sat down as well.

"Welcome to the team, Miss Wylde," Clive said.

"Bloody fucking bollocks!"

20

AND THE ROOM ERUPTED

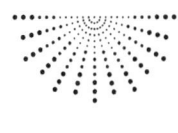

MIMI

A temporary Novitiate. But I was in. RATS approved, but on probation. More of a probation than the likes of Groves or Malcolm. But it would have to do.

I was getting my sister out of that man's clutches anyway I had to.

"You're mad if you think I'll let you do this," Jack growled in my ear.

We were walking down the corridor towards the cafeteria; I needed to eat. He did too, but I doubted he could stomach anything right then.

"You think you can stop me?" I asked.

"I think I'll bloody try."

"Well, you can't. I'm a Novitiate. I'm authorised to fly."

"Don't get smart with me, Miss Wylde. I *am* still the Surgeon in that scenario."

I stopped in my tracks and rounded on him. Finger out, pointed at his chest. He looked like he wanted to step back.

"You may be the Surgeon, but you have no right to ground me."

He stepped closer; chest to chest. Looking down at me, he said, "If you wish to play this game, I will match you, Miss Wylde. Move for move. Are you ready? *Really* ready for how I play?"

"You make it all sound like a game," I snarled. God, this man frustrated me! "This is my sister we're talking about."

He shook his head grimly.

"No, Miss Wylde. This is a RATS team, an expensive Orion, and the entire world watching our every move. We are accountable for our actions. Trust me; your sister is a low priority."

"Not to me," I growled and started walking.

I heard him sigh behind me, but he kept pace.

"Must you argue every point?" he asked, sounding aggrieved.

"She's my sister, Jack."

"And you're..."

I stopped again. Looked up at him. Shadows hid his eyes, but I could see the firm set of his lips.

"I'm what, exactly? What am I to you, Jack?"

He said nothing.

"You said you'd tell me what the dreams mean," I pressed.

"I said no such thing."

"That was before," I ventured.

"Before you stranded yourself in my time?" he queried.

"You're the one who brought me here," I pointed out.

He looked at me, really looked at me; searching my face for something, but I had no idea what. Eventually he said, voice soft, but not the gentle tone he used to reach me, this was different; sad and a little lost, "Maybe I shouldn't have."

And then with those words, he walked past me, past the cafeteria doorway, and out of sight. I stood there, uncertain, alone again, just a little lost myself.

And that's how Sally found me.

"There you are!" she announced with exuberance. "You're the talk of the Academy. Come on, let me show you off."

"Um...I'm not sure that's a wise idea, Sally," I mumbled, but couldn't prevent myself from being dragged bodily back into the still packed to the brim cafeteria.

"Nonsense," she said with a laugh. "You think I'm giving up my position on the totem pole of knowledge to some other RATS freak?

Not a chance."

What?

She pulled me into the middle of the cafeteria, and wrapped an arm around my waist, hauling me into her side. I stared at this prim and proper woman, her hair in an immaculate bun, her orange flight suit neatly pressed, bright hazel eyes shining.

"Everyone!" she said loudly, but not quite loudly enough to stop the multitude of conversations currently being carried out around the room. "Excuse me!" she tried. They all ignored her. "Oi!" she offered, but only a few turned to look.

I sighed. Then slipped two fingers into my mouth and whistled. Ear-piercingly loud.

"Oh," Sally said, looking at me. "You'll do all right."

The room quietened, and all eyes stared unblinkingly at the both of us. Sally cleared her throat.

"You've got questions," she said. "You have five minutes."

And then the traitor stepped to the side.

"Sally!" I hissed.

"It's OK, Mouse," she whispered back. "Trust me. It's better to get this over with."

Trust her?

You can't trust him, Mouse. You can't believe a word that he says.

I was sure my sister would extend that to all of RATS. I realised then that it was just like Jack had said, back on the pier. Carrie had picked her side. She'd chosen. I couldn't help thinking she'd been coerced. But then, who's to say I hadn't as well?

"What's your name?" someone called out. Accent unknown, but not British. I worked not to immediately mistrust them for that reason alone. But Carrie's words were on repeat in my mind.

I didn't trust any of them.

"Mouse," I said reluctantly.

"Mouse?" someone else repeated on a sneer. "You're in the wrong place, sweetheart. We're all lions here."

Laughter welled up, like a wave crashing to shore. It rushed over me, making my skin prickle and a blush steal up my cheeks. Strangely,

I'd never been truly embarrassed about my nickname before. It was me. It was who I was. And it was a damn sight better than Mimi.

If they couldn't handle Mouse, then they could go get effed, for all I cared. I crossed my arms over my chest, cocked my hip, and stared back at them dispassionately.

"Yeah," I said. "Mouse. Deal with it."

The laughter petered out.

"What time are you from?" someone asked.

Dr Crawford hadn't said I should keep quiet. He'd given no further instructions than, "Keep your head down and do as you're told." If he'd wanted his RATS Surgeons to be kept in the dark, he would have said.

But somehow I didn't think this show and tell was exactly what he'd had in mind.

"The 21st century," I offered, daring them to comment on my being out of time with a hard glare.

A few muttered to themselves, some blew out harsh breaths, but no one said the obvious.

I relaxed a smidgeon. If one more person said those words to me…

"How did you get here?" someone asked, their question delivered expertly, right in the middle of a lull. Several people nodded their heads, murmuring their eagerness to know that answer as well.

I looked around the room, taking in the people that watched me, studying them like they were studying me. There was a mix of emotions on their faces. Some were keen to have answers. Some were excited. Others scared. There were a few who were angry. None of them looked like they wanted to be friends.

But I wasn't here to make friends. I was here to find Carrie.

"I hitched a ride on an Origin Event," I offered, shrugging a shoulder as if it was nothing.

"Why?" someone asked.

"You're crazy," another offered.

"She doesn't look like she got fried."

"I'm not touching her just in case."

"You do it," someone said. "Go on. See if she sends out a zap."

"Touch me, and you're dead," I replied.

Silence.

Sally shuffled on her feet, looking uncomfortable. I offered her a raised eyebrow. She *had* started this.

"I like her," a voice suddenly announced from the back of the room. "She's got balls."

"Er, thanks?" I said, trying to get a good look at the person.

"I think the five minutes are up, Sally," the same voice said.

"Oh, yeah," Groves agreed. "All right, you lot. Showtime's over. You've seen her. Talked to her. Know that she's not crazy."

"I wouldn't say *that*," someone mumbled.

"Well," Sally snapped, "you know that she's human, then."

"What else would I be?" I asked, genuinely intrigued. Maybe things were different in this time.

"Argh, you know what I mean," Sally growled. Then instantly smiled. "Hungry?"

I was famished. And Sally Groves was kind of bonkers. I smiled back.

"Starving."

"Great!" She started heading towards the serving area, bypassing the bulk of the still avidly curious crowd.

I followed behind her, holding my head up high, just like Carrie would do. Feeling all kinds of nervous. I thought I was doing well until a woman stepped in front of me, blocking my passage.

She looked down her nose at me, her blonde hair straight as an arrow down her back, her high cheekbones lightly dusted in bronzer, her plump lips - now in a turned down snarl - liberally covered in cherry red lipstick.

I knew immediately that she was good friends with Harding. I swallowed my sigh.

"Hey," I said in greeting.

She didn't make a sound. I shrugged my shoulder and went to walk around her. She sidestepped, blocking my path.

It didn't take a genius to figure out what was going on. And I'm far from unintelligent. But how to avoid a confrontation once a challenge has been set is an impossibility for me. People assume that my nickname means something. It doesn't mean a bloody thing. I just hated being called Mimi. And "Mouse" worked. At least, it worked for me.

"Excuse me," I tried. One last attempt at civility.

"Mikaela, let her past," Sally said fearfully from behind the Amazonian.

"Shut up, Sally," the woman replied threateningly. Sally, bless her heart, shut up.

I resigned myself to a confrontation, sweat beading my brow, clamming up my palms, making it a little hard to breathe.

"Hey," I said again, this time not in greeting. "Don't order Sally around."

"You know who I am?" she asked.

"Wouldn't have the foggiest."

"I'm an Intern. A *doctor*." She waited for me to be suitably impressed. I just stared blankly at her. "You address me as Dr Pratt."

Of course, I laughed. Who wouldn't? And they think "Mouse" is amusing? I laughed harder. Actually doubling over, holding my stomach, snorting unattractively through my nose. Too much. Mikaela Pratt. *Doctor* Mikaela Pratt. What an effing prat, Pratt!

Laughter sounded off to the side. I was too busy wiping beneath my eyes to see who had joined in on the frivolity. Someone else made a sound in the other direction. I sucked in a breath of air, attempting to stop smiling. Another person chortled. I blew out slowly, still chuckling. Someone else coughed into their hand, but it was *so* laughter. I could tell.

Finally, I stood upright and got myself under control.

"Sorry about that," I offered. "It's been a very long forty-eight hours."

I didn't see the hand coming. But I sure as hell felt it hit the side of my face. I spun, letting out a squeak, and landed with a splat on my arse. Ow! I'd once laughed at something a kid had written on the blackboard during break once. It was stupid; I shouldn't have done it. It wasn't even funny. I don't know why I laughed. Bob Marley does indeed rule. Of course, he does. But I'd laughed all the same. I still remember the bruise I received on my upper arm for that one.

It hadn't hurt nearly as much as this slap to the face.

I glared up at the woman and said the first thing that came into my head.

"What are you? *Twelve?*"

This time, the laughter exploded; so much more forcefully than before. The room came alive with cackles. But I wasn't feeling particularly jovial right then. And Pratt had turned an unhealthy shade of red. I scrambled to my feet. Ready to face off against her. I'd even raised my fists. No girl slapping for me.

But a guy stepped between us, holding up his hands, a wide grin on his face.

"Gotta admit, she got you on that one, Mickey."

"Don't call me Mickey," Pratt growled.

"Come on, Pratt," the guy urged. "It's all good for a laugh, eh?" I realised he was the one who'd spoken earlier. From the back of the crowd. Telling Sally the five minutes was up. Telling everyone I had balls.

He spoke with a British accent, East End or Essex; I can never really tell them apart. He also wasn't wearing an orange flight suit, but a white one. It made his dark skin look luminous. But the mischievous glint in his eyes said more about him than his skin colour or accent ever could.

"You've got no say in this, gearhead," she snarled. "Go back to your cave."

"Haven't you 'eard, Pratt?" the guy said, seemingly unaffected by her calling him names. "I've got an all-day pass. A release from gaol. I've just as much right to be 'ere as you."

"Not in this you don't," she snapped. "Stand down."

"You really gonna do this 'ere?" he asked, lowering his voice. "With everyone watchin'."

Pratt looked around the cafeteria and blinked. Every single person was looking back at her. Some had their arms crossed over their chests. Some had implacable façades. Some peeked out from behind protection. But they were all watching Mikaela Pratt.

She growled low in the back of her throat; quite impressive really. And then turned to stare down at me.

"Watch yourself, Mousey," she said with a sneer, and then walked past, shoving her shoulder into my arm.

I rubbed at the bruise forming absently, as I watched her storm out of the room, wondering what in the effing hell I'd done to deserve this. Silence stretched, and I prepared for the next battle. It was like being back in bloody school.

Well, it *was* called an Academy.

I stifled the snort and looked up at my saviour. He smiled, showing a row of extremely white teeth.

"Now, if I were you, luv, I'd watch me bleedin' back. That one 'as a screw loose, she does."

Sally rushed forward. "Thank you so much, Dean," she said on a burst of air. "I'm not sure how that would have gone without you here."

"It was nothin', Sal. Nothin' at all," he said, suddenly shy, as others came closer and offered their own agreement. Bolstering him up and in the process rubbing shoulders with me.

In less than a minute, I was surrounded by a huge group of RATS employees. Some in orange, some in white like Dean, and others in blue and green. But all of them wearing jumpsuits. I felt a little out of place in my mini.

But I realised, I no longer felt so out of time.

Voices rose, and conversation flowed around me. Some asking me more questions, others offering to show me around. Even a few laughed at me. So normal. Facing off against Pratt had clearly made me equal in their eyes. Being singled out by the bully had allowed me ingress to their club, it seemed.

Somehow, I'd thought that people in the future would be different. That they would be more refined than those in my time. But Harding had been a bitch, and Pratt had been a bully. Perhaps a little imma-ture, but still the same. There had been bitches and bullies in my time, too.

A few minutes later I was sitting at a long table eating "bangers and mash". Every single seat taken. The noise was defeating. But I learned a lot.

Dean worked in engineering, maintaining the Orions. He also had a rather obvious crush on Sally. Unfortunately, he wasn't aware of Sally's crush on Fawkes.

The white overalls were for technical support staff. The orange for flight crews. The green for hospitality. The blue for security. I wondered just what sort of security a place like RATS needed. And then I remembered Lunik. When I tried to direct the conversation towards Ivanov, I was consistently steered away with an anecdote or point of interest. RATS, for instance, was over one hundred years old, but parts of the even older building were only ten; like the hangar. Sometime in their recent past, someone had blown up bits of the previous Academy.

I guess that answered the security question. Or maybe pointed a finger at the techies. It would hardly have been the green overall wearing kitchen staff who did it. But one thing was obvious; RATS had personality.

I'd walked into a living, breathing, collective of eccentric people. The type of place my parents would have adored being part of. The type of place Carrie would have loved to see. The conversations were blusterous. The personalities extreme. The mix of characters and backgrounds astounding. There was even a Surgeon from Haiti.

I sat back and watched it all unfold, wondering what my life had been like last week. What my life had been like last year. Had I ever seen such vivaciousness as this? Had my friends at university ever congregated around a cafeteria table sharing jokes and planning pranks and thinking up the unthinkable?

Home seemed so very far away. Not that RATS felt like home to me yet. But it did feel alive. I couldn't remember when Auckland had last felt that way. When I hadn't been studying or stressing or trying to keep everyone in line.

It left me feeling slightly disassociated. Slightly adrift from the laughter and bustle that surrounded.

Then someone brought out an MP3 player, attached it to speakers, and proceeded to introduce me to the latest songs. Someone else tried to entice me to drink a funky looking, psychedelic coloured, electrolyte replacement until Dean quietly pushed it away from me with a short shake of his head. Someone else brought out a pack of cards. Old school they said. To help me assimilate into their time.

And that's how Jack found me. Teaching the Surgeons of RATS how to play strip-poker in their cafeteria, half the staff - who were meant to be back at work - egging me on.

I was down to my bra and mini. Several of the others were far less covered than that. Sally was singing at the top of her lungs. *Ah, that's where the electrolyte drink went to.*

It was almost as bad as it sounds.

And then I lost the hand we were playing…and the room erupted.

21

I HONESTLY DON'T KNOW, MISS WYLDE

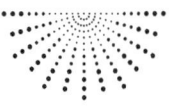

JACK

I shouldn't have left her alone. Anything could have happened. God alone knows there are a few aggressive people in the Academy. A few who took their position a little too far. Like any learning establishment, there was a tiered system of hierarchy. Not just Surgeon, Intern and Novitiate. Even within those ranks, there was a pecking order. And I'd left Mimi alone to field that battle.

I was such an arse.

The halls were unnaturally quiet. As though the place was on lockdown or a big flight was planned. I'd just come from Dispatch, so I knew no one was flying today. Ours was scheduled for tomorrow after we'd had our obligatory downtime between flights. Even RATS obeyed the occasional law. So, where everyone was, was a mystery.

Until I heard the noise.

"Strip! Strip! Strip!"

"What the hell?" I muttered, picking up pace, and then finally running full tilt towards the cafeteria.

I'm not sure what I thought I'd walk in on. But I *had* prepared myself for it involving Mimi. Everything seemed to involve Miss Wylde.

But there was no way I was prepared for what faced me.

The entire staff seemed to be congregated around the longest cafeteria table, all shouting and pumping fists in the air, as a group of six sat at the table in various states of undress. I noticed the electrolyte, in an off-hand kind of way. I spotted the playing cards; old school, how could I not?

But my attention, really, wasn't on any of that.

It was all for Mimi.

Who sat at the edge of the table, in the thick of the action, shouting back at all the hecklers…in nothing but a bra and mini skirt.

"What the hell?" I said again. And strode across the room.

It took a few seconds for the crowd to notice me, but when they did…

Silence.

"I think I've proved my point," Mimi was saying. She didn't sound drunk. "I really believe this lesson has gone too far." Bloody right it had. What lesson? "Must I really remove my skirt?"

Fuck.

"Nah, just your bra, luv," Dean Jordan said. His eyes met mine from across the table. Mimi's back was to me so she couldn't see the scowl. But Jordan did.

He so bloody fucking did.

He smirked back.

"I think I'll go with the skirt," Mimi announced, standing up from her seat and reaching around behind her waist to the zip. Her fingers weren't even trembling.

I crossed my arms over my chest and stood back, seeing how far she'd take this. Jordan snorted, and then covered the sound with an over-the-top cough into his playing hand.

"This game is better than I expected," he offered, trying valiantly not to laugh.

A few people shuffled nervously on their feet; some even snuck out of the room altogether; taking the opportunity while they still had it, I should think. Sally twisted in her seat beside Mimi, perhaps finally registering the tension in the room. Her eyes widened. She gasped. It sounded quite loud in the stillness.

"It's just a skirt, Sal," Mimi said. "I've got knickers on, don't worry."

Someone smothered a laugh.

Jordan looked like he was about to explode from holding his in.

Enough!

I took a step closer. My fingers covering Mimi's at the base of her spine, my lips to her ear as I said, "Would you like a hand, Miss Wylde?"

Mimi froze.

Jordan burst out laughing.

I think I might have growled.

"Don't you all have work to do?" I said pleasantly. The room evaporated. "Not you, Jordan," I ground out.

Reaching down, I picked up Mimi's blouse and handed it to her. She wouldn't meet my eyes. I wasn't surprised, I was rather angry, right then. My fists kept clenching at my sides. My fingers itching to help her dress.

This possessiveness was driving me wild.

I ran a hand through my hair and scratched at my jaw. My fingers found my scar. I worried it absently as my eyes drilled holes into Dean Jordan.

"Explain," I said, once Mimi was dressed and seated again.

"Strip poker, Doctor," Jordan advised. "Mouse was teachin' us how to play it."

"I see."

"It's quite a laugh," he added, digging himself a bigger ditch to get buried in. "You should try it."

I didn't say anything.

"We meant no harm, sir," Groves supplied, quietly. "A bit of a release, really."

"Really."

She nodded her head.

"It was my idea," Mimi announced, voice steady.

"I'm sure it was," I offered. Bloody hell, the woman hadn't been in any danger at all. Apart from a danger of embarrassing herself. I huffed out a breath of air.

No. Mimi wouldn't have embarrassed herself; she would have made herself the sole focus of every male in this facility. An enticing mental picture for them to all enjoy after hours.

Bloody fucking bollocks!

"This is not how RATS staff behave," I pointed out.

Mimi crossed her arms over her chest, a sure sign that she was firing up the boosters and about to launch us all into space.

"So far, I've noticed a decided lack of manners, strong evidence of malpractice, and a leaning towards a thug mentality. I'd hardly say a game of poker..."

"*Strip* poker."

"...corrupted anything."

We stared at each other.

Sally cleared her throat. "No offence was meant, Dr Evans."

"No offence was taken," Jordan offered.

Mimi and I didn't break eye contact.

"She fits in well, don't you think?" Jordan added. "Just like a bonafide Surgeon."

"Everyone thinks she's great," Groves offered as if that was a consideration when doling out punishment.

"Everyone who isn't a prude," Mimi added.

"I'm not a prude," I immediately replied.

"Could have fooled me," Mimi argued.

"You know nothing about me," I pressed.

"I know you're a prude."

"I am *not* a prude, Miss Wylde."

"Prove it." She promptly sat down and started to shuffle the cards.

I was aware of Jordan and Groves watching on avidly. Heads swinging from Mimi to me and back again. Like a bloody tennis match at Wimbledon. I stared down at Mimi's bowed head, her fingers and hands moving smoothly and rapidly as the cards slid over her palm and slipped out of sight in the pack. It was mesmerising.

But hardly appropriate.

"This is hardly appropriate," I repeated aloud. Mentally shaking my head at myself.

"See," Mimi declared. "Prude."

"I'm not doing this, Miss Wylde."

"What are you afraid of?" she asked, dealing out the hand. "A bit of nakedness?"

"I'm a Surgeon."

"A Surgeon who's a prude."

"Would you stop saying that!"

"I will when you stop acting like one."

"Bloody hell, woman! You are the most infuriating individual I have ever met."

"And you're the most prudish individual *I've* ever met."

"What the hell do they do in your time?" I demanded. "Argue someone to death?"

Her hands stilled. The cards fell softly to the table.

Damn it.

"Go back to work, Mr Jordan," I said, my eyes on the back of Mimi's head.

"You gonna be all right, Mouse?" he asked, before standing. She just nodded her head. "Come find me some time, eh?" Another nod of her head.

A glare from Jordan to me. But at least he left.

"Miss Groves," I started.

"I'd rather stay, sir." Now she grows some balls?

I shook my head.

"Mimi," Groves called. "Do you want me to stay?"

Mimi finally moved, turning to face Groves. The smile she gave the other woman was small, but beautiful. Everything about this frustrating woman was beautiful.

Damn those bloody fucking dreams.

"Go, Sally," she said. "I can handle the good doctor."

Yes, *that* was what I was afraid of.

"If you're sure," Groves said, not sounding convinced.

"I'm not as mousey as they think," Mimi offered.

"No," Groves agreed. "You're one of the fiercest people I've ever met." And then she stood and walked from the room.

Mimi watched her leave, a stunned look on her face. I was sure no one had called her fierce before.

Did she not see herself as I did? As others did? Fierce when needed. Bold when required. Caring at all times.

I let a slow breath of air out.

"Are you going to ground me?" she asked softly.

"I should do."

"But you can't. You need me."

In more ways than one, it would seem.

"What on Earth made you choose strip poker?" I finally asked, taking a seat at the table beside her.

"It seemed like a good idea at the time," she murmured.

I laughed. It was fairly short lived. She'd almost been bloody naked.

"Don't do that again." My voice was low but hard as steel.

She turned in her seat to look at me, a puzzled expression on her face. I couldn't blame her. I had sounded like a bloody Neanderthal.

"It's unbecoming," I found myself saying. Of course, I did. A grimace followed. Her eyebrows rose up her brow, disappearing behind the fall of her hair completely.

"Really?" she challenged. "And your behaviour right now isn't?"

I turned in my seat to face her, our knees almost touching. Still, I leant forward, my body attempting to get closer.

"There's nothing wrong with my behaviour," I argued. "I wasn't the one stripping."

"But you are the one acting like a pig."

Christ, she had me there. I opened my mouth to say something; I'm not sure what, but she beat me to it.

"Chauvinism is so unattractive."

"Chauvinism?"

"No, that's not right. Egoism maybe?"

"Egoism?" This just got worse.

"No, that's not right either. What's the word?"

"I honestly don't know, Miss Wylde."

She smiled at my sarcastic tone, all sweetness and light.

"Sexism. That's it."

"I have absolutely no problem with your sex."

She looked at me from under those long lashes; a temptress that I should resist. No, I had no problem whatsoever with Miss Wylde and sex.

I'm not sure who moved first. But somehow we aligned ourselves just right. My fingers found her hair. Hers gripped my suit. And our lips collided.

22

THIS IS HAPPENING

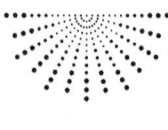

MIMI

*I*t was still angry. But I liked how he kissed. Anger suited him. Jack was full of rage; it boiled up and out through his kiss; it seared me to the core; it melded me to his body; it lit a fire inside I had no hope of dousing.

I wasn't sure what it was about this man that attracted me so much, but I knew it was big. Bigger than me. Bigger than I could handle. Jack Evans was a supernova.

His lips left mine; I felt their absence immediately. A hot trail scorched a path across my jaw, down the side of my neck. He inhaled deeply, his lips pressed to my skin, his nose buried in the hair at the base of my skull. His fingers tangled in the strands as he devoured me in a way I had never been devoured before.

A hand slipped under my blouse, heat unfurled in my belly and spread out; *everywhere*. A hot palm pressed against the underside of my breast, and I arched back; blatantly inviting further contact.

His deep chuckle broke the spell, even if it did sound sexy. I gasped, as though I hadn't breathed in hours, and then attempted to push myself away, fists to chest.

"Don't," he murmured against my skin, his hold tightening.

"Let me go!" I ground out, embarrassed to hear the breathless tone of my voice.

"Just give me a minute," he rasped. "I need...I can't..." There was just no way of telling what he would have said, but I thought I could anyway. I felt exactly the same way.

I needed more touch.

I couldn't pull away.

It was as if my body had a mind of its own.

He growled low, his thumb stroking the sensitive skin over my ribcage. Hot breath came out in a huff against the side of my neck, making me shiver.

"Stop moving," he murmured. "You're making it worse."

"Making what worse?" I demanded, curving my spine like a wanton hussy.

"Much worse," he muttered.

"What?"

He sighed but didn't pull away.

"The need to fuck you, Miss Wylde."

Oh. I wasn't sure what to say. But my body knew how to move when given such an invitation. My hands suddenly wrapped around his nape, my breasts suddenly pressed themselves against his chest. And I suddenly found myself straddling his lap.

I squeaked when the press of his erection found a home. His eyes came up to my face, amusement and chagrin both present in that darkened whisky hue.

"Please tell me this isn't your first time."

"We're not doing anything," I blurted. "So it couldn't *be* my first time."

"If you think this isn't going where it looks like it's going, then you're fooling yourself."

"Such a compelling argument to entice me into your bed," I snapped.

"I was thinking of yours, actually."

Why? Because he'd dreamed it too?

The thought of the dreams did a better job than I think a bucket of cold water could have. I shifted back on his lap, and he let me. Then I took it one step further and stood up. His hands fell away, resting on his thighs, as he watched me from beneath hooded lids.

"I don't understand what's going on," I said, in a fit of honesty I immediately regretted.

He tipped his head back and looked at the ceiling of the cafeteria, letting out a long, slow breath.

"My apologies," he murmured to the roof.

"Why are you apologising?" Did he regret kissing me?

"Because it seemed warranted."

"Just tell me what it is I'm feeling," I demanded. Hyde was very close to the surface. But then, he always was when I felt self-conscious.

Jack's head came down, and turbulent eyes met mine.

"What do you think you are feeling?" he asked. The man was incapable of giving a straight answer.

I swallowed past the dryness of my throat, fervently denying the desire to run and hide from all of this. Carrie. I had to remember Carrie. She was the only reason why I was here. Whatever was going on between Jack Evans and me was irrelevant. Or superfluous to reality.

I closed my eyes and shook my head, feeling infinitely tired.

"Sit down, Miss Wylde," Jack said softly. That tone. The one that made me obey his every whim.

I opened my eyes and looked at him, already reaching for a nearby chair.

"You've just had your tongue down my throat and your hand up my shirt, I think we can dispense with formalities."

He laughed so hard and abruptly; it was almost a snort. He covered it with a cough into his hand, which he immediately ran through his hair. I smiled to myself. It was good to ruffle him. Good to turn the tables now and then.

He watched me settle into the chair and then tilted his head to the side, studying me. It was almost as exhilarating as sitting on his lap. That sort of undivided attention did things to the inside of my body.

The look of potential that crossed his face made it difficult to breathe.

"Travelling through Time has side effects," he suddenly said. I sucked in air. "The more you do it, the more the side effects manifest themselves. But for some, it can be invasive from day one."

I didn't like where this was going.

He crossed his legs and sat back in the chair as if getting comfortable for a long conversation. I should have been relieved; I'd wanted answers. But all I felt was anxious.

"It's the reason why I didn't want you to know too much," Jack went on. "The reason why bringing you back to our time was the last resort." His chest rose and fell with a breath full of meaning. "But you're here now, and I'm guessing you've already had the dreams."

He didn't know that. He couldn't. I'd only been pressing him because he'd admitted to having dreams of me. But he saw something on my face, and a brief flash of satisfaction crossed his own. Gone in an instant, but I could have sworn I saw it. Replaced with an equable mask.

"More than one?" I didn't move a muscle. Just stared. "The same scene?" I gave him nothing. "Becoming more real?" Shit. "The haziness is your mind adjusting. The more vivid the dream, the more...accurate the prediction." He paused, seeming to decide something. Then said, "Mine have become crystal clear."

Eff me.

"Prediction?" I asked, my voice a mere rasp from how dry my throat was getting.

"We travel through Time, Miss Wylde. More often than not, backwards. But we are capable of forward travel, as well. The future is malleable; rips tend to not appear there. So, the majority of our flights are into the past. The dreams are our minds' way of balancing out the electrical signals they receive."

He shrugged his shoulders as if he wasn't describing something surreal.

"For every action, there is an equal and opposite reaction," he said. "Simple physics."

Not so simple for me.

"Prediction," I repeated. He smiled; I wouldn't have said it was particularly mirthful. But I was betting I was amusing him to some degree.

"Yes. Prophetic Dreamscape Realisation. It has a name and everything."

Huh.

"Prophetic," I found myself saying. I couldn't seem to manage more than one word every time I attempted to speak.

"You seem fixated on this point," Jack remarked. "Could it be you've had multiple dreams?"

"They're just dreams." Great, I was up to three words now.

"Dreams of the future."

"A possible future."

His smile turned pitying.

"Dreams of the future directly connected to where you have been."

"What the effing hell does that mean?"

"It means, Miss Wylde, that when we travel into the past, we dream of the future that will balance that particular action out. More often than not, but not always, that dream will include a person we travelled into the past with. For beginners, this is often the case. For seasoned travellers, there's more scope for variety."

The longer I did this; the more *varied* my dreams would be. Effing eff me.

"Now," he said, shifting in his seat, "this is where it gets complicated. And controversial. The dreams are prophetic, but the future is still malleable. Some debate that the dreams can be...refused. They believe it is possible to deny them. Some argue that the dreams are too closely woven with our genetic makeup. Therefore denying them would be as impossible as denying what skin colour you're born with. And then there's the third group."

"The third group?" Brilliant, back to three-word sentences. And parroting.

"Yes, the third group. This collective of people believes the dreams are prognostic. That by having them, we get caught in a causal loop of sorts. The future wouldn't occur the way the dream shows us unless we have the dream."

"Chicken and egg."

"Not exactly. The egg can exist without hatching." OK, if you say so. "But this third group believes that there is no avoiding the dream's outcome, once the dream manifests. They believe by having the dream, you make that particular future possible, and therefore every move you take towards that dream outcome only transpires because of having had *that* dream."

I was getting a headache.

"It's a lot to take in," Jack admitted. Maybe seeing the strain on my face from trying to reason this all out?

But that seemed to be the problem with time travel; there was no reasoning it out.

"So," he said. "Back to your dreams."

"I never said I had dreams."

"Please, you're turning an unhealthy shade of white as we speak."

"That could just be because of the potential to have them," I offered.

"Stop arguing."

"Stop bossing me about."

"Mimi. You've had dreams."

"How can you be sure?" I whispered.

His eyes searched my face, but I don't know what he saw there. I don't know what made his own face soften and a small smile tip up the corners of his lips.

"Because," he said after some time, "I know you." I shook my head. "And because," he added before I could open my mouth to argue, "my dreams are clear."

"The more vivid the dream, the more accurate the prediction," I murmured.

"Precisely."

"What did you dream?" I asked, surprised I'd found the courage to ask that question.

"You first."

"Ah-ah," I said, shaking my head.

"One of us has to," he said with a crooked smile.

"No, we don't. We can deny them."

"Is that what you want?"

Was it? To never touch Jack in the way I touch him in those dreams? To never share the sort of intimacy that we shared? To never feel the way he makes me feel inside a dreamscape? To never laugh and love and fly free as I did in his arms in that bed?

I couldn't say I would want to miss that.

But I couldn't accept a dream as being real.

"What do *you* believe?" I asked. "Which group of thought are you in?"

Jack let a slow breath of air out and ran that hand of his through his hair again.

"It depends on the dream."

"That's hardly scientific."

He smiled. "I'm a little more adaptable than your average scientist."

"Are you saying I'm not?"

"What was in your dream, Mimi?"

"What do you believe, Jack?"

He stilled. His eyes holding mine. His entire presence keeping me captive. I watched every minute shift of his features. Savoured every rise and fall of his chest. Anticipated every nuance as it developed. I could stare at this man for hours and never grow bored.

"I've had a recent change of heart," he murmured. "Prior to 1969 I would have said I am in the first group."

I frowned. "The one that believes we can refuse the dream?"

He nodded his head.

"And now?"

He smiled ruefully, as if to himself, not me.

"Now I find myself believing we are too intrinsically tied to our dreams. That maybe our DNA is somehow involved."

I shook my head. It had been a stretch for me to believe time travel existed at all. If I hadn't witnessed it for myself, I may never have comprehended that an Orion MPCV could surf dimensional waves through Time. But this...this was asking too much.

I was certain my reaction to Jack was *only* because of the dreams. Somehow they affected me. Somehow they made me want him when I should not. Somehow they elicited emotions and reactions in me that were not my own. They were the dreams' emotions and reactions. Not mine.

How else could I explain the way I threw myself at him? The way we fought and ended up kissing. There wasn't another explanation, as far as I was concerned. The dreams were fucking with us, that's all.

"I'm sorry," I said. I'm not sure why I apologised; I was doing nothing wrong. "But I don't believe that. I'm placing myself in the third group," I announced. "None of this would be happening if I hadn't had those dreams."

He didn't seem too upset by that admission. His smile stayed glued to his face. It was small, but then, Jack didn't often let himself go to any degree; a small smile was him practically laughing.

"So, you've had more than one?" he queried.

I didn't think denying it now would matter. I nodded agreement.

"And they were of you and me?"

Another head nod.

"What were we doing?"

My cheeks blazed red.

"Ah, we were...kissing?" I frowned. "Making out?" I rolled my eyes. "In bed." I bit my bottom lip. "Naked," he whispered. I just breathed. "Making love." I couldn't look at him. "Were we fucking or loving, Miss Wylde?"

"Does it matter?" I croaked.

"Humour me."

I cleared my throat. And then had to do it all over again before enough saliva coated the back of it to enable speech.

"We were making love," I whispered.

"As if we'd done it before."

"Yes." It was barely audible.

"As if we planned on doing it again."

I nodded, my eyes coming up slowly to find his. He was watching me, an entirely inappropriate look on his face.

What was it?

Smugness. That's what.

I straightened in my chair. "It's irrelevant. It won't happen."

"You said you were in group three."

"I said none of this would be happening but for the dreams. My reaction to you is affected. It is not mine. Therefore it is not real."

"But it is happening, therefore it exists."

I frowned at him. He just smiled benignly.

"I...I'll deny it, then," I rushed to say. "Group one. I'll refuse to let it transpire."

"Which is it, Miss Wylde? Group one or group three?"

"Both! Some of one and some of the other. A mix of both philosophies."

He laughed. Damn him for finding me amusing!

"You're a scientist," he said between chuckles. "You can do better than that."

"I can not!" Yeah, that argument worked.

He stopped laughing. Then moved forward, crossing the distance between us slowly, but steadily. His eyes held mine; a question there. His hand rose, fingers outstretched, and then as if I couldn't stop him, didn't have the will to stop him, he simply reached forward and stroked my cheek. Ran a finger down the side of my neck. Cupped my nape. Rubbed a thumb over my pulse point.

I shivered.

"Does it feel real?"

I closed my eyes.

Then felt hot breath coast over my lips.

I licked them.

He licked them.

"Does it taste real?"

"Stop. Please!" My words were mere whispers, feathers floating on the breeze.

"Deny it," he whispered back. "Fight it. Refuse it."

"I..I..."

He disappeared. My eyes flicked open to a coldness that had no right to exist but chilled me to the bone. Jack sat watching me.

"It's real."

"But..."

"You have a twin," he murmured. Carrie? What did she have to do with this? "Both of you were picked up on a flight through time." I stilled. "Monozygotic. As close to genetically identical as one can get." No. "Your DNA and hers are practically inseparable. Perhaps timing played a part. You were both in the right place at the right time, but you cannot deny that had your genetics also not played a part, then chances are you *both* wouldn't have been picked up on consecutive fly-bys."

He sat there waiting for me to say something. But what could I say to that?

Jack knew me. He knew how the scientist in me worked.

"Three days ago, I would have agreed with you," he said softly, gently. "Today, I can't."

I stared at a spot on the floor between us. Silence stretched.

Group two. He said he was now in group two. He said that the dreams are too closely woven with our genetic makeup. Therefore denying them would be as impossible as denying what skin colour you're born with.

"This is happening," I whispered.

"This is happening," he repeated with a small smile.

23

THE REST IS UP TO YOU, JACK

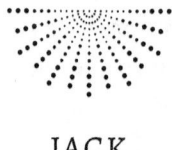

JACK

*I*t wasn't exactly how I'd planned for things to go. I'd envisaged discussing the dreams with Mimi while working toward them. As in, naked, in her bed, having just had fantastic sex. The first of many sessions with the woman.

The fact that I couldn't stop thinking about stripping her bare, or about lying in that bed I knew was in her assigned room, or about her pearlescent skin, shining brightly under a full moon as it softly glowed through her window, was alarming. The curve of her breasts. The dip at the base of her neck. The soft skin behind her ear. Dark blonde hair fanning out over a white pillow.

The images were more than vivid now; they were evocative. Suggestive in a way I couldn't stop fantasising about. I'd never had dreams become so realistic in such a short amount of time before. The rapidity with which they had crystallised inside my head was foreboding. A portent of things to come.

Of course, my body chose to tell me those things were going to be spectacular, but the Surgeon in me urged caution. Since when had dreams felt like destiny? Since when had I believed them dangerous?

Because they did feel that way. As if the longer it took to fulfil them, the more danger Mimi and I were in.

I walked her back to her room in silence. There was so much to say. The words clumped together in my mouth as if caught in a verbal traffic jam between my teeth. Sometimes it felt like kissing Mimi was the only way I could be honest with her. When I tried to speak, it all turned to hell.

But God, she was glorious when arguing.

We stopped outside her room, and it took me a minute to figure out what had consumed her attention. The entire walk back from the cafeteria I'd been acutely aware of her constant glances towards me. As if she couldn't stop herself from looking. I'd stoically kept my gaze face forward. But I'd been aware.

I was always aware of Mimi.

Now she stared at something else.

A bronze plaque had been attached to her door, just like the bronze plaques on all of the flight crew's rooms. *Novitiate Mimi Wylde.* It was official then. Clive had authorised her tag.

Part of me wanted to rejoice that she had a legitimate place here.

Part of me feared how much more dependent on her I would get before she was gone.

She'd find her sister, rescue her from Sergei's clutches, and then return to her time. She was an Origin Event. How could she not?

She was also one of the most determined women I had ever met. If Mimi said she'd do something, I was sure she would.

How did I protect myself from this?

"That's cool," she whispered, stroking the plaque. "Do you have one?"

"Yes."

"Does it say 'Surgeon'?"

"Yes."

Her eyes flicked to mine, then returned to the plaque.

"Jack Evans, Surgeon," she said with a small twist of her lips. It was a smirk, I realised. A bloody smirk.

"Actually, it's 'Surgeon Dr Jack Evans,'" I corrected. What an arse.

Mimi snorted softly and then turned her full attention to me. She looked up at my face and said nothing. I swallowed, but the words wouldn't form. My eyes darted to her still closed door. My mind conjured the picture of her bed from my dreams.

And then, of course, the whole reel was playing. I closed my eyes and let out a slow breath of air.

"Do you want to come in?" Mimi asked.

My eyes flicked open while my heart attempted to jump right out of my chest.

Yes, I wanted to come in. I so bloody fucking well wanted to come in that room.

"There's time, Mimi," I found myself saying.

"Time for what?"

I reached up and slipped a loose strand of her hair behind her ear. My thumb danced across the smooth skin of her cheek. I cupped her jaw. My eyes taking in every single inch of her perfection. Her hair was like spun gold. Her eyes were the deepest of oceans. I lost myself for a few seconds.

"Jack?" she pressed.

"Hmm?"

"Time for what?"

Oh. "Time for us to get to know each other better."

Her look called bullshit on that. And then reality came rushing back in. She'd be gone as soon as she found her sister.

I pulled my hand back and not knowing where to put it, thrust my fingers through my hair. I wanted to pull on the strands. I scratched my whiskers instead. I needed a shave badly.

Fuck. I needed fresh air.

"Sleep well, Miss Wylde," I said and turned away before she could answer.

The smell of cigar smoke hit me first; I recognised it. Then spent a few seconds debating whether to walk toward the sweet scent of tobacco or away. I sighed and moved through the formal garden, finding Clive sitting on his favourite bench. The heavy boughs of a chestnut tree provided cover from the moonlight, making his relaxed form a mere shadow in the dark.

"Jack," he said in greeting. "I thought you'd be in your bed."

So did I, but not *my* bed. Mimi's.

I leant against the trunk of the tree and crossed my legs. Picking a leaf off a branch, I ran it through my fingers, starting to tear it to pieces before I could stop.

"Couldn't sleep," I murmured.

"Something on your mind?" He puffed out a ring of smoke, seemingly unperturbed. But nothing got past Clive Crawford.

"The flight tomorrow."

"Fawkes will be fine; he was trained by the best."

I accepted the praise without comment. Fawkes wouldn't be wherever he was if not for the Wylde twins.

"This is uncharted territory," I offered.

"Not something you are unfamiliar with."

He was wrong. I was way out of my league.

"The girl," Clive said, flicking ash off the end of his cigar. "Is she up to it, do you think?"

"Mimi?"

Clive's eyes darted to my face immediately.

"Is that how it is?"

I cursed the familiarity the dream had brought.

"She'll be fine," I chose to say instead of defending myself. "She's very determined," I added.

"He may not give up the sister kindly."

"She's aware."

"And if he does fall for the trap? Are *you* ready?"

"Of course."

Clive rested his cigar down on the edge of the bench, glowing end hanging over the side, dripping ash. He ran his hands over his trousers as if brushing the wrinkles out of them. Then lifted aged eyes to mine.

"You know why I chose this time?" he asked.

I'd never thought to ask. Clive Crawford had started RATS over a century ago. Then abandoned it for several decades. He'd been back, reforming it, modernising it, for only a decade. For only as long as I'd been qualified to fly.

"No," I said, "I don't."

"Strange that you never asked," he said. "But I guess it's to be expected. You respect people's privacy, Jack. Even if it can end up blindsiding you."

"Will this blindside me?"

He laughed, a barrel-chested bark of laughter.

"Not so much as amuse, I should think."

"Then out with it, Clive. The suspense is killing me."

He chuckled at my melodrama. Then sobered.

"I dreamed of a girl." How apt. "With blonde hair and blue eyes and a sharp tongue." He looked directly at me. "She spoke with a Kiwi accent."

"Mimi?"

"Her sister. Although, I must admit, when I first laid eyes on your Miss Wylde I did wonder. But no, my dream girl was called Carrie."

Christ, how did this play out? In what way could Carolyn Wylde be connected with Clive Crawford? In what way could she cause him to travel forward through time to now?

"I'm sure we'll laugh about this eventually," I offered. "But for now, I'll be honest; I'm a little concerned."

"How could two sisters, twins, have such an impact on us?" Clive chuckled again. I was glad one of us was finding this amusing. I feared what sort of omen these dreams actually meant for RATS. "I have no idea what you dreamed, Jack, but I assure you mine was quite benign."

"Then what on earth made you shift times?"

His sad eyes met mine.

"She asked me to."

"I don't understand?"

"No, I suppose you wouldn't."

"Clive!"

He sighed, then picked up his cigar, which had almost burned down. He flicked off the remaining ash and then just stared at it.

"I'll have to quit these," he commented mildly. I shook my head, not recognising this version of the man I'd known for ten long years.

"I'd always wondered where you'd sourced them from," I offered. Maybe if I humoured him, the Clive Crawford I knew would return.

"I have my secrets." I was thinking he had a hell of a lot more secrets than I'd ever known.

"Clive," I started.

"It's all right, Jack. RATS will be fine."

"How do you know?"

He looked up at me, placing the remainder of the cigar between his teeth, and smiled.

"Because I built it to survive."

"Clive, you're worrying me."

He pushed himself to his full height, grabbing his walking stick while he was at it. The cigar in one hand, he leant on the stick with the other. The man I'd shared too many whiskies with on too many nights stared back at me. But I wasn't sure that I knew him at all.

"It's out of our hands now, son," he said.

"What is?"

"The future."

"What did your dream Carrie say, Clive?"

"I told you," he replied, starting to limp off. "She asked me for help."

"And reorganising RATS in my time helps Carolyn Wylde out how?" I called after him.

He stopped several feet away and looked back at me.

"I hired you," he said simply, and my lungs ceased working. "I made her sister a Novitiate," he added, and I felt lightheaded all of a sudden. "The rest is up to you, Jack."

And then he was gone. And I was alone in the dark under the boughs of a chestnut tree feeling like I was spotlit by a blazing sun.

24
AND IT WASN'T MINE

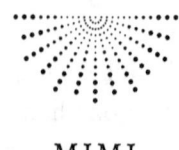

MIMI

*J*ack was in a foul mood. Thankfully, Rafe wasn't. But the Orion seemed so much smaller than usual, even without the presence of Sally. I sat in the third seat; the Novitiate's seat, and watched as Jack thumped in coordinates on the dashboard, one digit after another. I was sure his finger would go right through the plastic keys before too long.

Rafe watched on warily, flicking the odd reassuring smile my way, and then narrowing his eyes at the man in charge. Jack, for his part, didn't even seem to notice us. I stared down at the orange flight suit I was wearing, searching for that initial surge of excitement I'd had when I'd first put it on. But it was gone.

Jack had chased it away with his temper.

"Door," he suddenly barked.

Rafe got up from his seat with a silent sigh and approached the entrance to the module. I glanced around his body at the launch pad, noting a few white overalls in the distance. A couple of blue-clad security guards stood off to the side, as well. I was unsure if their presence was because of me, or because of the weight of this flight.

Orion Two was missing. And it was our job to find it.

Carrie, as Jack had said, didn't even matter. Not to RATS. Not to the various coloured jumpsuits out there in the launch pad hangar. Not even to Jack himself.

I bit my lower lip as Rafe accepted the module door from a techie and secured it with a large, hollow thud.

It sounded just like the beat of my heart.

I turned back to the console and wiped my sweaty palms on my thighs. Rafe was just as silent returning to his seat as he'd been getting out of it. Jack was an ominous dark cloud. For my first official flight in an Orion, I'd expected a different atmosphere. Not one thick with tension and the impending thunder of a tropical storm.

"Coordinates?" Jack asked.

"All checked...sir," Rafe muttered. Jack didn't even spare him a glance.

"Then let's do this," he said, about to hit the ominous looking red button before the command chair.

"Do we have a plan?" I blurted before I could stop myself. Jack's hand hovered over the button. He slowly turned his head toward me.

It was the first time he'd looked me in the eyes since we'd boarded.

"I was under the impression this was your plan, Miss Wylde," he said mildly.

"Shouldn't we discuss it?" I pressed. "Ensure we're all on the same page."

"This is your story," he argued. "Your page. We're just along for the ride."

Is that what he thought?

"You're the Surgeon," I snapped. I almost added, *Act like one.* But that wouldn't have gone down well.

"I am aware of my role, Miss Wylde," he countered, moving his hand to the red button. "Be sure you remember yours."

The Orion roared to life, the nebula-like cloud engulfing it outside, the stars shimmering through the coloured swirls of dust on the external camera screen. I felt weightless for a split second, then heavier than I had ever been. When silence surrounded us, I held my breath. Only releasing it when the world rushed back in again.

The Vehicle touched down without so much as a bump.

"Textbook landing," Rafe announced. "Well done."

Jack just grunted in reply.

"Time matches," Rafe added as if nothing was wrong. "Location as well. We're in 1969 at the Cocoa Beach Pier."

We both looked towards Jack. His eyes were glued to the sine wave on the main screen.

It was blue. Not orange.

"He's not here," Jack remarked.

"Give him time," Rafe offered.

Both men turned to look at me.

"Perhaps a walk, Miss Wylde?" Jack suggested. "God knows it was while you were on the bloody thing that Miss Groves disappeared."

I nodded my head. There wasn't much I could say to that. I was the outsider; they were the qualified doctors. He'd been wrong before. This was their story, and *I* was the one just along for the ride.

We changed into clothing appropriate for the era, taking turns in the bathroom as required. I stared at myself in the small mirror above the sink and wondered just what the effing hell I had gotten myself into here. I was travelling through Time chasing a Lunik vessel with the equivalent of an angry Rottweiler for a companion. If Sergei Ivanov was crazy, then what was I?

At the last minute, it was decided that Rafe would actually remain with the MPCV, as we were attempting to replicate prior events as closely as possible. Of course, Sally wasn't with us either. But that was also intentional. Why give Ivanov another person to target? We wanted him to target me.

In truth, though, it was *Carrie* we wanted. It was Carrie we wanted to target me.

That thought left me reeling and not just a little sick of heart. I was finding it increasingly hard to breathe.

The sun beat down on us as soon as we took our first steps outside, the scent of sea salt and brine wrapping around our frames. We walked in silence to the end of the pier, expecting an ambush at any minute. But nothing happened. No nebula. No stars. No space-like silence. Just gulls and crashing waves and the odd shout of a surfer out in the water. By the time we reached the railing at the end of the pier, I was a nervous wreck; sweating profusely; jumping at the merest creak of wood beneath our feet; heart beating erratically inside. Jack's perpetual silence only exacerbated everything.

I hadn't realised I'd come to rely on his gentle tone and softly offered support so much. But there you have it. Brooding Jack left me feeling all kinds of disconcerted.

Brooding Jack had had quite long enough.

"What's going on, Jack?" I asked, resting a hip against the railing. He stared out into the ocean as if not seeing a thing.

"What do you mean?" he asked. "And you should address me as Dr Evans whilst on a mission," he added.

"OK then," I said. "What's going on, *Dr Evans?*"

He flicked dark eyes to me, then back to the scenery.

"I don't know what you mean, Novitiate."

Oh, so it was like that, was it? My fingers clenched around the railing. Something inside my chest squeezed.

"You know, you've had a stick up your arse from the moment we entered the Orion," I said evenly. How I managed to stay calm was beyond me. "I was wondering what or who might have put it there...Doctor."

"That is hardly appropriate language, Miss Wylde."

"Would you prefer if I said, 'Bloody fucking bollocks'?" And there you have it, not so steady.

He closed his eyes slowly and then let out a deep breath. I felt his disquiet keenly.

"He's not coming," he said. Completely avoiding the topic of conversation. Completely avoiding facing me.

"No," I agreed, feeling acutely disappointed. With him. With the whole situation. With myself, in all reality.

I expected more from Jack than he was obviously capable of giving. He'd had me believe in the dreams. And maybe that was the problem; the familiarity; the fantasy; the intimacy.

The dreams were meant to be part of us, but every time I began to think that, every time I let that thought win, something happened to make me disbelieve.

"Perhaps we could try the Holiday Inn," Jack suggested quietly.

I packaged up my hurt and smiled.

"That could work," I offered. Sergei *had* approached me there. Would he again?

Would Carrie?

Jack turned to walk back down the pier, but I reached out and stopped him.

"Tell me," I pleaded. Why I don't know. Maybe I'm a glutton for punishment.

"This isn't the place or…" he began.

"You'll feel better if you do."

He smiled. The first real smile I'd seen the entire morning.

"I'm not so sure," he murmured.

"Something's bothering you, and until you face it, you'll never beat it."

"Very perceptive, Miss Wylde."

"I can be," I said with a small smile. *Speak to me.*

He stood statue still and just stared. Neither of us saying a word. If Ivanov had chosen that moment to appear, we would have missed him. Thankfully, the Russian wasn't heeding our call.

Yet.

"It's all right, Mimi," he finally said, voice soft and gentle. I'd missed that tone. "It's nothing you need concern yourself with. It's something I must accept on my own."

"You're not making any sense. And why do the rules not apply to you?"

"What rules?"

"*'You should address me as Dr Evans whilst on a mission,'*" I repeated in a mimic of his much deeper voice.

He chuckled. The tightness in my chest eased. "I'm the Surgeon, Miss Wylde. I get to make up the rules."

"And break them."

His hand moved as if to reach for me. I held my breath. Then he stopped it part way between our bodies. Returning it to his side eventually with a sigh.

"I'm breaking them all with you," he murmured, and then started walking back towards the beginning of the pier, somehow making my heart ache and my eyes fill with tears.

I dashed them away and followed behind him, unable to bring myself to walk at his side. Jack was deep in some sort of misery, one I couldn't seem to reach him in, even when I tried. The thought I should have understood what was going on entered my head, but for the life of me, I had no idea what would have made him so quiet.

It involved me; I knew that. And it upset him, of that I was certain, too.

Neither thought made me feel right.

"There is a chance," Jack said as we walked down the main street, passing by the diner we'd visited on my first trip back in time, "he will reappear at the origin of the tear. The Holiday Inn was where he first attempted to draw us. Where he approached you for that first time."

It made sense, but I couldn't seem to voice my agreement. Jack's mood had affected mine.

"Keep your wits about you, Miss Wylde. Our previous selves will be present here; we must stay out of sight."

"What happens if we don't?"

"A confusion of sorts."

"Which means?" I demanded.

"Which means we may devastate this time. The dimensional wave may become inoperable. Unlike a rip which we can repair, a muddled temporal dimension becomes impossible to navigate. So, we tread with care."

I nodded my head, unsure how we'd achieve that and why we'd returned at all if it was that dire.

We found a place off to the side to watch the scene unfold in the Holiday Inn car park. My eyes were automatically drawn to the astronauts. Once a NASA nerd, always a NASA nerd. I watched Neil Armstrong joke with reporters. I smiled wanly when they smiled. I imagined being him, being an astronaut, and imagined the weight of command, the weight of the impending flight on my shoulders. A new found respect for what they undertook settled deep in my bones. There had been other manned Apollo flights into space before this one. Orbiting the moon. Returning safely to Earth again. But this was the first time an Apollo crew would land on the surface. The first time man attempted to land on a natural satellite to Earth. A feat worth being in awe of.

But somehow, even though I felt it, imagined it, the awe didn't really reach me.

It was Jack who spotted Abe Silverstein first; clearly, I was too distracted. But along with Silverstein, we found the shooter. It was easy to extrapolate the order of events after that. But not so easy to see myself as it all unfolded. From our vantage point we couldn't make out the face of the person shooting, shadows left all but the most basic outline visible. They weren't tall or broad of shoulder, but they fired the pistol with a steady hand and lethal eye.

I sucked in a breath when the previous time's Jack bounded over the Corvette's bonnet. I stifled a yelp when Mr Silverstein went down. The crowd panicked. It seemed more chaotic than it had when I'd been in the middle of it. Even watching from outside, I felt every cry, every stumble, every scream, as though mine.

When Ivanov appeared at the back of the me we were watching, my hand reached out and found Jack's. He didn't deny me the contact; whether that was a concession he'd make any novice Novitiate, I wasn't sure. But I was thankful for his warmth and firm grip back.

I searched for the shooter again, but he'd vanished. Just like he'd vanished the first time, we'd been here. I wasn't sure how that was possible, how we could fail to see where he went even as we were looking for it the second time, but the events mimicked our original visit.

In every way bar one.

Sergei Ivanov, his gun pressed into the side of the earlier me's ribs, looked up and over my shoulder directly at us. The present us. Watching from our hiding place, trying not to be seen.

"Christ," Jack muttered. "How the bloody hell does he even know we're here? Now?"

I shook my head, seeing the hatred in those dark eyes directed right at me. Or us, I'm unsure. Seeing the intelligence behind the man. Seeing his intent. Feeling it all.

"Does it matter?" I asked, voice scratchy. "He's here. Can't we catch him?"

Jack glanced down at me, his lips pressed into a thin line, his brow furrowed.

"Are you ready for this, Miss Wylde?"

How could I not be? This man held Carrie.

How could I be, as well? I was out of time.

I nodded my head as Ivanov responded to my earlier attempt to emasculate him with my elbow and knee. And then we were running, and he was punching the earlier me in the stomach, and landing a particularly nasty blow against my temple with the butt of his gun. He looked up at our approach, watching us dispassionately, taking his time...and then ran.

It was all too easy, really. But it happened so fast, that we couldn't prevent what happened next. We rounded the side of the Holiday Inn, our breaths panting, our steps too loud, and came face to face with a Lunik. The door was open. The Vehicle was lit up on the inside. A nebula was already forming.

Through the open access way, I spotted a replica of our Orion, right down to the number of chairs. And in one sat my sister.

The world narrowed to just us, to just this moment, to the desperate need to reach her.

"Carrie!" I yelled. But she didn't even turn her head.

And she wasn't alone. In the command chair beside her sat Sergei Ivanov, his eyes on us, his hand on the console of the Vehicle. He hit a button. The door began to close. I ran harder, my heartbeat frantic, my breaths laboured, time seeming to slow.

Then I was leaping, screaming, reaching for the inside of the Lunik, as Ivanov raised a gun, pointing it at my head.

Stupid! I'd known he had a gun. I'd known he wouldn't hesitate to fire. If I was honest, I'd known his agenda was far darker, far more reaching, than we'd feared.

I squeaked. Carrie still didn't move. And Sergei Ivanov simply smiled.

Then Jack appeared out of nowhere, shoving me aside, grunting with the force of his actions, just as Ivanov pulled the trigger.

The Lunik door closed, the Vehicle disappeared in a star-studded blue and green and gold cloud, and the roar of rockets met my ears, mixed in with the distinct sound of gunfire.

I landed on my side, breathless, aching, already crying, as silence reigned and Jack fell to the ground. Hard.

It took a second. Maybe two, and then I saw it.

Blood. So much blood. And it wasn't mine.

25

DON'T LEAVE ME, JACK

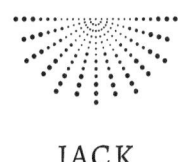

JACK

loody fucking bollocks, but that hurt like the blazes. I sucked in air and let out a wretched breath, feeling every muscle burn as oxygen coursed through my aching body. The world spun lazily around me, the ground warping in and out. I swallowed back bile, willed my heart to stop thumping its way out of my chest, and tried to blink my vision clear.

"Jack!" Mimi cried. She sounded frantic. I struggled to sit upright, trying to reach her, even though, for the life of me, I couldn't see a bloody thing right then. But if Mimi was shouting my name, she must have been in trouble.

"Oh God, Jack," she said, this time as though the words were wrenched from deep within her.

"Are you all right?" I asked. "Where does it hurt?" My hands found her; I scrabbled to get closer; somehow I managed it. My fingers running over her short skirt, finding smooth skin underneath, unblemished, and moving on in a heartbeat to her torso and chest, and finally her face. I cupped her jaw, my vision finally clearing, and saw the tears streaking down her cheeks.

"Shh," I murmured. "It's all right. You're all right." Damn it all to hell, why did she have to be in danger like this?

"There's so much," she whispered. "What do I do? What do I do?"

"It's OK," I murmured, wanting to hold her. The world tilted slightly. I shook my head. "We need to call the Orion."

"Oh, yes!" she cried, relief coursing through her entire frame. I watched on as she reached for her shirt hem, pressing the communicator inside.

"Well done," I offered, wanting to give her encouragement. Wanting to apologise. Wanting so much right then. I thought perhaps the apology was for our atrocious conversation on the pier. And then I thought it might well be for the fact that Clive Crawford had embroiled her in this mess because of a bloody fucking dream. And then I wondered if it was instead because I was such an arse and I was always making her cry.

"Lie down," she ordered.

"Why?"

An amusing growl emitted from the back of her throat and I thought her adorable.

"Just do it, Doctor."

"Doctor is it?" I said smiling.

A ripping sound reached my ears and then something was pressed into my side. Oh, bloody fucking hell that hurt.

"Sorry!" she squeaked.

"Don't, Mouse," I whispered.

Space warped. Time jumped. The dimensions collided. And then everything went dark for a while.

When I opened my eyes, I was on a cot on the floor of the Orion. Rafe was sitting off to the side, watching, a look of concern and impatience on his face. And Mimi was leaning over me, checking something on my side.

"It looks good," she said, but I realised it wasn't to me she was speaking. "That's truly very impressive," she added. "Why can't we carry that fix-it thing with us when we leave the Vehicle?"

"Gotta preserve Time," Rafe mumbled.

"What if you hadn't come when you did? He could be dead."

"He's tougher than he looks, Mouse."

"Well," she said, sitting back on her knees, "I don't want to test that theory."

"I sure as hell do. He was an arse."

I blinked, my lids drooping. Neither noticed I was awake. I smiled to myself, and closed my eyes, listening to Mimi's soft voice gain an edge to it.

"Don't be so hard on him, Rafe. Something has clearly happened."

"Something like getting out of the wrong side of the bed, you mean."

Mimi laughed. "Yeah, well, he was a bit of a grouch."

"Arse, Mouse. Say it."

She giggled. That was quite enough of that.

"Is there a reason why you're inciting insubordination, Dr Hoffman?" I asked.

"Oh, and he's back in the land of the living. Super!" Rafe muttered.

"I'm so glad you care."

"How are you feeling?" Mimi asked. My eyes found hers. For a second I couldn't think straight.

"I'm fine. You?" I finally managed.

"You gave me a scare."

"Just a scratch, Miss Wylde."

"We had to dig the bullet out," Rafe advised.

Silence met his words.

"Ah, well. I see," I muttered.

"He shot at you, Jack," Rafe persisted, his own voice gaining an edge. "He shot at a Novitiate."

I gingerly sat up, feeling the bandage on the side of my chest. My shirt had been removed. A sheet was all the cover I had. I let it fall to my waist, too tired to wrestle with it. But even tired I enjoyed the way Mimi's eyes widened slightly and the fact that she was unable to look away.

I leant back against the cabinets and let out a slow breath, feeling exactly like I'd just been shot. There was only so much a med-device could do. Seal the wound. Rebind tissue and muscle. Stop the bleeding. The pain, not so much.

Surgeons avoided painkillers; they tended to make the dreams too vivid.

"He's out of control, I agree," I said, my eyes closing as I battled fatigue.

"The bullet is out of time," Rafe offered quietly.

"Fuck," I muttered. How careless was Sergei getting? No wonder rips were appearing across the dimensions. Most of them were due to Lunik.

"What does Crawford say?" Rafe asked. "You must have talked to him about all of this."

My fists clenched and I gritted my teeth. I did *not* want to discuss Clive Crawford.

"He's aware," I ground out. "He's put certain actions in place."

"What actions?"

"I can't discuss them."

"That's bullshit," Rafe spat. "How the hell are we to do our job if Crawford keeps playing with the chess pieces behind the scenes?"

I almost defended him. I *would* have defended Clive in the past. But my lips remained sealed. I was too fucking angry with the RATS Chief Surgeon to back his actions right then.

My eyes opened, and I found Mimi. She was watching me. Intelligence sparked behind that clear blue gaze. Putting the puzzle pieces together?

"So, what's the plan?" Rafe asked, giving me my silence on the matter. That's why I liked flying with Rafe Hoffman; he knew when to shut up.

"I need some time to recover."

"Do we go back to RATS?" Mimi asked, both Rafe and I shook our heads.

"The less we travel the dimensions, the easier it is on our bodies," Rafe offered. "If we're to rescue Orion Two, and trap Lunik while we're at it, we need to plan our next flight accordingly. Traipsing to and fro through space waves only causes havoc."

"I'm at a loss as to where we could pick his trail up next," I admitted.

"Orion Two went missing around this time," Rafe replied. "I've checked the link; it's severed. And I can't locate them at our last rendezvous point as well."

"Bloody hell," I muttered, running a hand over my face, scratching my scar. "Where could they be?"

"Beats me, Jack," Rafe replied. "And if Sergei has them, he's not using the ace up his sleeve."

"He doesn't have them." I was sure of it. I knew Sergei Ivanov, and not gloating over such a coup was impossible for the Russian. He'd have been dangling Orion Two in front of our faces by now if he'd had them. Not firing potshots at our heads to scare us off instead.

No. Something else had happened to Orion Two. Something unpredictable. Something that caught them, and us, unawares.

My eyes found Mimi again. The unpredictable event slap bang in the middle of this.

Where did this all fit in? And when did Clive have that dream about Carolyn Wylde? Was she with Sergei in it? Or was she safe and back home in her own time?

I rested my head back against the cabinets and closed my eyes; I couldn't reason this all out. And Clive's penchant for the mysterious was only adding confusion to the midst. Rafe was right. We couldn't operate on such limited information. But returning to RATS would increase the danger to our dreams. The more we dreamt, the wilder the dreams became, the more chance of the future being altered to suit our dreamscape.

It didn't matter what school of thought you were in, it all boiled down to one thing. Dreams affected us. Psychologically. Emotionally. Physically. It was unavoidable. And the bane of our existence.

"Send a probe back," I said, forcing my eyes open. God, I was tired.

"What do you want it to say?" Rafe asked, already activating a probe to return through the dimensions to RATS.

There was no easy way to say this, and if I could have moved and entered the words myself, I would have. But I was stuck on the floor, exhausted, aching, and not just a little fucked off at Clive Crawford.

Let him fight his own battles.

"Address it to Crawford," I said, my voice sounding tired, giving away too much. "Tell him I need to know everything."

"Well, that's not at all cryptic, Jack," Rafe muttered. "He gonna understand that?"

He'd choose not to. I smiled, it was no doubt bitter.

"Tell him; I need to know everything about the dream."

Mimi sucked in a breath of air. My smile turned genuine as my gaze met hers. I saw the exact moment her own dream flushed her cheeks pink. I chuckled. It fucking hurt the side of my chest. A grimace emerged.

"You should rest," she whispered.

"You too," I offered.

"Get a room," Rafe muttered, under his breath.

Mimi rolled her eyes.

I should tell her. I should come clean. Prepare her for her sister's involvement. Because sure as eggs, Carolyn Wylde was in this up to her bloody neck. I needed to protect Mimi.

I needed to protect myself first.

"Probe sent," Rafe announced. "Now what?"

"Now we wait."

"Here?"

"Might as well. Maybe there'll be something in the reply that will make sense." It was a long shot, and Clive would be cagey, I was sure. But what else did we have to go on?

"This rip," Mimi said softly into the quiet of the Orion.

"Yeah?" Rafe asked, bringing up solitaire on his screen and shuffling the virtual cards.

"It started here in 1969?"

"Sergei's involvement in the press conference at the Holiday Inn," I agreed.

"Is it mended now?"

"Pretty much," Rafe added. "Fawkes clearly stitched it before he and his team went missing, 'cause it's not out of alignment now." The sine wave had returned to blue again since Sergei had left.

"But Orion Two wasn't here, this second trip," Mimi offered.

"Temporal paradox, Miss Wylde," I said, shifting to get comfortable.

She nodded her head, clearly working it all out in her mind. Time travel was not easy to grasp. I was impressed so far with her ability to stay abreast of our conversations. There was absolutely nothing slow about Mimi Wylde.

"Then Sergei won't be back," she said.

"No," both Rafe and I replied. "Unless he plans to mess with this time again," Rafe added.

"Even he wouldn't be that mad," I grumbled.

"May I remind you about the bullet," Rafe offered, deadpan.

I just grunted in reply. He had a point.

"Then staying here is a waste of time," Mimi said.

"'Wasting Time.' That should be our new RATS motto," Rafe quipped.

"Royal Academy of Time Surgeons," I said. "We don't just make Time; we waste it!"

"Sounds like we're pulverising it with a blaster," Rafe said on a laugh.

I chuckled. Mimi offered a small smile.

"Get some rest, Miss Wylde," I said. "We all need it. Tomorrow we'll attack it from another angle."

"With blasters," Rafe offered.

Mimi nodded and turned her chair away.

I was watching her, so I saw the second the thought appeared in her mind. Her head tilted to the side, her hand came up to her lips, and then she sat bolt upright.

"What is it?" I asked. She spun in her seat to face me.

"The rip didn't start here," she said.

"Yes, it did."

"Well, maybe the rip was here, but it started further along the timeline."

"What do you mean?"

She shook her head; uncertain. *Come on; you can do it.*

"My time," she said. Rafe stopped playing solitaire. His eyes met mine.

"The Origin Event's time," he said.

"Yes," I murmured. Mimi's Time. Carolyn Wylde's Time. "The rip didn't start here," I said.

My eyes met Mimi's. This woman was beyond clever. This woman was miraculous. Ingenious. Marvellous.

"Set a course, Dr Hoffman."

"On it, sir," Rafe replied.

I smiled at Mimi. "I guess this means we're taking you home." Bloody hell, those words hurt.

She smiled back. It was tremulous at best.

I could have sworn I could read the words in her tear-filled eyes.

Don't leave me, Jack.

But I wasn't sure it was me doing the leaving this time.

26

THE BEGINNING

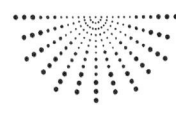

MIMI

*T*he second the MPCV touched down, I was out of my seat. But the door to the Vehicle remained resolutely closed when I tried it.

"Relax, Miss Wylde," Jack said from the command chair. "We can't exit until we confirm we're actually here."

"Time matches," Rafe offered on cue. "Location as well. OE: Alpha 1; Cape Canaveral. We're in the vicinity of the VAB."

I raised my eyebrows at Jack. He just sighed. It had been a tense few hours, but he'd needed time to recover, and we'd all needed rest and to eat, so despite my fervent arguments to the contrary, we hadn't flown straight away. I'd been forced to remain seated when all I'd wanted to do was rescue my sister out of the clutches of that lunatic.

There's only so much pacing you can do in an MPCV.

But Jack had denied me.

He was checking a few things on the console now, his eyes darting up to the yellow-green sine wave on the screen.

"Time has been tampered with," Rafe commented, his own eyes glued to the sinusoid as well. "But it's not a rip."

"It's an Origin Event location, it will always be slightly different than anywhere else," Jack replied steadily.

"Is he here, though?" I asked.

"Difficult to say, Miss Wylde. The rip was caused by our previous unscheduled stop in this time, but the rip itself has been repaired. If he is here, and not tearing the dimensions apart, then the wave won't register a colour difference."

The unsaid being, why would he be here at all? The flyby had been unplanned; Ivanov had chosen Cocoa Beach in 1969 as the time to draw an Orion out and deliver his message, not the VAB in my time. It was uncertain if any Orion would have sufficed, or if he particularly wanted Jack Evans'. And then there was the fact that he'd picked up Carrie on the trip through this year, as well. Had it changed his plans? Had he adjusted his strategy to better accommodate that windfall?

Was she a windfall at all?

He'd threatened her life, but that had been when he'd thought her one of RATS' own. He'd thought I was too. But he must know better now. And Carrie? She'd been the one to issue the second ultimatum. On the pier at Cocoa Beach. She'd been the one to demonstrate Lunik's new abilities, picking up Sally and returning her within a matter of minutes.

Carrie was as much a part of Ivanov's plan now as I was a part of RATS' plan to rescue her.

But we weren't here for Carrie, I realised when Jack tapped the screen excitedly and said, "They're here!"

"Bloody hell!" Rafe added. "Mouse, you're a genius!"

No, I was stupid. I was so effing stupid. Coming here wouldn't bring us closer to Carrie and Ivanov. Coming here simply traced the rip to its origin, thereby chasing down Orion Two.

Somehow they'd got caught up in the original tear; maybe repairing it had caused this unforeseen outcome. Trapped in my time, just as the Lunik and Orion One had been drawn here. But as they'd been travelling to another destination when they flew through here, they'd simply skimmed the surface of the wave and bounced right off it.

Orion Two clearly had not.

Of course, this was all speculation on my part. But it hadn't failed to register with me, though, that I seemed to have an infinity for all of this. My science degree, no doubt, helped. But I had a sneaky suspicion it was more than that. What exactly, I couldn't yet say. But my understanding was too swift, too clear, too accurate.

Even for me, a self-declared NASA nerd.

My shoulders slumped, just as Jack's and Rafe's postures became animated. I stepped aside, allowing them access to the door of the Vehicle. The door I had moments before been only too eager to open. I wasn't sure I wanted to face Bryan Fawkes and his team now. Facing them would mean one thing.

It was time to go back to RATS.

And going back to RATS meant leaving Carrie wherever she was. I couldn't do that. I just couldn't. And the battle that would surely come between Jack and me when I announced this was going to be epic.

I wasn't in control here. I was barely a certified Novitiate.

And, let's not forget, I was also out of time.

"Tether attached?" Jack asked over his shoulder, his eyes on Rafe.

"Attached and linked. They've just changed dimensions to match ours."

"Excellent," Jack said, opening the door to the Vehicle and taking a step outside. Rafe pressed a few more buttons on his console and then stood from his seat. He was still in his orange flight suit, Jack and I were in clothing circa 1970. But that didn't seem to phase him.

"You coming?" he asked when he noticed I hadn't moved an inch.

"Sure," I said. "After you."

"There'll be a party at RATS tonight, Mouse. Mark my words. And you'll be the guest of honour."

He stepped down the ladder and onto a concrete pad. I stood still a moment longer and then let out a slow breath of air. Hiding away in here wouldn't solve my problems. And a part of me still believed that Lunik might appear.

It was wishful thinking, I knew. But hope is an addictive beast. Once you cling to it, it's hard to let it go. Even when logic says it's already vanished.

I was grasping air and I knew it.

Carrie was gone.

"What the bloody hell is *she* still doing here?"

I looked up at the enormously tall building that surrounded us, immediately recognising the inside of the Vehicle Assembly Building and the Space Launch System still being constructed on its enormous stand. The hole from the earlier MPCV flyby was still gaping, but security measures had been put in place. Clearly, we'd timed our arrival after the event, but close enough to still be part of the original tear.

My eyes finally landed on Harding. I'd purposely stalled; a childish reaction. But hey, we can't all be saints.

"Miss Wylde is a Novitiate for this flight," Jack replied dismissively, making Harding sneer.

"Good God," she said. "She's out of time, unqualified, a walking disaster, and possibly an Origin Event, and you made her a Novitiate?"

Jack stopped his sideline conversation with Fawkes and turned his full attention to Harding.

"The Chief Surgeon appointed her, Dr Harding. I'd reconsider calling his actions into question if I were you."

"Don't mind, Jess," Fawkes announced. "She's just been holed up inside an MPCV with Malcolm and me for days on end. The gal's gotta let off a little steam now she's escaped the confines of our home away from home." He chuckled to himself. "Home. Makes you wonder. Just what kind of things we all got up to in there."

"I slept," Malcolm offered.

Harding just scoffed at him.

"I'm sure Dr Crawford has his reasons, Dr Evans," she allowed. "But not calling them into question would be the bigger mistake, I believe."

"Always so quick to argue a point, Jess," Fawkes drawled. "Sometimes you miss the obvious." I wondered just what he meant by that. "It's been an entertaining couple days, I'll tell ya," he added, more jovially and for the benefit of all of us. "But I can't deny, I'm goddamned glad to be outta that thing."

"What do you think happened?" Rafe asked.

"Damned if I know. One minute I'm stitching. The next we're surfing waves. And permanently stuck in one."

"Do you think Sergei had anything to do with it?" Jack asked.

"If he did, I didn't see him deal the cards."

"How else could we have been sent to here?" Harding demanded, looking around the VAB and sneering. Her default facial expression, at a guess.

"What made you come for us, Jack?" Fawkes asked, ignoring Harding. I wondered how often he'd had to do that in the past few days.

"Miss Wylde's suggestion, actually," Jack said, and if I wasn't mistaken, that was a hint of pride I heard in his tone.

Immediately drowned out by Dr Harding.

"What the bloody hell would a contemporary know about time travel?"

"Intelligence is not an invitation only club, Doctor," Jack replied, and then turned back to the rest of us. "The rip began here."

"Really?" Fawkes asked. "I didn't catch that."

"Lunik picked up Carolyn Wylde in this time while travelling to 1969," Jack explained. "Whatever caused it to drop out of the wave into this dimension followed his trajectory to Cocoa Beach in '69. The tear appeared there because he tampered with Time. But would he have, if he hadn't picked up Carolyn Wylde?"

"He wanted you to notice him," I said. All eyes turned to me. Plus one sneer. "Carrie may have altered his plans, but they didn't originate with her. He wanted to get your attention, to deliver that message. I don't know why he chose that time and location."

Jack considered that for a moment, then said, "He chose the location because it's an Origin Event. Cocoa Beach as much as Cape Canaveral. Separating them is quite impossible in terms of history; so many NASA employees lived there. Abe Silverstein being one of them."

"But had he been after Silverstein at all?" Fawkes asked. "I thought you'd ruled him out as a target."

Jack's eyes landed on me. "I haven't ruled anyone or anything out as yet."

"Then where to now?" Malcolm asked.

"He's not likely to come back here," Rafe offered. "The message has been delivered."

"And he won't part with Carolyn Wylde so readily," Jack admitted, his eyes holding mine. Then softer, he added, "He knows who she is now."

"Who is she?" Harding asked, and even though I always heard the sneer in her tone, the question was valid.

Who was Carrie to Sergei Ivanov now?

"That's the question, isn't it?" Jack murmured.

"Well, I'd sure as hell like a hot shower and a cold glass of beer," Fawkes announced. "So, if you have no objections, I'd like to return RATS."

"And what about her?" Harding asked. "Surely you're going to leave her here, in her *own* time. Now would be the obvious chance for success on that front," she added eagerly.

What a bitch.

"We're dimensionally out of line," Jack announced. "Or hadn't you noticed the lack of people here, Dr Harding?"

Oh, so that's how it worked. I'd thought we'd arrived at night, but come to think of it; it was still sunny outside the MPCV hole. Much like it had been when Orion Two picked me up on its flyby through this time.

"Well, that's easily solved," Harding advised. "We'll shift dimensions, drop off your cargo, and then head back. Simple."

I wanted to say something. But I couldn't seem to utter a word. I decided I hated this woman. She was as much a bully as Mikaela Pratt. I was sure my original assessment had been right. They were definitely friends.

"Miss Wylde will be returning to RATS," Jack said, not offering further argument.

"But surely…" Harding started.

"End of story, Dr Harding. Drop it."

"This is where you say, 'Yes, sir,'" Fawkes helpfully supplied.

"I don't know what the bloody hell is going on, but I intend to find out," Harding announced under her breath, and then stormed off to climb inside Orion Two, thankfully moving out of sight.

"Charming, isn't she?" Fawkes said. "Try spending forty-eight hours with her inside an MPCV. She only gets better."

"Better?" Rafe asked doubtfully.

"Well, let's just say, she's a little like aged cheese. She matures."

I tried not to smile.

"Grows on you," Fawkes added.

A laugh slipped out.

"Like fuckin' mould."

I choked back a sound. Fawkes offered me a wink and turned toward his Vehicle.

"You tethered us?" he called over his shoulder.

"Of course," Jack replied.

"Don't lose us this time, Jack."

"Wouldn't think of it, old man," Jack said, just as Rafe muttered, "A couple more hours of Harding and you'll be right."

Fawkes flipped him the bird and disappeared inside his Vehicle. Malcolm offered a small smile and followed. We stood silently, watching as he reached out of the entrance and gripped the door, swinging it closed behind him.

"Is she always like that?" I had to ask. "What a bitch."

"Microphones, Miss Wylde," Jack admonished. Damn, I'd forgotten about them.

"But Fawkes..." I said instead.

"Dr Fawkes is a Surgeon," Rafe explained. "He can get away with murder."

"Nice," Jack muttered, as he swept past. "I'll remember that, Dr Hoffman."

Rafe offered me a big grin and then added, "Just making sure you know your options, sir."

"And murder is one of them?" Jack asked as we entered the Orion.

"Murdering Harding could be," Rafe helpfully supplied.

Jack let out a sigh as he sat down in his chair. He looked shattered. Exhausted and still favouring his side.

"Well, we found them," he said quietly. "Let's get them home, then."

I stood in the entranceway to the Orion and bit my lip. I didn't want to do this. I didn't want to admit that she was gone. That she was further away than she'd ever been. The longer I left her with Ivanov; the more Carrie would change. She'd changed so much already. Even if I could make time and reach her before this all began, I somehow doubted it would be enough to save her.

This felt final. This felt like a conscious choice to walk away. Leaving our time. What had Rafe called it? OE: Alpha 1? Carrie's and my time. The place where the rip that started it all began. The location of the Origin Event that tied it all together. Why had Ivanov chosen here? Sentimentality? The Orion vessel he would have flown back on from the ISS, the one he'd stolen with time travel capabilities at the beginning of the twenty-second century, would have originated here. At the VAB. At Complex 39A of the Kennedy Space Center.

His journey was in my future, but the groundwork had been laid in my time. Why had he come here?

"Miss Wylde?" Jack's voice said, reaching me somehow through a tumult of emotions. "The door?" he asked, his voice a soft caress, tempting me.

I almost took a step backwards.

"There's nothing we can do, is there?" I asked. The words sounded tiny. Mousey. The old me.

But he knew what I was saying.

"For now. That doesn't mean, though, that we can't find her again somehow."

I shook my head. This was it. The turning point. The moment I chose one path and ignored all the rest.

"I can't go with you," I said. Staying here in Cape Canaveral seemed like the only way to fix this mess.

"She's not in this time, Mouse," Rafe said softly.

My eyes darted to his face. I felt the sting of unshed tears. He offered a reassuring smile. I swallowed the sob and blinked repeatedly.

"If you stay here, there's no way to travel through Time," Jack said steadily. "If you stay here, it'll be years before Orion even flies." And decades before it manages to surf dimensional time waves.

But if I left, I'd lose the one solid tie I had to Carrie.

"He could return her," I tried.

"You don't believe that."

"I don't know what I believe."

"But you don't believe that." No, I didn't. And Jack knew me.

"What does he want with her?" I asked.

Jack frowned, then reached up and scrubbed his scar distractedly.

"It's hard to say," he finally said.

I nodded. I was searching for impossible answers. But not all questions were unanswerable.

"What do *you* want with *me*?" I asked. I almost tagged his name on the end. I was thankful that I hadn't. This way, he could choose to take the question as meaning RATS. Not Jack Evans.

What did RATS want with me?

But Jack was no coward, even if his temper and moods could swing.

"I want you safe," he said quietly. "I want you where I can keep you that way."

And in this time he couldn't.

"Come with us, Mimi," he whispered. *Choose me,* the look in his eyes said.

It wasn't as easy as that. Jack and I shared something in those dreams.

But Carrie and I shared a history.

I closed my eyes and tried to make a choice. I fisted my hands and just breathed.

I heard the door clang shut.

I heard the computer accept the coordinates.

I heard Jack and Rafe secure their harnesses.

"Mouse?" Jack said. I'm not sure why it mattered, but it did.

He'd called me Mouse.

I opened my eyes and met his steady, amber and whisky gaze.

"I don't know what to do," I admitted and saw the disappointment on his face.

He schooled his features immediately, but I'd seen it. The letdown, the sorrow, the disillusionment.

He undid his harness and stood from his seat, walking the short distance to reach me. Rafe turned his back to us and pretended to be busy with the coordinates. But it was all an act. He heard everything.

Jack's hand slipped into mine and squeezed. His other cupped my jaw and tilted my head back, palm cradling my nape, fingers tangled in hair. Our eyes connected.

"I promise we'll find her," he whispered, thumb stroking over my pulse point. "I promise I'll help you." Blood thundered in my veins. "I promise this isn't the end."

I searched his face, but he seemed sincere. He meant every word, I was sure of it.

So, why did I feel deceived?

"Then what is this?" I asked.

His forehead came down and rested against mine, hot breath fanning across lips and cheeks. It was intimate. Private. And entirely too familiar.

He'd done this as well in our dreams.

"It's the beginning," he whispered, voice low and slightly rough. "Our beginning," he corrected.

But all I could think was it was the beginning of the end.

For Carrie.

And possibly for me.

27

THE SOONER, THE BETTER

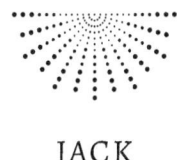

JACK

*M*imi hadn't spoken in hours. She'd retreated inside herself; protecting, hiding, evading confrontation. For a fleeting moment, I wondered if she was always like that. I wondered if when things got too hard, Mimi Wylde ran away. But no, I'd seen her courage. I'd seen the fire beneath the cool façade. What was ailing her now had to have been monumental.

I feared I knew what it was and what it would mean in the long run.

We'd been greeted with raucous enthusiasm in the launch pad hangar when we'd arrived. The return of Orion Two was indeed cause for celebration, and under normal circumstances, I might have joined in the festivities, but Clive's staunch refusal to discuss his dream with me and Mimi's almost stoic silence in the face of such frivolity had both left me reeling.

What the bloody fucking hell was Clive playing at?

And how the bloody fucking hell did I reach Mimi?

I wasn't sure which problem to battle first, but I did know they were both connected. Mimi had lost her sister, and she felt, with every minute of delay in going after her, that the chance of rescue was becoming slimmer. And Clive knew something. He knew where, if not when, Carolyn Wylde spoke to him in that dream.

Had it happened in reality already? Or was he just biding time until the dream came to fruition?

"If you stare at her a moment longer like that, she's likely to go up in smoke," Bryan Fawkes said from beside me.

"I'm not staring."

"You're doing something," he argued. "Drillin' her with your eyeballs. Tryin' to get inside her head with laser beams. I don't know. But people are starting to notice."

"And?"

"And," he said slowly, "you're a Surgeon. Surgeons don't fraternise with Novitiates."

"Bollocks," I spat, thumping my beer glass down on the table in front of me. "That's not a written rule." Maybe it should have been.

But then there were the dreams.

"It's an unwritten one, and a moral one, and an ethical one, and you know it."

I turned slowly in my chair to face the current pain in my arse. He raised two rather bushy eyebrows at me and blinked.

"You know it," he repeated more steadily. "At the very least, if you pursue this, palm her off on another Surgeon."

"Speaking from experience, Fawkes?"

"Damn straight I am."

"So what exactly has gone on with you and Miss Groves?"

"I ain't discussing that with your sorry ass."

"But something has, I take it. And you palmed her off on me?"

"You're a good Surgeon."

I smiled. "I'm also unlikely to fall for her charms." My track record had been stellar. I rarely got involved with co-workers. Despite having had interest from a few in the past.

My eyes scanned the crowded cafeteria automatically, finding my last entanglement if you could call what had transpired between us an entanglement at all. If Mimi knew Jessica Harding and I had locked lips on a stressful flight back in time to the French Revolution, she'd no doubt never speak to me again.

I found myself not relishing that idea.

"You keep to yourself for the most part," Bryan said cordially. "Sally could do worse for instructors."

"You didn't think Sebastian was the better route to take?"

He made a growling sound in the back of his throat, making it extremely clear what he thought of that idea. Sebastian Winchester was not as circumspect as I was where it came to co-worker fraternisation.

I quickly checked to make sure he wasn't bothering Mimi, but his current conquest was none other than Dr Harding. I huffed out an amused breath. God help the man.

A shudder quickly followed.

"But it's not me we're talkin' about," Bryan added.

"More's the pity," I muttered.

"Are the dreams clearing?" I nodded. "Same one?"

I let out a breath of air. I trusted Bryan Fawkes. Like Rafe, he knew when to keep his mouth shut and let things lie. For some reason, though, something about Mimi bothered him. That didn't mean he'd shout it from the rooftops, but it did mean he'd get me to face his concerns if nothing else.

In the past, I'd have valued both his discretion and his innate ability to get you to see things from a different point of view. Perhaps I needed that clarity now.

"No. There's been more than one," I admitted, refusing to show how that affected me.

"How many?"

"I'm not sure. Some seem a continuation of the original. Some not. It's only been a few days."

"Exactly, Jack. This is happening too quickly."

He was right, of course. But part of me refused to believe Mimi wasn't already mine.

"What do we know about the girl? Bring me up-to-date," he

ordered. From anyone else, I'd baulk. But this was Bryan Fawkes. An experienced and dedicated RATS Surgeon.

I forced myself to talk.

"Carolyn Wylde is her identical twin. The sister disappeared first, picked up by Lunik. We picked up Mimi chasing Sergei. Sergei threatened Carolyn's life, then in the next confrontation had Carolyn deliver the ultimatum. Mimi just wants to rescue her. That's all she can think about. The less likely that becomes, the more determined she gets.

"She's courageous, more so than you'd think. And extremely intelligent. She's taken to time travel as though made for it. She has a base understanding that most people take years to find. A natural." I shook my head. "She continues to mystify."

"A natural," Bryan murmured. "Don't you find it unusual that both sisters were picked up on flybys?"

"Absolutely. It's the one thing I can't reconcile inside my mind. The chances of one being picked up on a flyby are astronomical. But both? I wouldn't have thought that possible. I've a theory, though," I added. He nodded his head for me to continue. "It's in the DNA."

"I was thinking the same thing. What has Clive said?"

"Clive," I replied on a heated breath of air. Bryan's focus sharpened. "Clive has always believed our genetic makeup is involved when it comes to the dreams."

"Well," Bryan said, looking out over the cafeteria as if seeing nothing. He wasn't though. This was Bryan Fawkes. The American always saw everything. "If that ain't an endorsement for the twin DNA angle, then I don't know what is."

"But what does it mean?"

Bryan scratched the back of his head, his gaze steadying on Sally Groves as she talked to Mimi.

"It means, my friend, that she's the key. The rip's been mended, but not everything has been put back the way it should be. Both she and Carolyn Wylde are out of time. We return one; maybe the waves won't rebound or break apart. We keep them both out of their original time, then sooner or later, the dimensions are going to buckle.

Nothing this significant, this monumental like an OE, can be left untended, Jack. She *has* to go back, even if we can't locate the sister. Sergei won't do it. That leaves us."

He turned to look at me.

"The dreams," I argued. I didn't like where he was going with this.

"You have to make them happen. The sooner, the better. Once the dreams are realised, Time will settle. Then returning her should put a lid on all of this."

An awful feeling expanded inside my gut. A sickening sensation of doubt and guilt and desire and shame. This was not how I had envisaged things going with Mimi. I am not a manipulator. It's not in me to play such games.

Especially with someone like Mimi.

Someone full of such brightness and hope. Such sparks of intelligence and beauty. Such a courageous being forced to face disastrous odds. I was in awe of Mimi Wylde. But taking this path would ruin everything.

"What about Carolyn?" I asked, scrambling to grasp another argument. Anything that would prevent me from doing what Bryan had suggested.

"Carolyn is already lost," he said decisively, immediately followed by a small, shocked gasp from over our shoulders.

We both turned in our seats to see who had made the sound. For my part, I was stunned she'd approached so stealthily, that both Bryan and I had failed to see that Miss Groves and Mimi had moved at all.

Sally looked equally as shocked at what Bryan had just said, but underlying her shock was outrage.

Mimi just looked broken.

"Miss Wylde," I said, standing from my seat. Bollocks!

She shook her head. Let out a small sound of misery. And then she was running.

From the room. From the confrontation. From me.

It took a mere second for my feet to follow. My heart thudding painfully in my chest. My mind running on automatic; images of our dreams cascading across my eyes, followed swiftly by Bryan's unwanted warning.

You have to make them happen. The sooner, the better.

Time demanded we fix this outage.

My heart said, bugger that!

I had no idea which would win. But history has a habit of repeating itself. And I'd always, *always*, done the right thing.

2 8

UNTIL IT ISN'T

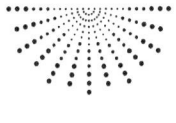

MIMI

I should have known. RATS was only concerned with one thing. Time. Fixing it. Mending it. Stitching. Catching. Making. It didn't matter how, as long as Time survived.

It would have been a noble cause, in an utterly unbelievable way, if not for Carrie. I was fighting a losing battle, and I had no one on my side to aid me. RATS was too stuck in its ways to see things from any other point of view. Carrie and I were out of time. Therefore we needed to be put back accordingly.

But what if we were meant to be out of time? What if putting us back negated all the good that we'd done?

That made me laugh. A snort of derision escaping as I gasped for air. In what way had Carrie made things better? Clearly, RATS and this time were doing just fine, thank you very much. But Carrie being here, delivering ultimatums for RATS to close or else, couldn't be construed as a good thing any which way you sold it.

And me? What was I? A scientist who obsessed over space travel. A nobody from a different century.

I rounded the corner of a beautifully manicured box hedge and found sanctuary under an old chestnut tree. The heavy boughs inviting me into the shadows beneath. I pressed a hand to my stomach, trying to still my wretched breathing, trying to dislodge the sensations of defeat and despair.

Reaching out, I rested my hand against the rough bark of the tree's twisted and gnarled trunk, and then simply collapsed, in a highly undignified heap, on the stone bench beside it. What was I going to do? How did I convince these people that rescuing Carrie was all that mattered?

It was all that mattered to me.

But all that mattered to RATS was mending Time.

Stitching. Catching. Making.

"You shouldn't have run," a voice said from out of the shadows.

I lifted my eyes and met steadying whisky-amber out of a concerned looking face. He was breathing freely, not struggling for every lungful as I was. But he would have been just as swift as I had been to get here so soon after I'd left the cafeteria. Jack Evans was super fit.

"I didn't run," I argued, and watched the side of Jack's lips tip up in a smile.

"What do you call it then?"

"A strategic exit."

"At full speed?"

"I can run faster."

He stepped out of the shadows and moved to sit beside me on the bench seat. I stiffened. I wasn't ready to face reality - or the dreams - just yet.

"You can't run from this, Mimi."

I stared down at the leaves strewn across the ground at my feet; colours turning for autumn. I didn't even know what day it was here. What year. I'd only guessed the century.

Damn, I was so far out of my time.

"Dr Fawkes was only stating his opinion," Jack said softly.

"His opinion seems a fair representation of RATS' own."

"You don't know that." There's a lot I didn't know. "I don't believe it."

I turned to look at him. He was watching me from behind carefully shrouded eyes. Truth or lie? I didn't know him well enough to be sure which, even if my mind, my dreams, knew his body intimately.

I shifted on the bench and sucked in a breath of air to steady myself.

"What *do* you believe, Jack?"

He leant forward and rested his elbows on his knees, staring off across the garden. I'm not sure he saw its beauty, I certainly wasn't paying it much attention. But he took his time staring at nothing before he spoke. Choosing his words carefully.

"I think this has all happened for a reason," he finally said.

"What reason can there be for Carrie being with that man?"

His head shook from side to side slowly, as if clearing his mind of an unwanted thought.

"I don't know," he admitted. "But I dreamt of you before I met you, and I'm not the only one here at RATS to have dreamt of a Wylde twin."

I stood up from the bench seat abruptly, rounding on him, hands fisted on hips, mouth open; words failing me for a second.

Had someone dreamed of Carrie? Who? Fawkes?

Jack lifted up his hand, palm open, to calm me.

"Easy," he murmured.

"Don't you 'easy' me, Jack Evans!"

"I'm just saying; there's no need to get upset."

"Isn't there? What's with you Surgeons and dreaming? What's with these effing dreams anyway?"

"I've already explained the dreams, Miss Wylde."

"Oh, and I'm Miss Wylde again!" My hands flew up in the air, and I turned away, pacing a good distance; putting space between us lest I strike out and hit the man.

Or knee him.

"Mimi," he said softly, that gentle tone from just over my shoulder. I hunched my back, sinking in on myself. But that wouldn't make him go away.

"I feel like I'm the only one who wants to find her, Jack," I whispered. "Like I'm the only one who cares about Carrie."

"That's not true. I care."

"And the person who dreamed of her?" I turned to look up at him. He was only a few feet away. Hands in his trouser pockets, a worried expression on his face. "Who dreamed of her, Jack?"

"It's not for me to say."

"Then why mention it?" I demanded.

He sighed, ran a hand through his hair. Scratched at his scar. I stared at the small mark; wondering where he'd gotten it; how he'd gotten it. Why he reached for it when things got too heated.

"The dreams mean something," he said. "To dream of you both before we met you for the first time...it's not a coincidence. Our dreams are prophetic, but rarely are they unrelated to our travels through Time. I've had countless dreams, Mimi. Over the years perhaps hundreds. And every single one of them involved a person I already knew. Had travelled with."

"Why are you and Carolyn so different? Why did I dream of you before we met?"

I shook my head. He took a step closer.

"And the type of dreams," he said in a quieter voice. "The intimacy." I blushed, praying the shadows kept the telltale sign from my cheeks. "Not just what we were doing, but the fact that we'd done it before. Enough times for us to feel comfortable. To feel safe. Content."

He took another step closer, this time bringing himself to within a foot from me. I didn't move, but I did look down at his shoes, noting the distance, or lack thereof, between us.

"You felt it too, didn't you?" he asked. "Mimi? You felt it too, that intimacy," he stressed.

I wished he would stop using that word. But I had to admit the word did feel right.

Intimacy. Intimacy which as strangers we shouldn't be feeling.

"How do you do this?" I asked out of desperation. "How do live with these dreams making you feel something that isn't right?"

"In what way is it not right?"

I looked up at him and shook my head.

"We barely know each other, Jack. And yet I know exactly how you like to be touched. How you like to touch me. That's *not* right."

"I don't agree."

"Of course you don't. You're a man."

He arched a brow at me and smiled.

"So glad you noticed, Miss Wylde."

I huffed out a breath and waved a hand at him, taking a step away.

In moves too quick to catch, he reached out and stopped me; hot palm to the side of my neck. Another intimacy he should not have had. I rounded on him, moving with the pull of heat from his fingers, stepping into an embrace I had no intention of completing. His fingers wrapped up in my hair in a move I recognised immediately.

Was the recognition from the dreams or the few times we'd actually kissed in reality? It was all getting so confusing.

"Mimi," he murmured. I pressed my fists to his chest, trying to halt the progression of the caress. "In a year's time, the dreams will make sense," he whispered into my hair, his arms so much stronger than mine.

I hesitated, waiting for his explanation. Giving him an opportunity I shouldn't have.

"We're merely jumping ahead of ourselves in this one regard," he murmured, his free hand soothing down the centre of my back.

Heat unfurled from in front of me, sparks of electricity fired up and down my spine. I was sandwiched between an inferno. My body reluctantly relaxed. He took advantage; pulling me closer; drawing me further in; cinching the embrace.

"As Surgeons of Time," he murmured, "that doesn't seem such an unbelievable thing, does it? When you think about it, it actually makes sense. We surf dimensional waves from one time to another. Sometimes we visit things before they have even transpired. Why not feel them sooner too?"

"It's not natural," I argued, but my words were muffled by the front of his shirt. My cheek pressed against his chest, my breath making the material beneath my lips moist already.

"Why can't it be?" he pressed. "If time travel exists, then why not this?"

"Time travel is not right either," I argued, for the sake of arguing I think.

His chest rumbled as laughter bubbled up from deep within.

"I love your contrariness," he said between chuckles. "I love that you question everything."

Not many people did. Carrie, for one, often grew frustrated with me. Having to wait until I'd argued every side of a thing before I'd proceed. My sister was spontaneous by nature. I was the cautious one.

And yet here I was, wrapped up in the arms of a stranger I knew with every beat of my heart.

"It can't be right," I whispered. It was almost a plea. His shoulders relaxed, even as his arms tightened. He ran a hand through my hair and then bent down to kiss my forehead.

"You've seen such amazing things in the past few days," he said softly. "You've had your whole outlook on Time altered. You've handled it with a level of decorum most wouldn't have possessed. And yet you doubt this?"

"Did you always believe in the dreams?" I challenged, knowing the answer already.

"Not always, no."

"How long before you began to see them as being real?"

"A few years," he admitted reluctantly.

I snorted and pulled back to look up at him. "And you expect me to accept all of this within a few short days?"

He smiled. "You've set a high standard, Miss Wylde. You've made it all look so effortless." I doubted that completely. "One can't help but be surprised that finally, something has thrown you off kilter."

I couldn't stop it; I smiled. He stilled. And then in the next breath, his lips were pressed to mine. My body responded immediately. The familiarity of the act making it impossible to deny. But I couldn't tell if that familiarity was due to the dreams or the fact that I'd kissed Jack Evans several times now. Each time more exquisite than the last.

The dreams had me knowing things. Things I shouldn't have

known yet. But the reality of a kiss from Jack Evans made the dreams pale in comparison.

I'd feared there was nothing of discovery left. I knew his body. I knew the sounds he made when he lost himself in the act of making love. I even knew how he tasted. But actually kissing Jack made me realise how small those sensations were. How tiny they were compared to reality. How insignificant they were to what Jack actually made me feel when he kissed me in truth.

I couldn't imagine what differences there would be when we finally made love. Familiarity mixed with intimacy coated in the reality of Jack.

He'd always seem so much bigger than a dream to me, I was sure of it. Even as I battled what the dreams made me feel when apart.

I moaned as his tongue delved deeper, my lower back arched over his arm, exposing myself better to his attentions. One of his hands was wrapped up in the strands of my hair, tugging, directing, controlling; a move I was very familiar with in my dreams as well. He pressed the length of his body down the curve of mine; fitting himself against me as if a missing puzzle piece. He devoured my mouth, cupped my hip against his frame, rocked his body into mine.

Jack did nothing by halves.

I wanted to climb up him. I wanted to climb inside him. I wanted him to climb inside of me.

He moved us, somehow maintaining our connection. Our lips locked, our tongues entwined, our bodies begging each other for more contact. I felt the coolness of the bench beneath my butt cheek, and then I was up on his lap, my legs spread either side of his thighs, his erection pressed into my centre. Rocking. Moaning. Pleading. Tasting. It was almost too much.

And then not nearly enough. I knew what else he could offer.

"Jack," I gasped when he pulled away to suckle on the side of my neck.

"Fuck," he murmured against my heated skin. "I want you so badly." His voice was beyond a rasp; desperate. "I know exactly how good it will feel and yet I don't know if anything can better this. Can better you. Here. Now." His lips moved across my skin, tracing a heated trail over my jaw, my chin, finding my lips again in a blistering kiss.

He groaned into my mouth as if pouring himself inside there. He gripped me tightly around the waist and pulled me hard down on top of him, rubbing me in exactly the right spot, reminding me what lay pressed against my stomach. What was there for the taking. His hand tightened in my hair, tilting my head exactly where he wanted it. He consumed me. He owned me. He laid all past experiences to waste.

I'd never been kissed like this.

I'd never be kissed like this again by anyone else.

Jack ruled my body from his lips. I was his at that moment. I tasted heaven. I touched paradise. I forgot everything else but this.

"Mimi," he said. "Say yes," he begged.

Say yes to him. Say yes to realising the dreams. Say yes to mending Time by sending me back without Carrie.

You have to make them happen. The sooner, the better. Once the dreams are realised, Time will settle. Then returning her should put a lid on all of this.

I'd heard every word Bryan Fawkes had said.

And I was not giving up on Carrie. Even if RATS did.

I pushed against Jack's hold; for a moment he resisted. Too consumed by an inferno, we shouldn't have started. I scrabbled backwards when he finally released me, almost falling on my arse on the ground at his feet. Not exactly attractive. He reached out to steady me, but I only hissed out a breath and sidestepped.

Standing beneath the heavy boughs of the chestnut tree, I gasped for breath and sanity.

Jack looked devastated.

"Mimi," he said. It broke my heart; the desperation; the desire; the disbelief.

I sucked in a breath of air and slowly shook my head. RATS had a plan. A plan to fix Time by returning me to mine. But those dreams were preventing that from happening. For now.

So, for now, I'd use them. I'd deny them. I'd stop them from becoming a reality.

And then I'd figure out how to get my sister back.

"Don't do this," Jack begged.

"It's not real," I whispered.

He huffed out a breath, hands fisted on his thighs, jaw set.

"It's as real as it gets, Miss Wylde. Until it isn't."

And then he stood up and walked away, leaving me wondering just what the effing hell that meant.

Leaving me feeling like I was losing something precious. Maybe even more precious than my sister.

29

ONLY TIME WOULD SEE

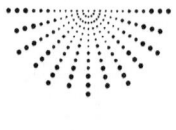

MIMI

I realised it was cold. That the golden leaves on the ground at my feet were a message. RATS was in England; even I could tell that. I half expected the Academy to look like Westminster Palace; my go-to reference image for that country. It didn't, but its Christopher Wren styling did prove one thing; it was definitely in England. And in England, in this time, it was autumn. It was cold.

I wrapped my arms around my body and hugged myself tightly, but for the life of me, I couldn't make myself shift from where I stood. I was in England in an unknown time, well past the time that I should have been in. I was miles away from Cape Canaveral; where it was warm, and the air was moist with the promise of an afternoon thunderstorm.

I was on my own. Out of time. Out of options. So far out of my league. And I missed my sister. I missed her so very much.

For the past several months she'd been my rock. She'd been the only thing in my life that had kept me grounded. When our parents hadn't returned from their holiday in Russia, Carrie had been the one to hold me tight. When we'd taken phone calls in the middle of the night from the New Zealand Embassy in Moscow, Carrie had been there holding my hand, keeping me strong, pressing for information on their possible whereabouts. When we'd seen the last pictures taken of our mother and father at a peasant commune - happy, entranced, alive - Carrie had been the one to cry with me. To grieve with me.

No one else understood that level of loss.

I hadn't been able to find my parents; I was determined I would find Carrie. But how?

I stared up at the RATS building, wondering where I could start. How I could get them to go after Sergei. And not send me back to my time. I needed a plan. I needed allies. I needed a certain Surgeon to help me out.

I wasn't sure I could count on any of that.

I was on my own. But I have never been one to shy away from a challenge. Just that my challenges in the past have been of the scientific variety. Not the life and death reality I was currently starring in.

A sound startled me from my thoughts, and then the bitter laughter of an unseen observer overrode all other noise. For a second, I thought perhaps Sergei had found me. However, the laughter was too high pitched to be male. But the notion that he'd be acting alone was also ridiculous; even I had to concede that Carrie was aiding the Russian now.

I spun in a tight circle, but whoever was watching me was keeping themselves hidden. The chestnut tree was not the only aged plant in the garden. Something came out of the bushes to my right, arcing through the air and whacking me on the shoulder. Something else rocketed toward me from another direction. Hard, spiky, accurate.

I took a step backwards, my head sweeping from side to side, my breaths too fast and loud, my ears ringing. I rubbed at my upper arm and glanced down quickly, trying to determine what the projectiles were. Not bullets. No gun had been fired. And all I could see on the ground were yellow-gold leaves and the odd chestnut burr.

Chestnuts. They were throwing chestnuts at me. I shook my head in disbelief.

A chestnut whacked me on the side of the face. That one stung considerably. And was a little too close to my eye to have been thrown in jest. Another hit me mid-section, making me double over slightly to protect my vulnerable belly. Then several were thrown at once, bouncing off my back and head, hitting my cheeks and chest, glancing off my legs to land in pattering thuds on the leaves below.

"Cut it out!" I yelled, picking up a prickly chestnut and hurling it back in the direction of one of the mysterious attackers. I received a satisfying "Oomph!" for my efforts. "Two can play that game!"

"You have no idea how to play the game," came the reply. I recognised the voice immediately.

Pratt.

"You really are an adolescent," I growled, picking up a chestnut just in case I needed it.

She stepped out from behind a bush, a sneer on her face that seemed familiar. She glanced down at the chestnut in my hand and raised a blonde eyebrow.

"You going to throw that, Novitiate?"

My eyes darted to the object in my hand, but before I could lift them to her face again, a chestnut hit me on the forehead. That was it! I hurled the chestnut directly at Mikaela's face just as a flash went off blinding me. I blinked as the bright white light kept flickering, making spots appear before my eyes, and heard Pratt grunt out a sound of distress as the chestnut hit home.

Silence followed. My eyes took a second to adjust. And then Pratt was grinning.

"See?" she said. "You have no idea how to play the game."

"What game?" I said, utterly confused now.

She just smiled, and then turned on her heel and walked away.

Twice now I'd been abandoned under this chestnut tree, but this time I wasn't so sure about what had just transpired. Mikaela Pratt was a psychotic, immature bully. She was crazy. And somehow she'd decided to play games with me.

"This is ridiculous!" I muttered, forcing myself to start in the direction of the RATS building. I glanced over my shoulder, making sure no one was following me or lurking in the shadows, but the entire walk back was devoid of confrontation.

"What is wrong with these people?" I continued to mutter under my breath. "Effing chestnuts!"

"Is that some kind of new swearword or somethin'?" a voice said off to the side.

"Bloody bollocks!" I shouted, jumping out of my skin when Dean suddenly appeared. "You scared me half to death."

He grinned and said, "Now that's a swearword I've heard bandied about 'ere many a time. Did you know you sounded just like Jack Evans then?"

"He must be rubbing off on me," I growled.

"He has a tendency to do that," Dean agreed. "Where you been? We've been looking for you."

"Who's we?"

"Sally and me, of course."

"Oh."

"Yeah, oh! You're the guest of honour, and you're not even 'ere celebrating, but skulkin' around in the gardens as if up to no good."

"I wasn't up to no good."

"Weren't you? Shame."

I smiled. Dean Jordan had a way of making you do that. Jack made me swear. Dean made me smile. Mikaela Pratt...Eff knows what just happened with that psycho.

"Tell me something, Dean," I started.

"Anythin' for you, luv."

I tried not to smile. "How old are the Surgeons here? I mean, clearly the Surgeons are older, but the Interns seem rather young to me." Childlike in some cases. Crazy bitch.

"Ah," he said, looking a little uncomfortable.

"What is it?" I pressed, coming to a stop and turning to face him. I reached out and laid a hand on his arm; he seemed to need the reassurance.

"Well, you know time travel ain't a walk in the park, right?" I nodded encouragingly for him to go on. "So, there's been a few times that things 'ave gone awry."

"Awry?"

"Disastrous, more like."

"Oh."

"Yeah, oh." He scrubbed the back of his head. "A while ago, it was just the Surgeon and an Intern who flew the Orions. Then we lost several in quick succession."

"Lost them? Lost who?"

He held my gaze with a steady one of his own. "Several Interns. The Novitiates didn't fly back then. All their time was spent in theory. So when we lost all those Interns within weeks of each other, the Novitiates were bumped up to replace them, and a new class of Novitiates was brought in."

I was silent for a moment. Not much you can say to all of that. I'd thought Sergei had been an anomaly. Clearly not.

"How long was Novitiate training before this?" I finally asked.

"Four years. Interns need a further two to complete training. It takes six years in total to become a Surgeon. But most of those Novitiates raised to Intern back then hadn't even been 'ere more than twelve months. Straight from school."

I frowned.

"Don't they go to university first?"

"Nah, we teach 'em all they need to know 'ere. Time travel ain't a course taught at Oxford or Cambridge, Mouse. It's specialised like."

"Yeah," I said, unconvinced. "And they call themselves doctors."

"Yeah, well. It's been recognised by Parliament and all that. I don't know what it's called. Department of Education or somethin'."

"So, Mikaela Pratt and Jessica Harding?" I pressed.

He snorted. "Practically still in fuckin' nappies."

"And you?"

"You askin' me my age, Mouse?" I smiled. "I'm twenty-six. Got an engineering degree and all. Bet you didn't see that comin'?"

I laughed. "I've got a masters in science," I admitted.

"I know," he said. "Everyone knows. It's all they're talkin' about. How much like a Surgeon you already are. Done your time, so to speak."

I shook my head. "I haven't. I've been stuck in theory." Just like those former Novitiates.

"How did you lose them?" I asked after a stretch of silence.

"Lunik," he said. One word and it meant everything.

"I didn't know," I murmured. I'm sure there was much more I could have added.

"How could ya? It 'appened a year ago."

"Just a year?"

He nodded, thrust his hands in his white overalls and stared off over the garden behind us.

"It hit us hard. No one saw it comin'. Sometimes the Surgeons dream and we get a bit of a warnin'. But this time it 'appened out of the blue. Even Crawford was devastated."

"And they haven't been found?"

"We're still searchin'. Most of our flights now are to search for our lost. The occasional one to fix a new rip, like the rip you got caught up in. But every day an Orion flies back to those coordinates. Back to where we lost our people."

"The same time? I thought that was dangerous. To go back to a time you've visited often."

"It is, but they're our people, ya know? We can't just leave them there."

I shook my head. "They won't be there anymore."

He frowned down at me. "What makes you say that?"

"Sergei Ivanov has a plan. Something big that involves destroying RATS."

"Yeah, well, good luck to him. RATS Surgeons don't go down without a fight."

"Why would he need Interns?" I asked quietly.

"Fucked if I know."

"Why didn't he take the Surgeons?"

"Too knowledgeable?" I nodded in absent agreement. "Those last two years of trainin' must pack a punch."

Yes, I thought perhaps they did. What was Clive Crawford holding back for the final two years of training a Surgeon? And why did it make a difference to Sergei Ivanov?

"So, now ya know," Dean said conversationally. "RATS is a quagmire of risk. Danger lurks at every corner. You've missed out on some of the trainin', but one of the things they teach a Novitiate before they let them fly an Orion is how everything connects. How one slip 'ere can cause a rip there. How a butterfly fluttering its wings in China causes a tsunami in Australia. That kind of thing."

"So those lost Interns?"

He let out a long breath of air. "Those lost Interns caused Time to warp. We're travelling down a different dimensional wave now. The future has been altered. The past changed."

"One year," I whispered. One year ago in my time, things had changed. One year ago in Jack's it had too.

"What does Ivanov want?" I wondered aloud.

"What does any plonker with a time travelling device want, Mouse? To rule the fuckin' world."

Money. Power. It didn't make sense. Sure, both were commodities that an egomaniac would desire. But it seemed so paltry compared to death. He'd kill for both. If that's what he'd done to those Interns. He'd certainly taken them to affect Time. To change the past and alter the future. Had he killed them too? Would he kill Carrie?

I closed my eyes and breathed through the physical pain that thought brought with it. The world swam around me, making me sway.

"Hey, you all right?" Dean asked. "Come on, come over 'ere and 'ave a seat." He helped me to a low wall surrounding a well-maintained garden in front of the building. I sat down and let the world right itself, feeling not just a little lost myself.

Ivanov had changed - warped - Time by taking those Interns out of theirs. Carrie was out of time. I was out of time too. This was a quagmire of risk. No wonder Fawkes wanted to return me. No wonder Carrie wasn't a concern, but I was. They couldn't find their Interns. They couldn't find Carrie. But they had me. Me they could fix. Me they could use to help mend the lost time.

I understood Bryan Fawkes' motivation now. I understood Clive Crawford's as well.

But Jack's I didn't. Because he wanted to keep me here. He wanted to realise those dreams. Was it all a way to return me too? To trick me into something he knew I wouldn't fall for otherwise?

I didn't trust anyone here to help me. Dean wanted to be a friend, but that could have been for other reasons as well. Maybe he'd been put up to it. Explain the situation, get her on side, then she'd do what was right.

But abandoning Carrie was not right. It couldn't be. I wouldn't let it be.

The door behind us opened suddenly, and a shaft of yellow light shone down on the ground around us, making our shadows lengthen and warp on the paving stones, much like Time itself.

"Miss Wylde," a voice said over our shoulder. "Is this where you have been hiding?"

Dean and I turned to the owner of the voice, my heart sinking. What could Jessica Harding want with me now? I stood up, taking in her well-presented form, out of an orange jumpsuit and in skinny jeans and a midriff baring top. I noticed how young she was then. Younger than me, that's for sure.

Even if I wished I had a chestnut hidden in the palm of my hand right now.

A shadowed form appeared over her shoulder. It took a second to recognise it. Dr Crawford.

"Sir," Dean said, standing straighter.

"Best you be off, Jordan," Crawford said dismissively. "Rather nasty business, I'm afraid."

Dean frowned. "You want to speak to Mouse?"

Crawford blinked. "I wish to speak with Miss Wylde. An accusation has been brought against her."

Dean turned slowly to look at me but didn't make a move to leave. Jessica stood behind Clive Crawford and sneered. I hadn't realised the sneer had been missing until then.

I had a very bad feeling about all of this.

"Mr Jordan?" Crawford pressed.

Dean offered me an encouraging smile and shrugged his shoulders, then moved past the towering forms of Crawford and Harding to walk inside. We all waited for him to be far enough away not to listen.

I had a *really* bad feeling about all of this.

"Please tell me, Miss Wylde," Crawford began. "Did you happen to throw something at an Intern this evening?"

Oh, effing bloody bollocks.

"There's no point lying," he added. "The evidence speaks for itself, I'm afraid."

Crawford held a photo in his hand, thrust out toward me so I could see it. In it, a surprised and much abused Mikaela Pratt was receiving a chestnut to her forehead, clearly thrown from my hand, as the evidence showed in a blindingly bright white flash from an unseen camera. The photo was overexposed but undeniable.

My eyes met Harding's. The sneer was replaced with a self-satisfied smirk.

"You have got to be kidding me," I muttered.

"No, sadly this is not a joke," Crawford said, but I saw something in his eyes as he looked down his nose at Harding. I held my breath. "I'm afraid I must ground you, Miss Wylde."

"Ground me?" I queried.

"Yes, standard operating procedure for this sort of thing."

"You have a procedure for chestnut throwing incidences?"

He grimaced. "Surgeons are a rather volatile lot. Confrontations do occur."

I hated confrontations. I hated Jessica Harding and Mikaela Pratt more.

"I see," I said, refusing to lower myself to their level. For the second time in one night. "How long, sir?" I needed to find Carrie.

"Twenty-four hours should do it," he said cheerfully.

Harding started to splutter. "That's hardly long enough, sir!"

Crawford turned his big baulk to look at her, seeming to suddenly take up more space and air.

"Twenty-four hours, Dr Harding," he snapped. "Now if you don't mind, that will be all."

She ignored the dismissal. "Who will be flying with Dr Evans tomorrow?" she demanded. "I would gladly offer myself as second chair." Her smile was sickly sweet. I almost gagged.

"That won't be necessary, Dr Harding. The flight has been reassigned to Dr Fawkes. You will be accompanying him."

"Jack doesn't want the flight?" she asked.

"*Doctor* Evans has other concerns."

"Concerns?" I found myself saying. What sort of concerns? And did they involve me?

Crawford frowned at both of us and straightened his tie unnecessarily.

"That will be all, Doctors," he said finally.

"She's not a doctor," Harding snarled under her breath, offering me a sneer while she was at it, and then turned her back and left.

I let out a slow breath of air. I had landed in the *Twilight Zone*. Maybe that was what was wrong with this time. Ivanov was fucking with us, sending us back to grade school.

"I should be very careful of Drs Harding and Pratt, if I were you, Miss Wylde," Crawford suddenly said.

I looked up at him and saw the intelligence behind his ageing eyes. He'd not been fooled by Harding at all.

"I will, sir," I said in agreement.

"They have a superior belief in themselves and their place at RATS," he added.

I wasn't sure what to say to that. I wanted to point out that they were psychotic, but held myself back.

"Jolly good, then," he offered, clearly thinking I'd received the reprimand and warning as intended. And then he was gone.

He could certainly move for a man with a limp.

"That was bloody awesome!" Dean's disembodied voice announced from behind a bush.

"What a bitch," Sally offered in commiseration, stepping into the light.

I sighed. Clearly, I wasn't getting rid of them. Friends or foes, at least *they* hadn't abandoned me under a chestnut tree to face off against lunatic nut throwers.

"Come on," I said resignedly. "I need a drink."

"Mouse!" Dean exclaimed. "What a bloody fantastic idea. Why didn't I think of that?"

Sally whacked him on the back of the head and then wrapped her hands around my upper arm, starting to herd me inside the building.

"Ignore him," she said conspiratorially, then leant in to deliver the next words on a laugh. "He just wants in your pants."

"Not *my* pants…" I began to say, only to have Dean wrap his hands around my other arm and squeeze. Hard.

I started to laugh too, as they both pulled me inside RATS, each clearly with ulterior motives. I just couldn't decide what those motives could be.

Friendship? Or something else? Only time would see.

3 0

READY?

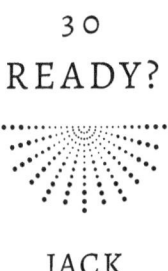

JACK

*T*he Orion had a fault. That was the only explanation I could see. A multi-million-pound dimensional wave surfing device didn't just up and vanish all on its own. Everyone was accounted for. RATS at full capacity. No one from our team had launched that Vehicle without clearance. It had obviously followed a previous trajectory when something electrical short-circuited.

"Well?" I demanded, hovering. I hate hovering. But damned if I could move away from the technician frantically tapping keys on his tablet screen.

"Nothin' out of the ordinary, sir," Dean Jordan declared.

"Are you certain?"

"Positive. It just up and vanished. All on its own-some."

"That is hardly a scientific hypothesis."

"You want scientific, ask Mouse."

"Miss Wylde would have no bloody idea what has transpired here."

"Well," Dean said, "Neither do we."

"Not exactly a ringing endorsement for your friend, Mr Jordan. Rather a sad indication of your own expertise."

Dean merely huffed out a breath but didn't reply. Wiser than I'd thought, then.

I scratched my day's old beard. I hadn't had a chance to shave this morning. The Orion had departed at half past three. All hands on deck afterwards. Clive was demanding answers. Orion Two was missing.

Thank God its crew was all here.

"Anything?" Fawkes asked as he approached from the other end of the hangar.

"Tech Support is coming up blank as well," I replied.

"So is Dispatch. Nothing in the logs."

"Crawford's confirmed everyone is accounted for."

"Then we've got a rogue Orion. How the fuck did that happen?"

"No idea," I said with force.

"Doctors," Dean called. We both walked over and hovered. "I've traced its last flight path, and there is a chance that it's gone back to Cape Canaveral. The Kennedy Space Center to be precise. I'm picking up a rip in 1969."

As soon as he said the words the Dispatch Centre's alarm began to sound. A soft *whoop-whoop* announcing a detected tear in Time.

"That'd be you, Jack," Fawkes declared. "I ain't got a Vehicle to fly."

"Sebastian's up next on the rota," I argued. "And one of my crew is grounded."

"Winchester's been assigned my flight plan. He's prepping for that already."

I let a slow breath of air out. Clive wouldn't let Mimi fly, not when she'd been officially grounded.

"All right then," I said. "Where's Miss Groves?"

"Cafeteria when I last saw her." I raised an eyebrow at him; since when did he keep tabs on Novitiates? He shrugged his shoulder. "Fair warnin', she's got a hangover."

"Brilliant," I growled and stalked towards Dispatch.

"Page Miss Groves, if you please," I instructed the dispatcher as soon as I walked in the door. The room was buzzing, as it usually is when a rip is detected. Not every day affords us the opportunity to do what we're trained for. Some days it's just another failed search and rescue. Today, we'd be Surgeons. RATS would justify its expensive existence. Clive would breathe easy for another twenty-four hours. Parliament would be satisfied until the clock shifted and the sun sank, and another night reminded us that we were all still here.

Worse for wear.

I strummed my fingers on a filing cabinet as I stared at the sinusoid up on the screen. International Orange. It shouldn't have surprised me, Cape Canaveral in 1969 was an Origin Event. And I was getting used to seeing that colour. But even so, it was a foreboding thing.

"Did you dream anything useful last night?" Rafe asked from beside me; I hadn't even heard him approach.

"No." I had dreamed. But I could hardly call Mimi and I entangled in bed sheets useful. "You?"

"Not a bloody thing."

"Then we do this the hard way."

"Maybe Mimi dreamed something?"

"She isn't flying with us, Groves is."

"Is that wise? Mouse is connected to this location more than any of us."

"She's grounded," I snapped. "Rules are rules, Dr Hoffman."

"How the hell did she get grounded? And where was I?"

"Chestnuts," I said succinctly. "And you were quite occupied."

He barked out a laugh. "What a night. Chestnuts, you say? Didn't see that one coming."

"Neither did Dr Pratt, apparently."

He guffawed a little longer and then brought himself back under control with the muttered words, "Can you blame her?"

I stared at him for a suspended moment and then sighed.

"It is most inconvenient."

"You would say that," Rafe replied. "Sally's not nearly as tempting to look at."

"Thank you, Dr Hoffman," Miss Groves offered from over his shoulder. "I do try."

Rafe grimaced obviously and muttered an apology in reply. Miss Groves just smiled sweetly. I was really beginning to like the girl.

"Miss Groves, you'll be with us this morning," I said smoothly. "Cape Canaveral. 1969."

"Not again," she complained.

"Well," I offered, "this time, let's get it right."

"It was hardly our fault we picked up a passenger last time, sir," Groves argued.

"Indeed. Maybe we'll pick up somebody else."

"God! Does Mouse have another twin or something?" Rafe demanded.

"Not as far as I'm aware," I replied.

"And we're not likely to pick up Carolyn," Groves supplied. Then flicked concerned eyes to my face. "Does she know?"

"Who know?" I was playing coy and we all knew it.

"Mouse, sir. Does she know we're going back without her?"

Silence. Then I manned up.

"No. And we're not going to tell her, Novitiate."

"Your call, sir," she said with obvious sarcasm. "That's why they pay you the big bucks."

"And give you a flash office," Rafe added.

"And invite you to all the fundraising balls," Sally offered.

"And polish your brass plaque every day."

"And let you sit in the command chair."

"That's enough!" I practically shouted. All eyes in Dispatch turned to look at us. "Why the bloody hell I put up with you two is beyond me."

"We make a good team," Rafe and Sally said together, then turned to look at each other, grin maniacally, and high-five.

I made a strangled sound of defeat and reached out to accept the flight plan from the dispatcher.

"Thank you..." Fuck! I'd forgotten her name again. I smiled - perhaps more of a wince - and stormed out of the room.

My flight crew obediently followed. Thankfully silent. Rip flights do that to you. Sober you up in a hurry.

The Orion sat on its launch pad softly gassing liquid oxygen. Dean Jordan was disconnecting the power supply that keeps the Vehicle powered while on standby and saluted as we walked past. He busied himself with the cord, not making eye contact. Perhaps I'd been a little rough on him earlier. But he had been the one to get Mimi rip-roaringly drunk last night.

I'd watched from the corner of the cafeteria, nursing a whisky and bad attitude. Clive had told me what had happened, and if either Harding or Pratt had dared to approach me, I would no doubt have been grounded as well. Instead, I'd sat fuming, at them, at Clive, at the whole bloody fucking situation. But most of all at Dean Jordan, who'd been there for Mimi when she'd needed him.

I had left before they did. But I'd seen enough.

And I hadn't seen Mimi since.

It felt wrong to be flying without saying goodbye. Without trying to mend the rift that had grown between us. It didn't help that my dreams had been crystal clear last night. That I still tasted her on my tongue. My fingers still twitched with the phantom sensation of her smooth skin. Even the scent of the soap she'd been using hung in the air as if she'd been here mere seconds before we'd walked in.

"Coordinates," Rafe announced, passing me a sheet of paper. I sat down in the command chair, ran a palm over the armrest, and stared at the dimensional numbers in my hand.

"This could be a rough ride," I said softly. "Anything could transpire."

Neither crew member argued that point.

"Are you armed, Dr Hoffman?"

"Yes, sir."

"Miss Groves?"

"Yes," she said quietly.

"Well, then," I said. "Let's do this. Let's find out what 1969 still has in store for us."

"Always liked that decade," Rafe supplied, confirming the coordinates.

I stood up and reached for the door from the technician outside. It was Jordan again. And he still didn't meet my gaze. I frowned down at him, but the door swung closed before I could gain his attention. Before I could see what look he was keeping from me in his eyes.

I shook my head as I locked the capsule portal and returned to my seat, buckling my harness.

"Ready?" I asked.

"Ready," both crew members replied.

I hit the button and the Orion warped. Stars and clouds and an infinite galaxy engulfed us, and then silence wrapped itself around our bodies and squeezed tight.

The Vehicle shuddered, rattled, and something in the bathroom thudded against the wall. Bloody Jordan had probably forgotten to secure it. With an earsplitting roar, sound returned and the Orion touched down with barely a jolt.

Rafe immediately started checking our location against the coordinates, as Sally flicked switches getting us a view of outside the MPCV. The Vehicle Assembly Building loomed over us, complete, intact, no sign of an Orion sized hole in its side. Sixties-era vehicles were parked outside, one of them a Corvette, as inside a Saturn V rocket was getting its final makeover.

An Apollo capsule already attached to its side.

I was about to unbuckle and open the Vehicle door when I saw it. Orion Two. Parked up inside the VAB, behind the shelter of scaffolding and tarpaulin sheets, in an area of the building that was obviously used to store equipment. At the moment it was devoid of people, but that wouldn't last long, I should think.

"There it is," I whispered.

"What's it doing there?" Rafe demanded. "In plain sight."

"Can we tether it?" Groves asked.

"Excellent plan, Miss Groves. Dr Hoffman?"

"On it, sir. Tethered and linked. It's empty inside."

"How the hell did it get here?" I wondered aloud.

"*Why* is it here?" Sally offered.

"I have no bloody idea," I replied.

"Would you like us to shift dimensions, sir?" Rafe asked.

"Yes, but keep us in this time. I want to find out why it's here."

"Shifting," Rafe offered, as the view from outside our Vehicle morphed, removing those people who had been working on the Saturn V.

We sat in silence, staring at the screen and Orion Two outside. Nothing moved. The entire VAB stood still. If things were happening in this time, we wouldn't see it. They would simply come into existence on our plane. Our brains absorbing the difference but not recognising that anything had happened at all. One shift in dimensional planes was all it took, to keep us present but out of the loop.

"OK," I said. "Miss Groves you're with me. Dr Hoffman, keep an eye on things. If Orion Two moves, I want you to follow it."

"And leave you, sir?"

"You can always come back."

"That's rather risky, Jack."

I automatically checked my communicator in the sleeve of my jumpsuit. I'd pressed it before even realising that's what I'd do. A red light flashed on the Vehicle's console; the Orion confirmed over the speakers that we were on board and accounted for, before deactivating the call sign in the next breath.

"We'll be in touch if we need you," I said to punctuate all of that. Rafe let out a slow breath of air as Groves sucked one in.

It *was* risky, but we were connected. We wouldn't be alone for long.

"All right, then," I said, looking down at Groves. "Ready?"

She lifted her chin and replied, "Ready, sir." I smiled.

And then the door to the bathroom opened.

31

I CALL YOU MOUSE IN MY DREAMS

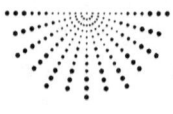

MIMI

"*B*loody fucking bollocks!" Jack exclaimed. I winced. This was going to go down like a cup of cold sick.

Everyone had been conspiring against me. Ruining everything. I'd been desperate. The longer Carrie was with Ivanov, the worse things would be. I knew it, even if I didn't know how I knew it. I just knew that Time needed to be mended. But not by Surgeons. By *me*.

I'd taken a risk. A *huge* risk. But worse than that, I'd pulled someone into the danger zone with me.

Dean could lose his job over this. But if I fixed Time, like I *had* to fix Time, maybe I could save him too.

Being grounded made that impossible. Having Pratt and Harding breathing down my neck had turned the tide. I did not respond well to bullies. For once in my life, I took the bull by the horns, and I shook the mother-effing shit out of it.

Carrie needed me, and no stick wielding old man and his infantile bunch of Time Surgeons was going to stop me. I'd had enough. The mouse had grown claws.

"Miss *Wylde?*" Jack shouted. "What the bloody fucking hell are you playing at?"

"Getting my sister," I said with vehemence.

His head pulled back, and he blinked.

"You organised this?" he demanded in a slightly lower tone of voice.

"I don't know how to fly these things," I admitted. "And," I mumbled, "I needed help."

His mouth opened, closed, and then opened again.

"Have you gone completely insane?" he finally managed to rasp.

I straightened my shoulders and tipped up my chin, staring him in the eyes.

"I will not stand by and watch you all arrange my return to the 21st century while my sister is with that man."

"You've gone completely insane," he surmised.

I took a step forward, aware Sally shrank in on herself, and Rafe kept his hand hovering over his gun. I ignored them, thrust out a finger, and jabbed it into Jack's chest.

"You think I don't know what you're all planning. You think I don't understand what it will mean for Carrie. RATS' only concern is for its missing Interns. Not my sister. And certainly not me."

"You know about the Interns?" Jack asked. And then he shook his head. "Of course you know about the Interns. Dean Fucking Jordan told you."

"Something else you wanted to keep from me," I growled. "First the dreams and now this. Ivanov has been playing with you for months. Not just the past few days. You had me believe this was all new, something unseen before. But it isn't. He has a plan, and now he has my sister. But you don't give a shit about that."

Jack stared at me as if he didn't know me; which was closer to the truth than anything else. Those dreams had fooled us both. But that was over now. I was destroying any chance of them being realised.

Part of me broke apart at that notion. But the part of me that loved Carrie rejoiced.

Jack slowly pulled himself up to full height, attempting to kowtow me. I offered him a roll of my eyes.

"You have no idea what you have done," he ground out. "Got a good man fired, that's what. Jordan won't be at RATS by the time we return." I stopped breathing. "Dr Hoffman, send a probe back."

Hoffman remained silent, watching from his seat, but not moving an inch to obey his Surgeon.

"Did you hear me?" Jack demanded.

"I heard you, Jack," Hoffman said carefully. "But let's not be hasty about this."

"Hasty?" Jack yelled. Then thrust a finger out towards me. "She stole RATS property, and Dean Jordan helped her."

"We don't know that."

"Of course we bloody well know that!"

"Actually, I got him shitfaced on Tequila and wheedled the answers out of him," I offered. Jack spun back and glared at me.

"I beg your pardon." Even irate he was polite.

I smiled. He grew enraged.

"I found out how to get an Orion to return to previous coordinates," I said with a shrug of my shoulder as if it was nothing. "Bypassing the failsafe when no one was on board. I couldn't be, you see because I don't know how to fly these things yet."

"And you sure as hell won't find out now," Jack muttered.

"And I might want to get back afterwards," I said, ignoring him. Again. "So I hid on board here, knowing you'd be the crew to trace it."

"How did you know that?" Jack asked mystified.

I frowned, not liking this next part. "Got to know Dr Winchester," I mumbled under my breath.

"What was that?" Jack demanded in a lethally soft voice.

"Flirted with Winchester," I snapped.

Rafe started laughing. Sally looked shocked, but also strangely impressed. Jack was beside himself.

"By flirting you mean *what* exactly?" The entire sentence was said between clenched teeth.

I waved a hand dismissively at him. "It doesn't matter. But I knew his crew would replace Orion Two on today's flight plan, and you'd be the one called up to follow the missing Vehicle."

"It's actually quite clever when you think about it," Hoffman offered.

Jack just glared at him. The seconds stretched.

"Bloody hell," he finally said in defeat. I let out a breath of air I hadn't realised I'd been holding. "You are quite remarkable, Miss Wylde."

"Thank you?"

"Oh, don't thank me," he rushed to say. "You're also in a wealth of trouble. I've a right mind to…"

He let the sentence hang.

"Mind to *what*, sir?" Hoffman asked mischievously.

"None of your bloody business, Doctor." Jack sighed and slumped back down in his chair. I noticed Sally immediately relax a little too. Hoffman just winked at me. I bit my lip and chewed on it a while, watching Jack for clues.

He hadn't immediately ordered a return flight, so there was still a chance he'd help me. The probe back to RATS hadn't been sent either. So we still had a little time. But further than that, I was at a loss.

I'd only planned this far ahead.

"What now, Miss Wylde?" Jack asked. Bastard. He could read me like a book.

I let a slow breath of air out and ventured toward the fourth seat. Jack leant back in his and watched me with a shrouded look. Contemplative. Wary. And was that amused?

I shook my head and sat down and then played with the zip on my flight suit.

"You haven't thought that far ahead, have you, Mimi?" Jack said.

I shook my head.

He huffed out a breath and stared at the screen. "Mend that rip, would you, Rafe?"

"Certainly, sir."

"Bloody hell, Mimi," Jack muttered.

"I had no choice, Jack."

"You had choices. Everyone has choices. But what you've done; I don't think I can cover for this."

I blinked. I hadn't expected him to cover for me. Jack was a rule follower; even I could tell that. And I'd just broken God alone knows how many of RATS' rules. I'd assumed he'd be honour-bound to uphold them. Hopefully after we'd found Carrie.

"Bryan Fawkes summed it up really," I said quietly. Jack met my eyes with a look of regret. "Once those dreams are realised, Time will settle, and returning me to my time will...what were his words? 'Put a lid on all of this.'"

Jack let out a long breath of air.

"We're Time Surgeons, Mimi. It's what we do. It's how we think. But that doesn't mean his was the only solution."

"I saw your face, Jack. I saw you recognise the truth in his words. The lack of further options. And then Dean told me about the Interns. The ones you can't find. And it all made sense. Your time is already out. Your future altered. Desperation makes us do unheard of things."

"Yes, I can see that," he offered.

"I didn't throw the first chestnut," I said, unsure why that came tumbling out.

He raised an eyebrow at me.

"But I sure as hell threw the last." Rafe almost fell off his chair laughing. Even Sally let out an amused giggle.

Jack fought a smile and won.

"Twenty-four hours," he said. "It was nothing. It was the best we could do given the circumstances."

"We?" I asked.

"You think I wasn't involved in your punishment, Miss Wylde? You're my Novitiate."

I glanced at Sally.

"Miss Groves is too," Jack said with a dismissive wave of his hand.

My turn to raise an eyebrow at him.

"You know what I mean." No actually, I was quite sure I didn't. But I let things lie as is.

"Twenty-four hours would have been too late."

"You don't know that," he argued.

"I do!" I pressed a hand to the centre of my chest. "In here. I know

246

it. I don't know how, but I do. If I don't find Carrie today, she'll be lost forever. I couldn't wait, Jack. I couldn't let Harding and Pratt keep me grounded. I couldn't let Carrie slip away."

"Then what's the plan?"

"You'll help me?"

He looked toward Sally and Rafe.

"I'm in," Hoffman offered.

"Me too!" Sally squeaked.

"You realise how this could go?" Jack queried. "You understand the consequences? Miss Groves?" Jack pressed.

Sally glanced towards me and smiled. "I believe in Mouse, sir. She's my friend. And friends help each other."

I let out a sharp breath, feeling it keenly, deep inside. Feeling it in that place that was hollow. The place Carrie usually lived. I struggled not to show how much her words meant to me, but I was certain she saw. Sally blinked and looked away, smiling softly to herself.

"Well then," Jack said. "I guess we're doing this. Whatever the bloody fucking hell this is, Miss Wylde. But you've got yourself a flight crew. Now, where the bloody fucking hell do you want us?"

Jack could also be very crude at times too.

I smiled. He shook his head.

"How about this?" Hoffman said. "We've tried Cocoa Beach and the VAB in '69. We've also tried Mimi's time, also at the VAB." He ticked off locations on a tablet screen as he talked. "We've visited '61 at the Lewis Laboratory, albeit we didn't exit the Vehicle, and we've travelled to South Beach, Miami in 1962. Ivanov or his Lunik was at Cocoa Beach and the VAB only out of all of those destinations. But there has been one other location his Vehicle has travelled to, or through, that we haven't rechecked."

"Launch Pad 39A," I said.

"Precisely," Rafe offered quietly. "It's our best bet."

"It's also back in my time," I pointed out.

Rafe had the decency to look abashed. "That's not why I suggested it, Mouse."

I nodded. Going back made sense. But leaving me there would save their skins when they returned to RATS.

No one offered a platitude to reassure me. It was an option they wouldn't dismiss.

"So do we do it?" Sally asked.

Jack and Rafe looked at me intently.

"This is your mission, Miss Wylde." I wished he call me Mimi. "Your flight plan, so to speak." Mimi meant he wasn't hiding something. "We'll go if you so desire it."

What choice did I have?

I nodded my head.

"Dr Hoffman?" Jack asked, keeping his eyes on me and not Rafe.

"On it, sir. Working the coordinates now."

"Do we drag Orion Two with us?" Sally asked, and still Jack didn't stop looking at me. Wouldn't look anywhere else.

"Send it back, Miss Groves. That'll give RATS something to contemplate."

"They could send Fawkes straight back out in it after us," Rafe pointed out. Jack held my gaze with a steady one of his own.

"We might well need him," he finally said.

Silence descended as the weight of what we were doing sunk in. Not just risking their jobs at RATS. But facing off against Sergei Ivanov. The man responsible for stealing the original Orion.

And for taking several RATS Interns. Possibly killing them.

The man who was doctoring Time to suit his needs. Needs we didn't yet understand.

He was unstable, unpredictable, and lethal. And we were hunting him.

Because he had my sister. Because I couldn't abandon Carrie. Because I wasn't RATS trained and didn't give a rat's arse about rules.

"Thank you," I mouthed. Jack ran a hand over his face and scratched at his jaw. His eyes never leaving mine.

"Don't thank me, Mimi," he murmured. "I can't help feeling I'm enabling you. I'm allowing you to do something monumentally stupid."

"Like rescuing Carrie?" I demanded.

He took one last look at me and said, "Like getting yourself killed out of time." And then he turned to the console, checking Rafe's coordinates, and preparing to hit the launch button.

"Buckle up!" Rafe announced cheerfully. Sally offered me an encouraging smile.

I fiddled with my harness, getting it wrapped around itself and somehow upside down. Jack's hands appeared from out of nowhere, untangling it all. My eyes darted up to his shadowed face. There weren't shadows in here; he just seemed that way.

"It'll be all right, Jack," I whispered.

His eyes met mine. A soft brush of his fingers across my cheek. A small smile.

"Just don't die," he murmured quietly.

"I don't plan to."

"There's a lot of things you don't plan, Mouse, and still you somehow manage to get into trouble."

"You called me Mouse," I said, stunned.

"I call you Mouse in my dreams."

And then he was gone, in his own seat, buckling up with efficiency, and hitting the button.

My mind stalled. Visions of my own dreams swamping me. As clouds formed and stars winked and a sonic bomb sounded.

In the silence of space, I realised something.

I was falling for Jack Evans.

3 2

A WOMAN LIVING OUT OF TIME

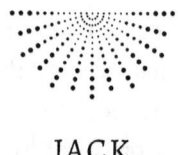

JACK

*I*f I'd thought I'd known what sort of person Mimi Wylde was, I'd thought wrong. Cautious, but once committed, recklessly so. That courage I'd witnessed, time and again, was tempered with a vulnerability that caused my chest to ache. A more impetuous creature I had yet to meet. Wild, rash, careless, misguided, she was all of those. But she was also determined, headstrong, dedicated, devoted, and loyal beyond anything I had ever seen.

Her heart was her biggest strength and also her biggest downfall.

And all I could think was I wanted to call her mine. To lay claim to this miraculous woman. To shout it from the rooftops that she belonged to me and no one else.

And all I could do was watch as she flew headlong into chaos, dragging every poor unfortunate soul who fell for her charms along with her, and try to protect her while she did it. But protecting her against Sergei Ivanov was a tall task indeed.

There were things she didn't know. Things even Rafe didn't know. Things only Surgeons were privy to.

"Touchdown!" Rafe exclaimed as the Orion softly landed in Mimi's time. Sally had the screen illuminated immediately, and we all looked out on an empty launch pad, the Fixed and Rotating Service Structures dwarfing us, the scorch marks of previous launches visible against a stark white concrete, shadows stretching long as the afternoon sun sank toward the horizon.

"Time," I said, forcing my voice to sound normal. Nothing was normal anymore. I was trapped in a dream; part beautiful and alluring, addictively sought every time my eyes closed for even a second; part nightmare, the certainty that death stalked us riding me hard, causing my heart to clench and my stomach to churn.

"OE: Alpha 1," Rafe said quietly. "If we shift dimensions we should see Lunik fly by and pick up Carrie any minute."

"Do it!" Mimi ordered as if she was in charge here.

"Just one moment, Miss Wylde."

"If we catch her before he does, we can put a stop to all of this."

"Everything has consequences," I pointed out. "Even corrections to Time."

She paused. Then, "What aren't you telling me?"

Too clever by far, this woman.

"What happens if Lunik fails to pick up your sister?" I asked. "You both leave here, undetected, and go about your lives unaware."

"I don't see a problem with that," she supplied. The knife dug in a little deeper.

"You wouldn't get arrested by the KSC security team," I went on. "You wouldn't get hauled into the VAB. And you wouldn't get picked up by this Orion."

"So?"

We wouldn't meet, I wanted to say. Instead, I said, "We've had the dreams. They can't be taken away."

"Why not?" I wanted to shake her. Then hold her tight and never let her go again.

"No Surgeon has ever managed to alter a dream once realised. Yet another nail in the coffin for dreams being connected to our DNA, wouldn't you say? Not only has the dream manifested, but it's also adhered to our genetic makeup and cannot be changed."

"I don't believe that."

"Always an argument, Miss Wylde."

She shook her head. "Has anyone ever tried this? Stopping something before it has happened? Taking out a key component to a series of events?"

"She's an Origin Event, Mimi," I said softly. "They're unpredictable at best."

"And at worst?"

"We explode this time apart. No more life in this time as you know it. Perhaps, no more Carrie in this time as you know her too."

"No," she said on a breath that sounded too close to a sob for my liking. "That can't be true. How do you mend Time then? How do you fix a rip?"

"We catch it. Stitch it. Or remake it," I said.

"But if we grab Carrie now, aren't we catching the rip before it's happened?"

She was grasping at straws, and she knew it. That bloody stubborn streak of hers beating herself to a pulp.

And cutting me to shreds while she was at it.

"The rip has already happened, Mouse," Rafe said from the side, reminding us both, I think, that we'd had an audience.

"Retrocausality," Groves added in a soft tone of voice. "The temporal paradox exists."

"And that can't be changed," I finished. "There are limits to what we can do," I added. "We can mend Time, and in certain situations, we can make Time, but we can never change Time. Not directly. Not like this."

"I don't understand," she whispered. "If you can make it…"

"Remake, Mimi. Consider us reconstructive surgeons. We can return a time to its original state, or as near as the talent of the Surgeon allows, *only* if the time succeeding it hasn't altered too far or travelled too long down the new dimensional wave created by the rip."

"What does that mean?"

I held her sorrowful gaze, let her see the regret on my face, even if part of me did not feel it, and said, "You know too much. You've been in our time too long. What makes you, you, has changed."

I closed my eyes and said aloud the one thing Surgeons are sworn never to repeat.

"Time has a failsafe switch. If tampered with outside of these parameters it wipes itself clean. Carrie is an Origin Event for this rip; you may well be part of that OE as well, I'm unsure. But if you try to meddle with this rip before it occurs, you may wipe Carrie, and yourself, from existence."

"I've never heard of that," Rafe said forcefully. My eyes met his, and he slowly shook his head. "Need to know basis, huh?"

"What do you think the widespread knowledge of this failsafe switch could create, Dr Hoffman?" I asked.

His lips pressed into a thin line, and he shook his head more vigorously, eyes boring into mine hard.

"Sergei Ivanov, that's who," I said.

"Motherfucker!" Rafe swore. Mimi grimaced, and Groves jumped in her seat. "That's what happened to them, isn't it? That's why we can't find them."

"Oh my God," Groves muttered. "No."

"Why didn't you tell us?" Rafe demanded. "Why let us think we could still find them?" Anger made the air thick.

"The fewer people who know this failsafe exists, the better," I offered.

"The better for who?" he shouted.

"For everyone!" I yelled back. "Have you any concept of what, *who*, could be extinguished if people flipped that switch? It's a clean murder, Rafe. One where, if done correctly, no one even remembers the person existed at all."

"But we remember them," Sally said, voice trembling.

"Which is why we're still searching. If Ivanov attempted to wipe them, he failed. Something went wrong. We cling to that hope. But letting you all know this is what we suspect would lead to retribution. Wouldn't it be simple if we just wiped Sergei Ivanov from existence?"

"Sounds like a bloody good plan," Rafe muttered.

"He created Orion," I said flatly. "If not created, he was the first to realise its potential. We wipe him; we wipe RATS. We wipe everything we know about our time completely."

"But that's not the only possibility, is it?" Mimi said, drawing all of our attention. "You wipe him; you return Time to what it would have been before he stole Orion. Is that not a possible future you could see yourselves living in?"

"Would you give us up so easily?" I asked before I could stop myself.

"I would do anything to save my sister."

Bloody fucking bollocks! I was in love with a woman who wouldn't feel a thing if she walked away.

I would damn it! And I'm not sure how that came to be. But I would feel *everything* if Mimi Wylde walked away.

"You wouldn't even remember me," she whispered as if she'd heard my thoughts directly.

"*You're in my dreams,*" I growled and punched the button to release the door lock.

I was up and out of the Vehicle before another word was spoken. I was halfway across the launch pad before I was able to breathe. The potential for widespread psychosis was astounding. Couldn't they see that? How many other dreams wouldn't be realised because Sergei Ivanov was wiped and RATS was never founded? How many people would they condemn to insanity?

I bunched my fists and stared up at the FSS, the red paint glinting low in the afternoon sunlight. The sound of a shoe scuffing behind me met my ears. I closed my eyes, but didn't turn to face her. Mimi's scent had already surrounded me.

"How certain are you...?" she began.

"Very. We've tested it. Lost a good man proving that dreams once realised are inherent to our being."

"We haven't realised..."

"Mimi," I said, turning to face her. "Others have. We are not unique." I started to laugh, shaking my head with frustration. "And we *have* started to realise the dreams."

"How?"

"I'm in love with you," I blurted. "I already *love* you. In the dreams, you're my world. Do you honestly believe you aren't already in reality?"

She looked stunned. Terrified. Lost. Awed. And then devastated in quick succession.

Not exactly the response I was looking for when I admitted my feelings.

"Then what do we do?" she whispered.

"We let the rip happen," I said. "We let him take her. And then we take her back."

"How, Jack? How?"

I stared across the landscape towards the Vehicle Assembly Building in the distance and said, "We make a scene. We make enough noise to draw the attention of every MPCV in the vicinity. We replicate an Origin Event episode that Sergei participated in and then hang around afterwards to see if he returns to protect it from the fallout."

Mimi looked towards the VAB where a hole had appeared out of nowhere in its side. It was happening. One dimensional shift away, her sister was being picked up in a nebulous cloud on this very launch pad.

"I think we can make that bigger," she said softly, a determined glint in her eye.

I huffed out a breath of laughter and slowly shook my head.

"Whatever you want that I can give, Mouse, you'll have it."

She turned to look up at me; so much emotion washing over her face I couldn't track it. Then she was in my arms as her body was pressed against mine, her heat engulfing me as her hands grasped, lips trembling. Her tears on the tip of my tongue as I kissed her. Deeply.

God help me, I was in love with this woman. A woman living out of time. The potential for disaster was enormous.

The possibility of heartache a given fact.

33

PLEASE DON'T KILL THE SPECIAL AGENTS, MISS WYLDE

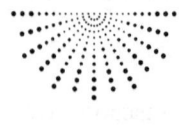

MIMI

I stared at everything and anything in the Orion except Jack. Exposed wires, bunched together in a twisted snake across the ceiling. Silver wrapped piping running like platinum tears down the side of the Vehicle. An array of red and blue and white lights flickering and glinting spasmodically across the console. An orange sine wave haunting us all up on the screen.

Was it bigger than before? Were we changing Time even now by replicating it?

He'd said he loved me. Was already *in love* with me. I was out of time, and the longer I was, the harder it would be to get back.

But did I want to get back to my time? Did I want to give up Jack and RATS and this surreal world I'd discovered?

For Carrie, I'd do anything. Or at least that's what I kept telling myself. I wasn't so sure the words were reaching me anymore.

Because he loved me. Was in love with me. The dreams were being realised even if we hadn't made love yet.

I bit my lip and sucked in a ragged breath of air as Jack pressed in coordinates on the console, and Rafe checked them, and Sally did whatever a real Novitiate did at times like these. Part of me wanted to watch everything; my last chance to take it all in before it was gone from my world, from my life.

Part of me was breaking apart every time I looked at Jack Evans.

I wasn't sure I could do this. I wasn't sure what was right anymore.

Carrie. I so wanted my sister back. It's all I could think about. It's all that truly mattered. If I got Carrie back, things would sort themselves out. Right?

"Ready?" Jack asked into the strained silence of the MPCV.

"Ready, sir," Groves supplied, offering me a worried look.

"On your mark, Jack," Rafe muttered.

"This could be a rough ride," Jack announced, looking back over his shoulder towards me. I looked away, feigning interest in a cabinet door. "We're matching the original flight path of Lunik as precisely as we can, but sometime after its initial crash course through Complex 39. In order to miss the original you, Miss Wylde."

I nodded, but couldn't bring myself to look him in the eye, instead I stared at the zip at the top of his jumpsuit. At the hollow in his neck where a small smattering of dark hair could be seen. At the rapid beat of his pulse just beneath his smooth skin.

Jack sighed, and turned back to the console, then lifted his hand to hover over the ignition.

"We're playing with Time," he said quietly. "We're one step away from what Sergei Ivanov is doing. I don't believe we've crossed that line, but we're standing pretty bloody close to it. Weapons stay inside the Orion. We tamper with this temporal dimension as little as possible. As soon as we land, I want you, Miss Groves, to monitor the rip we've caused, catching it before it goes supernova. Dr Hoffman, Miss Wylde and I will exit the Vehicle. Prepare for anything. It won't take him long to return and make sure we're not obliterating the good he's done here. This time, Mimi's and Carolyn's time, means something to Lunik's commander. Let's find out what exactly it is."

He hit the button before anyone could reply. Which was just as well, because that was one hell of a speech. Jack was playing hard and fast with the rules, all because of me.

It made my heart hurt. It my head dizzy. It made it hard to breathe.

The Orion launched in a hail of falling stars, shooting through a purple and red nebula. I felt weightless for a few seconds, and then much too heavy. Space came and wrapped itself around us, chilling our bones and crushing our breaths. Time stalled. Everything was quiet. Almost peaceful.

Then the silence broke, replaced by the roar of rocket-like engines, as the Orion shuddered and creaked and thudded its way through its landing. The harness dug into my shoulders and cut across my stomach. Cabinets flung open and their contents spilt out. The bathroom exploded, blue liquid leaking out from under the doorway. Lights flickered, alarms beeped, and smoke began to rise from behind the console. Then it all rolled to a stop.

I let out a little squeak, much like Sally's.

"All right?" Jack asked, but his eyes were on me and no one else.

"Fine," Sally managed to murmur.

"All present and accounted for," Rafe offered, patting himself down.

I nodded my head. Jack held my gaze for a few more seconds and then turned to the console, reaching under it to grab a fire extinguisher and proceeding to spray the entire surface in foam.

"That'll do it," Rafe said on a hacking cough.

"Check time and location on the tablet," Jack ordered.

"On it. Time matches, location...Launch Pad 39A via the VAB. Nice. Never seen anyone perfect a crash landing like that, Jack. Well done."

Jack huffed out a breath of air and then wiped the main screen clean with the sleeve of his flight suit. The sine wave was still orange, and the view outside showed an empty launch pad and service structures. This time having reached it by following Lunik's flight plan closely.

"Right. Miss Groves, you're on that rip. Keep an eye on it, but don't do *anything* until it's close to exploding."

"How will I know that, sir?" she all but squeaked.

"Sergei Ivanov will be here, and he'll be fuming." She nodded her head uncertainly and took the offered tablet screen Rafe handed her.

"You know what to do, Sally," Rafe said quietly. "You've trained for this."

"Not quite this, sir," she muttered.

"Come on!" he said teasingly. "They get you to simulate disasters all the time in that training module. This one's no different."

"This one's real and we made it," she replied, eyebrows arched.

"Then we're the ones in control," Rafe offered.

"I'm scared not stupid," she growled.

"Enough," Jack snapped. "You can do this, Miss Groves. I have the utmost confidence in your abilities. If it turns to custard, hit the return button, it's isolated. That will at least get you home."

Sally straightened her shoulders and lifted her chin. "Not without you, sir."

"Thatta girl," Rafe murmured, slapping her on the shoulder.

Jack offered what I assumed was meant to be a smile, but was more a grimace, and then turned to the door.

"Miss Wylde?" he said, without looking over his shoulder. He'd entered Surgeon mode. Commander mode. I wasn't sure if I was relieved or worried.

"Right behind you," I said and unbuckled. Rafe offered me a wink, and then we were climbing out of the module.

I expected to see Ivanov straight away, but we were the only ones present. I glanced around the now too familiar launch pad and followed the trajectory of our scorch marks back toward the VAB. I could hear sirens sound out in the distance. Smoke was wafting up from the side of the over-height building. A large groove in the grass leading up to the safety wire surrounding Launch Pad 39A had me turning back to the Orion to inspect it for damage. Jack was already walking its circumference, Rafe muttering to himself as he ran a hand over the burn marks on the underside of the MPCV.

There was a large dent in its side. The floatation ring had deployed. One of the parachutes was hanging forlornly down the side of the Vehicle. A landing booster had exploded completely, leaving a gaping hole into the innards of the vessel.

"Holy crap," I muttered.

"Yes," Jack said softly as he rounded the Orion. "We seem to have done a number on our Vehicle."

"Will it fly again?"

"Not likely." He looked up and saw the shock and fear on my face. "But we can fix it, Miss Wylde."

I swallowed, my eyes unable to look away from the new hole where the landing booster ought to be.

"Change of plans," Jack announced. His eyes were darting all over the launch pad. "Dr Hoffman, start repairs."

"Yes, sir. And you two?"

"We'll remain on guard, keeping a watch for Lunik. I shouldn't think he'll take long to appear, we've already been noticed."

I turned and looked toward where Jack had been staring and noticed a KSC truck and several black cars heading our way.

"We don't have much time," I said urgently.

"No. But neither does Sergei."

"How did he fly on after landing here like this?" I demanded, looking back at the state of our Vehicle again.

"Maybe he didn't," Jack murmured, glancing around the launch pad.

"But we saw him later at the Holiday Inn. He already had Carrie by then; he threatened her life."

"Hers specifically, Miss Wylde?"

I thought back and tried to remember Ivanov's exact words, but I couldn't be sure if he had mentioned Carrie by name. I shook my head.

"He held someone he thought was ours," Jack said carefully, his soft eyes pools of milk chocolate. "But it could have just as easily been a lost Intern."

I nodded, feeling more confused than ever.

"He did, however, have your sister on the pier." Yes, he did. "Which leads me to believe that he repaired his Lunik at some stage and made his way there to intercept us. That doesn't tell us how long it took him to fix the machine, just that he did, and is probably no longer here now, in this time."

"How long has it been since Carrie was picked up?" I asked, checking my watch and realising the futility of that gesture.

"Several hours. Your previous self should be in containment at the LCC by now."

"Which means..." I said squinting at the cars thundering along the roadway towards us, "we can expect Special Agents Dawson and Carter to be here."

"Oh, jolly good. I do believe we owe them a little something." I wasn't sure, but I think that might have been glee I saw in Jack's eyes. Mixed with a hell of a lot of fury.

"This is gonna screw with their heads," I muttered.

"Indeed."

"Isn't it also going to screw with this time?"

"Quite possibly."

OK, then. Jack was winging this sting.

We watched on as the cars grew nearer, glancing around the launch pad every other second. Rafe was banging and crashing and cursing behind us, the Orion was emitting liquid oxygen gas and the occasional clank which sounded ominous, and the sun was creeping lower and lower by the minute. Making shadows elongate and our vision become poor.

I swiped at a bead of sweat on my forehead and shifted my weight from foot to foot. The orange jumpsuit suddenly felt too tight. I ran a finger under the collar, and then out of desperation for more air, dragged the zip part way down my chest, leaving the whole thing gaping.

Jack flashed me a smile, his eyes darting to my cleavage and then away again.

"Interesting tactic, Miss Wylde," he murmured.

"Better than yours," I snapped back. "'*Weapons stay inside the Orion*,'" I mimicked. "We're effing sitting ducks here."

Jack chuckled, and then reached down and picked up a chunk of concrete the Orion had broken off the pad. "Please don't kill the Special Agents, Miss Wylde," he said, handing me the makeshift weapon. "Save it for Sergei."

"Gladly," I muttered, hefting the rock-like chunk in my hand and grinning maniacally.

"You really are amazing; you know that?" Jack whispered, fingering his own chunk of concrete.

"Don't," I whispered back.

"I can't help how I feel, Mimi."

"Not now, Jack."

"Always," he murmured in return, as the federal agents came barrelling through a gap in the chainlink.

It was strange to see them again. To know for me days had passed, but for them mere minutes, maybe an hour. They blinked when they saw the Orion, something clicking inside their heads, making their eyes narrow and their lips thin. They yelled out warnings to "Freeze" and "Raise your hands" when they spotted our orange flight suits, double fisting their very real guns.

They stilled completely when they recognised me.

"What the hell?" Carter exclaimed. "How the fuck did she get back here?"

"It's the sister," Dawson growled. "Down on your knees, Carolyn! Now!"

"Just a moment, Special Agent Dawson," Jack said conversationally. "You're being a little hasty here."

"Shut your mouth!" Dawson yelled, a vein almost popping on the side of his neck. "On the motherfucking ground now!"

"This is not Carolyn Wylde," Jack explained as if he wasn't about to receive a bullet to the skull. "This lovely woman here is, in fact, Mimi Wylde. I believe you know her."

"Shut the fuck up!" Dawson growled, tightening his hold on his gun.

"Easy," Carter murmured softly at his side. "Everyone, let's just calm down. What is that thing?" he asked, nodding towards the MPCV.

"Oh, this?" Jack said enthusiastically. "This is an Orion Multi-Purpose Crew Vehicle. I believe you would have seen one inside the Vehicle Assembly Building, am I right?"

"How did it get here?" he demanded.

"It travelled through a hole in the VAB," Jack supplied.

"It's ours?"

"Do you mean NASA's?" Jack asked.

"Yeah, dipshit, he means NASA's," Dawson growled.

"What do you think?" Jack asked.

"How did it get here?" Carter repeated.

"A malfunction?" Jack offered with a shrug of his shoulders.

"Who the fuck *are* you?" Dawson yelled.

Jack smiled. "Jack Evans. Surgeon." The smile widened.

"Jack," I warned.

"Any moment now," he murmured. He was stalling. Messing with agents because he wanted to. Because he wanted to fuck with their minds. But there was more to all of this. He was stalling, waiting for Sergei Ivanov to arrive.

"What if he doesn't show?" I asked, the agents watching and listening intently. Guns raised, fingers on their triggers.

"He'll show," Jack said softly. "I would," he added and then stilled completely, as if afraid to move a muscle.

I flicked my eyes to the side, tipped my head to look up at him.

"Jack? What makes you think that lunatic would do anything that you would do?"

He smiled, it was nothing like the grin he'd just given the feds. It was Jack's now familiar grimace.

"Can we discuss this later, Miss Wylde?"

My eyes darted back to the agents.

"You bet your British arse we will," I growled.

I heard him huff out a burst of laughter.

"What the fuck are you two playing at?" Dawson finally demanded.

"Our jobs, Special Agent Dawson," Jack replied.

"To sabotage NASA property?" he snarled.

"We didn't sabotage anything," I argued. "You've got such a one track mind."

"That's it!" Dawson shouted. "On the fucking ground now or we shoot you!"

Where was he? Where was Sergei Ivanov right now? Watching, a dimension away? Or ignoring us completely? Laughing his Russian arse off as he downed a shot of vodka and did God knows what to Carrie?

"This really isn't necessary," Jack insisted.

"Oh, but I think it is," Dawson growled back.

"Dr Hoffman?" Jack called.

"Shit Creek. Sir." Rafe shouted back.

"Who's there?" Carter yelled. "Show yourself." Rafe didn't appear. "Who else is here?" he yelled at us instead.

"My crew," Jack replied smugly.

"How many? Get them out here!"

"Miss Groves?"

"Yes, sir?" she called from inside the Vehicle.

"Get ready."

Sally remained silent, but I knew her hand would be shaking as it hovered over the return button. I wondered absently if she'd mended the rip yet. Maybe it hadn't got big enough to go, how did Jack put it? Supernova. Maybe that was why Sergei wasn't here.

I fingered the concrete slab in my hand. I took a quick look over my shoulder at the crippled Orion. It could go back to RATS without us, but it clearly couldn't do much else.

We could go too. We could run on board while they fired at our backs. We might even make it.

And then Carrie would be lost to Sergei.

I looked at the thrumming feds. At the bristling KSC security guards. At the shadows as they lengthened towards me like crooked fingers in the dark.

Please don't kill the special agents, Miss Wylde.

Well, someone had to rip this time apart.

I let the rock fly, watched as it arced through the air towards them; heard Jack shout out a warning, felt him throw his body into mine as gunfire sounded. Saw the ground rush up to meet me. With a bone-jarring crunch, we hit concrete as the special agents' bullets hit the Orion.

Time warped. I vaguely saw I'd missed both Dawson and Carter; the concrete wedged into the grille of their SUV. But their aim had been true. The Orion puffed out a cloud of gas, emitted a loud pop that deafened, and then caught on fire.

"Sally!" I screamed, just as a Lunik flashed into sight.

3 4
RETURN!

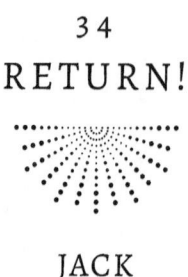

JACK

*S*he'd shattered this time. I was shocked at her audacity. And equally as proud. A 21st century bullet, or two, lay lodged into a 23rd century Orion. Time didn't like the conflict.

And neither did Sergei Ivanov.

Bullets flew in all directions as I crawled towards Mimi. Rafe rounded the side of the Orion, hurtled through the hatch, and hauled Sally Groves out. Smoke billowed up behind them, alarms bleeped persistently into the night, and the angry, confused shouts of the agents and security guards rose above it all.

And still, Sergei fired.

I rolled us towards the Orion, the only obvious source of cover, even if it was about to explode. My hands frantically checking Mimi for injuries, as I covered her head with my torso to protect her from any stray bullets.

"What the bloody fucking hell was that?" Rafe yelled as we grouped together behind the hatch door.

"A bullet," I replied, worry making my answer curt. Mimi hadn't moved, wasn't fighting my hurried assessment of her body. Her chest rose and fell, her eyelids flickered, but otherwise, she wasn't there.

I found the culprit when my fingers came away red from the back of her head.

"Oh, God," Sally murmured, rushing forward to check the injury. "I've got her," she offered. "Secure the vessel."

"Who's in charge here, Miss Groves?" I demanded, but her words had me moving, even if all I wanted to do was stay with Mimi.

"Can you get back inside and put out that fire?" I asked Rafe.

"I can give it a damn good try if you cover me."

"With what?"

He thrust a gun in my hand. "Sergei's from our time. Or has been for a while. Shoot back."

I lifted the gun, aimed, and fired. Rafe took the opportunity and slinked back inside the Orion.

"Watch out for Carrie," Mimi muttered from the ground, loud enough to hear, but still far too weak for my liking.

"Are you all right?" I asked.

"Peachy," she mumbled.

"Stay still. You've got a bruise forming," Groves growled, wrapping a strip of torn jumpsuit around Mimi's forehead.

"Nice," Mimi said, touching the bandage and wincing.

"Do as she says, Miss Wylde," I ordered, keeping my eyes on the battle ensuing.

At least Sergei had provided us with a distraction; his shots were now aimed at the KSC guards and the federal agents. We were momentarily forgotten, for now.

Mimi moved to a crouch beside me, peering around the edge of the hatch door. Her movements were stiff, but her eyes seemed clear and bright. Yet all I wanted to do was push her to the ground behind me and fire blindly at anything out there that moved a single inch.

"It's now or never," she announced.

"Now or never for what?" I demanded.

She blinked up at me. "I'm getting my sister, Jack. While the feds keep him busy, I'm going in."

"You'll do no such thing!"

"Watch me!"

She made to move, but her motions were still sluggish. I had an arm about her waist before she'd managed to cover a metre of ground.

"Argh!" she growled as she fought my hold. Feebly. Every struggle she gave made her face pinch in pain and her hands shake a little more.

"Calm down," I ordered. "For the love of God, Mouse, calm down."

She stopped fighting and just lay there panting. My heart nose-dived. My head reeled.

This was it. Let her go - or at least let her save Carolyn - and maybe lose her forever.

Keep holding her too tightly and lose her anyway.

Bloody fucking bollocks!

"We go together." She nodded her head slowly. "I'll cover you. You grab Carolyn. Then we retreat."

"OK," she said.

"Keep an eye on things, Miss Groves."

"Sure," she said unconvinced.

"Send a signal when Dr Hoffman has this Vehicle under control again."

"Yes, sir."

"Ready?" I asked Mimi.

"No," she replied. "But that's never stopped me before."

And that's why I loved her. That's why she was going to destroy me.

I nodded my head, checked the magazine in the gun, and then followed her out.

The scene was one I'd witnessed many times before, in many different times. Syracuse. Hastings. Orléans. Waterloo. Normandy. This was small on the scale of war, but death is death. And when delivered so brutally it has its similarities. The sounds. The smells. The taste on your tongue of gunpowder and flesh wounds and fire.

Someone had been shot, maybe more than one person, it was hard to tell. But Sergei was ripping this time apart, perhaps in self-defence; he'd been the one wielding a gun when he'd emerged from his Lunik.

The federal agents had turned their attention to the real threat and chaos had simply followed.

One shot from the Russian and the contemporaries retaliated.

One shot from them and Sergei returned fire.

It was a catch 22, but he wouldn't stay here for long. He'd retreat, regroup, and change his strategy. It's what I'd do. It's what I'd taught him to do. I pushed that uncomfortable thought from my mind.

But if we could get onboard his Vehicle while he was distracted, retrieve Carolyn Wylde and hit the self-destruct button, then we might just be able to save some lives and get out of this with something to show for our efforts.

That's if we didn't get hit by a stray bullet first.

Mimi ducked as something whizzed past her ear. The Lunik protested loudly. Gas mixed with smoke mixed with gunpowder. Sergei yelled out an insult in Russian. It might have had something to do with Dawson's mother.

We rounded the side of the Lunik, inching forward on our hands and knees, heads tucked down, eyes darting, gun hand at the ready. The door was open, providing an easy retreat for Sergei. The internal lights were on, and the console was active. Coordinates had been entered for a retreat location. My eyes took everything in in a split second. The sine wave on the screen. The warning lights on the dashboard. The smell of burned electrical wires and fire fighting foam. The soft grunt of someone working hard at something. The countdown on the centre console that indicated Sergei had a backup plan.

Evacuation in T-minus two minutes. All in Russian. All foreign to Mimi no doubt. But not to me.

And not to Carolyn Wylde.

I watched as she entered a command, using Cyrillic script with practised moves. I watched as the command was received by the Vehicle's computer and then a second countdown appeared. I watched as she lifted her hand over the red button, her eyes glancing over her shoulder towards the door, and landing on us.

"Mouse," she whispered. "Oh, no," she added. "You have to leave."

"Not without you," Mimi growled.

It was too late. My mouth became too dry to speak. My eyes too moist to see clearly.

This was going to hurt.

"Get out of here, Mouse!" Carolyn yelled. "Get back on your Vehicle and go home."

"I'm not going anywhere without you!"

"Can't you see?" Carolyn yelled beseechingly. "This is *all* for you. If I do this, he'll leave you alone. If I stay, I can protect you. It's what I've *been* doing. It's *what* I do."

"What the hell does that mean?" Mimi yelled back.

"Get outta here, Mouse." Carolyn turned back to the console and hit the button. The second countdown began as the computer issued a warning in Russian.

"Bomb activated. Detonation in t-minus three minutes."

"We've got to go," I said.

"Get her out of here, Rat," Carolyn growled. Then in Russian to me, she added, "I'll distract him, while you run. You've got less than three minutes."

I nodded my head and reached for Mimi. "What the effing hell?" she cried, her eyes all for her sister. And then they shifted, taking in the Cyrillic, flicking to Carolyn's fingers, and then the keyboard where she'd just been typing.

"How long?" she whispered.

"T-minus one minute to evacuation," the computer sounded in Russian.

"Too long," Carolyn replied.

"Come with us. Please," Mimi pleaded. "We can fix this."

Carolyn just smiled. "I'm the older sister now, Mouse. By more than three-hundred seconds."

"No," Mimi cried. "What has he done?"

"Nothing I didn't agree to."

"To save me," Mimi guessed.

"Let me do my job, Mouse. Let me keep saving you. Go."

"Mimi," I urged tugging on her jumpsuit. "Sweetheart, come on. It's too late."

She knew. Mimi's was one of the most intelligent, quick minds of her generation. Of her time and I was thinking, perhaps, of mine now too.

She knew it was too late for Carrie. Her sister had chosen her side. For good reasons, but it was long done now. Lost time is never found again.

"I love you," Mimi whispered. "I *will* find you," she vowed.

"Not if I can help it." Carrie lifted a weapon up from beside her and aimed it at my head. "Run!"

Mimi squeaked, tugged on my sleeve, and pulled me back out the hatch just as Carolyn Wylde fired.

The bullet flew over our heads, out of the entrance to the Lunik, and blindsided Sergei. He yelled, rolled, and came up firing. But not at the Lunik, at us, as we ran and dodged, and ducked and dived, and somehow made it back to the Orion alive.

I pushed Mimi through the hatch, rolling in behind her in a hail of bullets, and shouted, "Return!"

The door was latched behind us by an efficient Rafe, and the second the capsule was contained, Sally slammed her palm down on the red button. I didn't have time to be thankful for my flight team.

Lights flashed, sirens screamed, the Orion rocketed into space-time as if on fire. I was betting it probably still was. We rolled around on the metal floor unrestrained as rivets exploded, and cabinets doors burst off, and first aid kits came raining down. And a foul smelling liquid sloshed over our bodies, drenching us all.

With an earsplitting boom, we landed, barely breathing, barely moving, barely seeing straight at all.

I expected a technician to open the hatch, but none came.

I expected someone to contact us through the communicator now we were back at Shadowship, but silence reigned.

Just the ticking of our Vehicle and the soft *whoop-whoop* of internal alarms and the smell of electrical circuitry burning mixed with biological nitrates.

And the sounds of intermittent gunfire from inside RATS.

35

AND THEN SILENCE

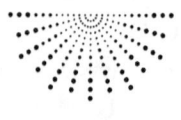

MIMI

I could hardly breathe. My chest hurt. I could hardly see. My eyes were full of tears. I could hardly think. My mind was reeling. Dear God, what had I done? I'd failed to rescue Carrie.

I couldn't get the image of her in the Lunik out of my mind. I couldn't stop seeing the foreign words up on the screen and her hands flying over the keyboard writing them. I couldn't stop hearing her say something to Jack in Russian.

This didn't make sense. None of it did. Carrie had only been gone as long as me. A few days. A handful of hours. This couldn't be happening.

But it was. Carrie could speak Russian. Carrie could operate that Lunik. Carrie fired a gun at Jack.

I rolled over, a moan escaping me; it could have been for all the bruises and scrapes I'd managed to acquire. Or just because my heart was aching. My palm landed in a puddle of blue liquid that smelled disgustingly like the toilet, successfully breaking my train of thought for a moment.

"Argh," I managed, as Sally groaned and Rafe muttered something indecipherable, but undoubtedly a swearword, and Jack remained motionless.

I wanted to move to him. I wanted to check he was OK. But my mind returned to Carrie, and my body refused to shift a muscle.

Carrie in the Lunik. Carrie tapping away on a keyboard that made no sense. Carrie ordering Jack around as if she knew him. Carrie lifting a gun up and firing at his head. If I hadn't pulled him backwards out that door would the bullet have hit home?

I was thinking, yes.

Carrie had shot to kill.

A sob escaped, and I felt Sally's hand come to rest on my shoulder. My ears buzzed. My head felt dizzy. My eyes couldn't seem to focus.

"Gunshots," Jack said from the floor, beginning to shift gingerly upright. "Someone's firing outside the Vehicle."

"At us?" Sally squeaked.

"No, they sound farther away. Not in the hangar."

"RATS is under attack," Rafe said quietly, pushing up to his feet and moving to a key code locked cabinet.

"Is everyone all right?" Jack asked, brushing his jumpsuit down absently. The orange was now coated in blue, making a strange pattern appear. He looked terrible.

He looked as bad as I was feeling.

But his heart wouldn't have been breaking, would it?

Oh God, Carrie. I'd failed.

Rafe had opened the cabinet and was pulling out weapons, handing them to Jack and Sally. I didn't know how to fire a gun, let alone long nosed rifle looking things like the ones everyone was grasping.

Carrie did, I should think. Carrie knew so much more than me. Where had she been? Where had the time gone? Why didn't she come with me?

And that's perhaps the one thing that hurt the most. Carrie refusing to save herself. Carrie choosing to be a martyr to protect me. Whatever Sergei Ivanov had promised Carrie she believed by staying with him she was keeping me safe.

I didn't need her protection, nor want it. I wanted my sister back.

"It's not your fault, Mouse," Jack said softly.

I looked up and found all three of them watching me. I was the only one still sitting on the floor in a puddle of blue. I wanted to cry. I wanted to scream.

It is my fault!

"It's not your fault, Mouse," Jack repeated.

"We were too late," I whispered.

"We were too late the moment she was taken," he said softly, gently. That tone. "You never had a chance of convincing her to leave him. The decision had already been made. He'd had her too long, Mimi. He's had her too long."

I didn't want to believe that. I didn't want to think my sister couldn't be rescued at all. I couldn't believe that. But what could I do?

Carrie was gone. And I was here at RATS. Time had changed. For us and for the Time Surgeons. Altered by Ivanov, aided by Carrie, sealed in its fate by me.

I was not returning to my time. I would not go back without her.

"Jack," Rafe said, moving to the door. "We need to find out what's happening out there."

"Yes," Jack said, his eyes still on me. "Mimi?"

This was it. This was me accepting my fate. For now, letting Carrie go. Letting this new time she'd helped create evolve. Choosing where I wanted to be in it. What side of the line I stood on.

Carrie was my family. My only living relative. I should have been with her. By her side. Keeping her safe.

But Sergei Ivanov was destroying Time not mending it.

My decision had also already been made.

I chose RATS. I chose this year, whatever the hell this year was. I chose these people, who were trying to save history and Time, not shatter it.

I chose to see what those dreams actually meant.

My eyes met Jack's. Not such a hardship. I'd lost Carrie. My heart would never fully repair. But I'd gained something else, something extraordinary. Something I had not expected ever to have.

I'd gained Jack.

I nodded my head and accepted the hand he held out to me. Accepted our fate.

It hurt so much, even as my heart accelerated in anticipation. Even as my fingers tingled with his touch. It hurt to admit defeat. It wasn't in me. I am not a quitter. This last year had been a challenge, for sure, but one I was about to emerge from. I would have returned to my doctorate. I would have returned to life in Auckland, New Zealand.

I would have returned to Carrie.

But Sergei Ivanov happened.

I took the pistol Jack offered me, thankfully not one of those stretched guns, and let him show me how to use it. The others were already outside the door to the Orion, scanning the empty hangar, listening out for approaching feet in between the sounds of explosions at the back of RATS.

"What if she's here?" I asked Jack quietly.

He lifted his head, his hands still on mine on top of the firearm.

"Then she's here, and you have another chance to convince her to abandon him."

All my breath left me in a rush. He couldn't have said anything better.

"You think I can still save her?" I asked, my voice trembling with too many emotions.

Jack's hand came up and cupped my cheek, his thumb swiping at my tears. "I think you'll never stop trying. It's not in you. I think there's always a chance if you never give up hope."

I nodded my head, tipped my cheek into his palm, and just breathed.

"But you have to be aware, sweetheart," he said softly, "that Time has changed. And so might Carrie. Sergei has seen to that. We've repaired the rips, we've done what we can to fix his mistakes, but I fear he's been playing with the failsafe. Expect the unexpected, Mimi. Then it can never surprise you."

"Jack!" Rafe shouted. "Get a move on! Our people could be dying."

"You can do this," Jack whispered. "Stick close to me." I nodded. "Miss Groves, you glue yourself to Dr Hoffman. Understood?"

"Yes, sir."

Jack met Rafe's eyes. "Let's move out. We've got surprise on our side, don't waste it."

"Agreed," Rafe said with a curt nod of his head. "Don't care who the fuck they are, they're shooting up RATS. This ends now."

That's what I was afraid of. This was getting out of hand. Ivanov. The rips. The failsafe. Time. It was all about to converge. And Carrie was right in the middle of it. On the wrong effing side.

"Please don't shoot Carrie," I whispered to myself. "Please don't hurt my sister."

Please God, let her survive.

The hallway was dark. Plaster and chips of wood scattered across the floor. A window had been shattered, a soft breeze bringing the smells of autumn inside the building. Our footsteps echoed as we jogged down the corridor, my heart setting up an accompanying beat. Sweat beaded my brow even though the temperature was cooling. Night had fallen, shadows stalked. Stars winked up in an unforgiving sky.

Somewhere out there was the International Space Station, or whatever acted as it in this time. Somewhere out there, up in the infinite vastness of space, was a Crew Vehicle like ours. Not surfing dimensional time waves, but space itself.

Somewhere out there is where it all began.

But we were finishing it tonight.

If Sergei Ivanov were here at RATS, then I'd shoot him. Damn Time and failsafes. Damn it all to effing hell.

I'd reached my limit, and so had Rafe. By the looks of Sally, who held her long-nosed gun with expert hands devoid of tremors, so had she. Jack was his usual unflappable self. But we'd been through too much already not to be prepared to do what's right.

I only prayed what we were about to do was right. And that Carrie was missed in all the crossfire.

We rounded the end of the hallway and came out in the cafeteria to a sight I never wanted to see again. Something had gone wrong in here. Something large and catastrophic. The night sky lit up the destruction through a broken ceiling. Tables and chairs were thrown haphazardly outward from one place. A shoe. The flash of blue clothing. A hand covered in blood.

"Oh, God," Sally whispered.

"Hold it together, Miss Groves," Jack ordered, leading the way across the room, gun muzzle swinging, body rigid but flowing through the debris with apparent ease, and hardened eyes.

Rafe and Sally covered the right-hand side, while Jack and I stalked through the left. There was more than one body. I stopped counting at ten.

My hand fisted the gun harder. My heart turned to ice. I wanted to face him. I wanted to lift my firearm and shoot him in the forehead. I wanted it so badly in that second that I could taste success. I could taste his blood on my tongue.

We came out on the other side of the cafeteria into more hallways that branched off in two different directions. The sound of intermittent battle could be heard farther ahead, but which direction to take was uncertain.

Jack hesitated. To the left were the offices. To the right the accommodation. Jack met Rafe's eyes and nodded. In silence, Rafe and Sally peeled off and headed towards the bedrooms. Their shadowed forms lost to the darkness within seconds making my breath catch uncomfortably in my throat.

Please God, let Rafe Hoffman and Sally Groves survive, I prayed. Adding their names to the mental list.

"Stay behind me," Jack whispered as we moved forward down our corridor. Darkness engulfed us; there was no light for shadows.

My ears rang with the silence, only shattered now and then with a small pop or muffled cry. Whatever had happened was nearing its end. Because there were no RATS survivors?

Damn Ivanov for this. Taking Carrie had been hard enough to swallow, but I realised in the darkness and unknown shadows filled with silence that RATS had a place in my heart as well. That this building with its eccentric Surgeons and surreal time machines was important to me. Not just because through them I could reach Carrie.

But because of who they were and what they did. Where was Dean? Where was Dr Crawford? Fawkes and Malcolm? What if something happened to Jack?

This was their home, their world, their time. This was all they knew. Jack had been right. Even to save Carrie I couldn't turn my back on any of them. To rescue my sister at the expense of RATS was not an option anymore.

My eyes landed on the back of Jack. His gun was raised, pointing forward in front of him, his head cocked to the side as he listened for threats, his steps sure and steady. He headed into danger without hesitation. He went forward when retreat was safer. He pushed on when things looked grim. He would fight to his last breath for his people.

He believed in RATS. He believed in what they were doing. If RATS didn't exist who would stop people like Ivanov? I knew the Russian wasn't alone. He had Carrie. He had a Lunik. Who's to say he didn't have more than that?

Kill Sergei, and we'd maybe buy us some time. But only if we didn't wipe RATS.

This was going to be so much harder than I'd thought. How the hell did we make sure we weren't killing an earlier version of Sergei who was needed in order for certain things in our time to transpire?

I shook my head, making a sharp pain start behind my right eye. I lifted a hand to my forehead, feeling the makeshift bandage Sally had made, and that's when they fired.

Thankfully not at us, but outside the window of one of the offices, we'd just cleared. Their guns pointed towards a contingency of blue covered security guards. RATS jumpsuits blending into the night sky, which finally made sense of the colour choice. Flashes of gunfire illuminated their determined faces for split seconds at a time. They were doing their jobs, but they were scared.

Jack rushed into the office in a low crouch, his hand out behind him motioning for me to get low to the ground as well. I crawled in behind him, coming up beside his vibrating form at the window ledge. The window was intact, making firing out of it a difficulty.

With infinite care, Jack slowly opened the latch and pushed the window up centimetre by centimetre, both of us holding our breaths.

But they didn't hear us over the rapid gunfire. And they didn't see us with muzzle flashes blinding their eyes. But we saw them.

Two people hunkered down by a Lunik.

The world froze. Time stalled. My eyes fixed on the couple as they fired at random, seemingly haphazardly toward the guards.

"Get inside," a male voice ordered his companion at the Lunik.

"That's not Sergei," Jack said and my world shattered.

No, it wasn't Sergei. I'd heard him speak Russian. He'd threatened my life in a whisper at my ear. I knew how he sounded now. I knew his non-accent.

It wasn't Sergei.

But I also recognised this new voice. Recognised this new twang. This new drawl.

My head shook from side to side, my eyes wide trying to focus, trying to see in the intermittent flashes of gunfire if what my mind was telling me was right.

It couldn't be. There was no way it could be. It didn't make sense.

I let out a soft cry.

"Mimi?" Jack said, swinging his gaze to me and not at the people attempting to flee on the Lunik. "What is it?"

I kept shaking my head. No. This wasn't right.

"Flick the switch!" the man yelled at his partner.

No.

I started to cry. Silent tears burning.

"Are you sure?" the woman replied. "I don't know!" she wailed, her hands wringing in a fashion I also recognised.

I started to hyperventilate.

"Mimi!" Jack said, dropping his gun on the ground and reaching out to cup my shoulders. He squeezed them, then shook me slightly. "Slow down!" he pleaded, the whites of his eyes too bright.

"This is for Carrie!" the man yelled, and I sobbed out a stuttered breath of air. "Do it, or she dies."

The woman rushed inside the Lunik; I watched it all in a frozen moment of utter terror and disbelief.

Don't shoot! I wanted to shout to the RATS guards.

Stop this! I wanted to scream at the Lunik.

No!

No words came out. The world kept on spinning. Time kept on surfing its own dimensional wave. This was happening.

I should have known by now: Time marched to its own beat.

A rumble started out across the grounds of the Royal Academy of Time Surgeons. The building shuddered and groaned. The floor beneath our feet lurched, making us lose our balance. Making me lose sight of the world outside. Dust rained down on our heads as windows shattered and walls collapsed. And screams went up into the night.

I heard the roar of rocket engines. I felt the electricity in the air. I tasted burned argon. And then silence.

Outside a nebula would have formed. Stars twinkling in a cloud of gas and light. Blue, red, orange, purple. The Lunik had taken flight.

And on it, my parents. My supposedly *dead* parents. The people I'd been mourning for the past twelve months.

36

TIME DROVE US ALL NOW

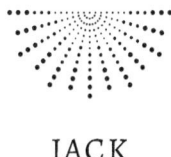

JACK

*T*here was no way to process this sort of loss. There was no way to comprehend its fruitlessness. Its inevitability. Its reality. Its emptiness. There was simply no way to accept any of this.

We'd counted twenty bodies. All ours. All RATS. And an untold number of injuries. Clive was alive, at least. So were Fawkes and his team. Sebastian and his. Mine. But we'd lost eight security. Five hospitality. Four technicians. And three flight.

Her name was Susanne. Two Ns and an E. I remembered it now. I would never forget. The dispatcher had been at her console when the attack had begun. She'd been one of the first to die.

Susanne. We all grieved.

But none so much as Mimi. I had never seen such raw grief before. Never felt it as if it was my own when it clearly was not. She wouldn't share. She wouldn't open up. She'd closed down, doing what was necessary to help the wounded, to find some order in amongst the chaos, to fortify our resources in case they came back.

No one could reach her; not even her friends. Sally and Dean had tried. Bryan and Rafe had tried. Hell, even Crawford had tried. But none could break through the ice she'd surrounded herself in.

I understood. She'd lost Carrie. But we'd lost twenty good women and men.

I watched her now as she took water to the injured, wiping their foreheads with a damp cloth, straightening their bedclothes, fussing her way across the infirmary. I watched her when I should have been strategising with Clive. Discussing options with the Surgeons. Addressing the elephant in the room.

They'd had a Lunik.

They'd had explosives from our time.

They'd spoken with a Kiwi accent.

Mimi had known them.

I bunched my fists and turned back down the corridor, making my way to the meeting. I was late. I was in a foul mood. I wanted to hit something. This was not going to go well.

As suspected, I was the last to arrive. Sebastian Winchester sat in the corner drinking a glass of whisky. It was far too early for that, but no one objected. Bryan Fawkes leant back in a chair tossing peanuts up in the air and catching them in an open mouth. Dave Sanders, head of security, watched from his lean against a bookshelf behind the door. And Clive had his back to the room, staring out of the window at the scorch marks on the green outside.

"You're late," he said when the door shut quietly behind me.

"Just checking on things," I murmured and took a seat beside Bryan.

"Checking on your Kiwi?" Sebastian asked. His would be the face I undoubtedly hit first.

"Three more have been released from the infirmary," I offered in reply.

Clive grunted but didn't turn to face us.

"We're almost back to full staff," Dave added, clearly keen to get on with this debrief. "Had a couple in training; I've raised them to full-time. You know, to cover the losses."

Silence. I shifted uncomfortably in my seat. Clive didn't move a muscle.

"Are we going to dance around the real issue?" Sebastian asked, swirling his whisky in its glass, making the ice clink annoyingly.

"They were Sergei's, no denyin'," Bryan offered. "A Lunik is a Lunik is a Lunik. Try sayin' that three times too fast," he added in a mock whisper to the side.

No one chuckled.

"But they weren't the Russian, were they?" Sebastian countered, his eyes boring into mine.

Clive turned to face us, his arms clasped behind his back, his chest puffed out, the walking stick nowhere in sight. He let his eyes roll over each of us in turn, making sure we saw him. Making sure we understood he was still in charge.

I was relieved. I trusted Clive Crawford. I trusted him to do what was right when I couldn't. When I wouldn't.

Right now, all I wanted to do was bloody my knuckles.

"What are we going to do about the girl?" Winchester demanded.

"What girl?" Bryan asked, all innocence.

"You know damn well, Yank, which fucking girl we're talking about. The Kiwi! One of four we know are embroiled in this mess."

"She's not embroiled in this mess," I said before I could stop myself. "She's as much a victim here as we are."

"Bullshit!"

"Enough!" Clive bellowed. "We are not school children fighting over a piece of candy in the park. We will discuss this as adults. Taking *all* evidence into consideration." His eyes met mine. "She recognised them?"

I let out a slow breath of air; it did nothing for my anger levels. "Yes."

"There you have it. She's a spy!" Trust Sebastian Winchester to go for the bloody convenient. We needed someone to blame. We didn't have Sergei Ivanov to hang. We didn't have the couple responsible for all the deaths to punish.

But we did have Mimi Wylde.

"Who are they to her, do you know?" Clive asked.

"No. She won't talk."

"Have you asked her?" Dave pressed.

"She won't talk at all. To anyone. About anything. She's shut down. Operating on automatic."

"All the better to avoid admitting duplicity," Sebastian offered.

I clenched my fists tightly.

"He's upped his game," Bryan supplied, drawing everyone's attention away from the ticking time bomb. If I could think straight, I'd have thanked him.

Not gonna happen.

"Two-pronged attack," he continued. "Cape Canaveral in Mimi's time. Greenwich in ours. He couldn't be in two places at once, so he used associates. I gotta say, boss, his associates weren't professional."

"They knew how to operate a Lunik," Winchester pointed out. "And how to plant explosives."

"They couldn't fire their weapons for shit," Sanders argued. "They missed more than hit their targets. The only way people were killed or injured was from fallout from explosions." He growled out the rest. "They had a fucking lot of those."

"Current explosives. Appropriate for our time," Clive said.

"How is that relevant?" Sebastian demanded. "So, Ivanov didn't want to wipe RATS, just rattle us. He needs us to exist."

"Exactly," Clive said, moving forward to finally take his seat. "He almost destroys Miss Wylde's time but not our time."

"That was an accident. Happenstance," I said. "The federal agents fired first, he retaliated. Sergei was never shy in coming forward."

"You should know," Winchester sneered. I ignored him. It was hard. My hands twitched.

"So, what does he want then?" Bryan asked.

"He wants to shut us down, not destroy us," Clive offered. "He wants us out of the picture for a while, but why? To what end?"

"He's certainly got something planned," Sanders agreed. "But I'm not sure he wouldn't be happy with us being destroyed as well. Those explosives were top of the line. They had over fifty on them. They deployed thirty."

"I wasn't aware thirty explosions went off," Clive murmured.

"They didn't. Fifteen did. They failed to flick the switch on half of them. Ineptitude at its best."

"Or a calculated risk," I offered.

"What makes you say that?" Clive demanded.

I wished to God I'd just kept my bloody mouth shut.

"If you know something, Jack, speak." Clive's hard eyes bore into mine.

"I'm not sure I know anything. Just a hunch."

"Then out with it, son. We need to know what we're up against."

I stared at the blotter on his desk.

"Protecting his lover, that's what," Winchester growled. "Nice bit of skirt that one, Evans, but fucking the enemy is low even for you."

I was up and out of my seat in a heartbeat. My fist planted in his face before the next beat had thumped. Breathing hard, I shook out my hand as Winchester laughed up at me from behind a bloody nose.

"Did I mention we'd discuss this like adults," Clive said deathly quiet.

"Call your Rottweiler off, Crawford," I growled.

"This is getting us…"

A soft knock interrupted Clive's words. All heads swung toward the door, and in the case of Sanders, a gun was drawn. Touchy the room certainly was.

"Enter!' Clive announced authoritatively.

The door crept open and a delicate hand wrapped around the frame. I closed my eyes and tipped my head back. And then snapped them open in order to protect her from oncoming threats.

"Miss Wylde," Clive said in greeting. "How may I help?"

"You're discussing me," Mimi said.

"Whatever made you think that?" Clive hedged.

She smiled. It was small and tremulous and broke apart the last of my failing willpower.

Mimi tapped the side of her head. "Finally had a new dream."

Oh, bloody fucking bollocks. Her eyes met mine. I held her gaze, willing her to see she wasn't alone in this.

Let me in, Mouse. Just let me in.

"And what did your dream tell you?" Clive asked.

Mimi took a step into the room and met the gaze of each of its occupants. Some were cordial. Some were neutral. One was a sneer. She held each one without blinking.

"You need me, Dr Crawford," she said boldly.

"We don't need jack shit from a spy," Winchester exclaimed.

I rounded on him, my fists bunched again, a threat clear in my eyes. He actually flinched.

"Stay down," I growled. Bryan chuckled. Clive sighed.

"Why don't you explain yourself, Miss Wylde," he said, motioning her forward.

Mimi crept into the room on silent feet, her back straight, and chin lifted. I couldn't have been more proud. I moved to stand closer to her, catching her eye with a small smile. Her lips twitched.

Was she laughing at me?

"Sergei Ivanov," she said, "has my sister."

"We know this, Miss Wylde," Clive replied, not unkindly.

She nodded. "He also has somehow…" she licked her lips, cocked her head to the side and sighed, staring at nothing. "Somehow," she repeated, her voice whisper quiet, "he's managed to get my parents."

I'd known it. Or at least, suspected it. How could I not? Kiwi accent. *This is for Carrie!* Mimi's shock and shut down.

I'd known it. But nothing prepared me for the fallout.

She'd thought them dead.

Oh, sweetheart. Why didn't you come to me first?

"Well, there's your proof," Winchester announced grandly, hauling himself off the floor and dusting himself off. He moved to pour himself another whisky as if everything had now been solved and put in its correct box.

"Proof of what exactly, Dr Winchester?" Clive asked.

"Proof she's as much a part of this as her sibling," Sebastian said as if speaking to a child.

"Are you a part of this, Mimi?" Clive promptly asked.

The room stilled. Mimi bit her bottom lip. "If you don't find him first, I will. And I won't miss. I won't stop. Until he's dead."

"Well, that's puttin' it out there, kid," Bryan said, crunching on a peanut. "You've got my backin'."

"It wasn't an answer," Winchester growled. "She can't even be honest with you."

"Evasion is not a lie, Doctor," Clive argued. "Miss Wylde? You need to be more precise in your reply. Are you part of Sergei Ivanov's attempts to bring down RATS?"

"No." I slowly released the breath I'd been holding. I think a few others did as well.

Winchester just sucked one in, preparing to fire.

"I thought my parents were dead," Mimi said cutting him off. "For the past year, I've grieved them. Carrie was all that kept my head above water. She was the reason I got up in the morning. The reason I tried to see past the loss and heartache. Carrie was the only family I had left.

"He's got them all," she said, shaking her head forlornly. Such a figure of complete and utter grief. "He's taken my family from me. He's got them all."

I reached out for her, taking the steps necessary to wrap her up in my embrace. I didn't care what they thought, what they saw, what it said about me. This woman was my world. I wouldn't, *couldn't*, let her go through this without me.

She held me back tightly, taking the support I offered, laying her cheek against my chest, clinging on with desperate fingers. I savoured the moment, knowing it would shatter. Knowing life was not this easy.

It was Mimi who pulled back. Who let reality storm in again. Not Winchester. Not Clive Crawford. But Mimi. My mouse.

She met my eyes, offered a small smile, and then turned to face the room.

"You need me," she repeated, her voice stronger, her fingers quietly slipping into mine.

I felt about ten feet tall.

"That's hardly an argument," Winchester offered, but his words were tempered a little now.

"Why Mimi?" Clive asked.

"Carrie doesn't know about our parents," she said. "She's doing all of this for me. My parents don't know about me. They're doing all of this for Carrie. Ivanov is playing them both. Two sides against each other. But he's forgotten something. He's forgotten about me. My love for Carrie. Carrie's for me. My love for my parents. Theirs for me. I'm their vulnerability. I'm the one thing that would stay their hands.

"He wants to send my parents in here to fuck with RATS? He's forgotten they won't if I'm here. If they see me. He wants to make Carrie fuck with our Surgeons and our Orions in various times? He's effing well forgotten about me." Her free hand thumped into the centre of her chest. "She can't. She won't. Because of me!

"You need me, Doctors. RATS *needs* me."

Mimi had summed it up beautifully. We did need her. Without her we were vulnerable. With her here, her family would be hesitant. Could be contained.

Could even be turned.

She was brilliant. Feisty and courageous. Utterly stunning. Coming in here and facing off against our anger and rage. She was miraculous.

But she'd forgotten one thing. One *vital* thing.

She'd forgotten that *I* needed her too. That I needed those dreams to be real.

It didn't matter that she'd made her choice to stick by RATS. To call it hers as well as ours. It didn't matter that she was trying to right the wrongs committed by her family. None of it did.

Because without Mimi Wylde in my life I would simply go mad.

I already loved her. I was already in love with her. She was already my world.

And I was determined to be hers as well.

"Well, then," Clive said to the room at large. "Any objections keeping Miss Wylde around for a while longer?"

No one raised their hand.

"Get her trained up accordingly, Dr Evans. We can't have our most precious asset unqualified. This is not the last we'll see of Sergei

Ivanov." Clive looked towards Mimi. "And not the last we'll see of your family either, Miss Wylde."

Something flickered in his eyes, something calculating and scheming. Clive Crawford at his Machiavellian best. And if I wasn't mistaken, it might just have involved a prophetic dream or two, as well.

Carolyn Wylde meant something to the Chief Surgeon of RATS.

Just like her sister, Mimi, meant something to me.

I didn't like placing our faith in dreams; for so long I'd denied them. But there was no denying Mimi. I couldn't. I *wouldn't*. She was already mine.

Time had already changed to accommodate her.

Time drove us all now.

But was it Sergei's Time or Mimi's?